Jonathan Bennett is a freelance writer and translator. His screen credits include film and TV drama, his travel writing has appeared in *The Guardian*, *The Independent* and *Time Out*, and he wrote the long-standing Roger de Flower column in *Barcelona Metropolitan*. He also writes audio guides for museums, castles and other damp venues.

AROUND THE COAST
IN
EIGHTY WAVES

Jonathan Bennett

SANDSTONEPRESS
HIGHLAND | SCOTLAND

First published in Great Britain and the United States of America
Sandstone Press Ltd
Dochcarty Road
Dingwall
Ross-shire
IV15 9UG
Scotland.

www.sandstonepress.com

Commissioning Editor: Robert Davidson

Maps by Helen Stirling Maps

The publisher acknowledges support from Creative Scotland
towards publication of this volume.

ISBN: 978-1-910124-88-8
ISBNe: 978-1-910124-89-5

Cover design by David Eldridge at Two Associates
Typeset by Iolaire Typesetting, Newtonmore.
Printed and bound by CPI Group (UK) Ltd, Croydon CR0 4YY.

For Karen and Cordelia

And for my parents, Sue and Geoff

Acknowledgements

I met many friendly, generous people both in and out of the water. Some are named in the narrative, others remain nameless. I would like to thank them all. I would particularly like to thank several who invited a bedraggled vagabond into their homes and gave him much-needed food, warmth and companionship: Jane and Toby, Mike 'Tup' Newman, Julian and Annika, Jim and his delightful family, and the artist couple in Bantham who enquired about the colour of my van one day. Blue, I told them, whereupon they invited me for lunch.

From start to finish, I relied heavily on two surf guides, Wayne Alderson's very thorough *Surf UK* (Fernhurst Books, 2000), and Chris Nelson and Demi Taylor's rather more discreet *Surfing Britain* (Footprint, 2005 and 2008). I can recommend both, preferably together.

I would very much like to thank Robert Davidson and Moira Forsyth, and everyone at Sandstone Press, for publishing this book, as well as Andrew Lownie for his encouragement and efforts. I would also like to thank the various people who provided me with somewhere to write it: Jon Markwell at Brighton co-working space The Skiff, Mike and Maggie Handley in Herne Hill, and everyone at The Lido Cafe, especially Dan, John, Anke, Nick, Danni, Sarah, Anna, Christine, and the many others who generously let me sit for long hours with a blank sheet of paper in front of me.

Many people have supported and encouraged my writing over the years, and I am delighted to be able to thank them in print for the first time. Suzanne Wales gave me my first break, and later was the first person to actually pay me to write, along with Richard Schweid and Esther Jones at Barcelona Metropolitan; Tara Stevens pushed me when I needed it; Jean Kitson was my first agent, for which I cannot thank her enough; and Lyn Washbrook gave me my first TV commission. Without their combined and cumulative contributions, I would still be starving in a Barcelona garret.

Others have been more generally supportive over many years. I would especially like to thank Angels Seix, Sarah Stothart and my sisters, Claire Bennett and Lucy Taylor. My long-suffering parents Sue and Geoff would have preferred their son to embark on a more secure career – possibly as a lawyer or the piano player in a brothel – but their resigned acceptance deserves recognition, even applause. Someone once said that home is the place where, when you have to go there, they have to take you in. Sure enough, when bad weather, poor waves or mechanical failure struck, they did so without complaint.

Finally, neither the trip nor this book would have happened had I not met Karen Livingstone, who gave me love, toast and Cordelia, and who still lets me go off surfing or writing far more often than I deserve. For this, and much, much more, words cannot sufficiently express my thanks. And yes, reader, I married her.

Jonathan Bennett
February 2016

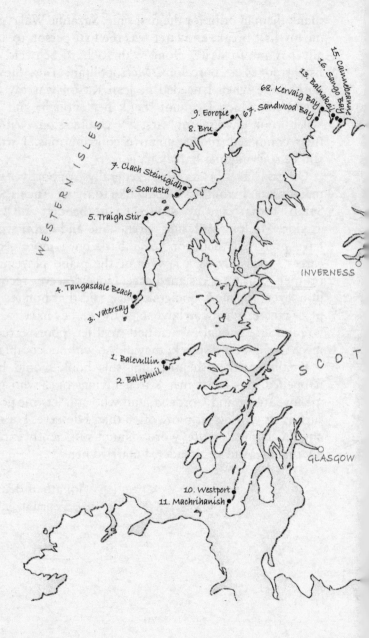

15. Cainndeanne
16. Sango Bay
13. Balnakeil
68. Kervaig Bay
67. Sandwood Bay
9. Eoropie
8. Bru
7. Clach Steinigidh
6. Scarasta
5. Traigh Stir
4. Tangasdale Beach
3. Vatersay
1. Balevullin
2. Balephuil
10. Westport
11. Machrihanish

WESTERN ISLES

INVERNESS

SCOT

GLASGOW

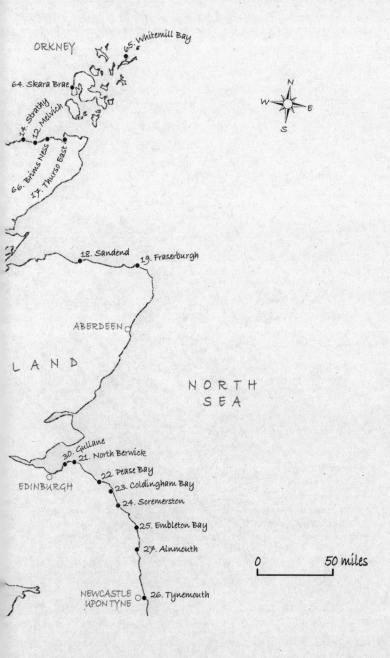

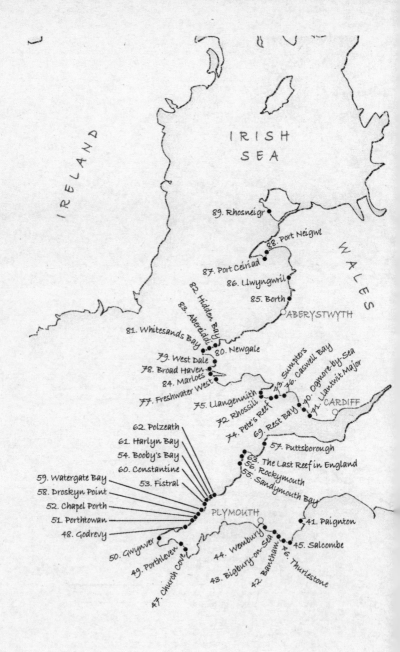

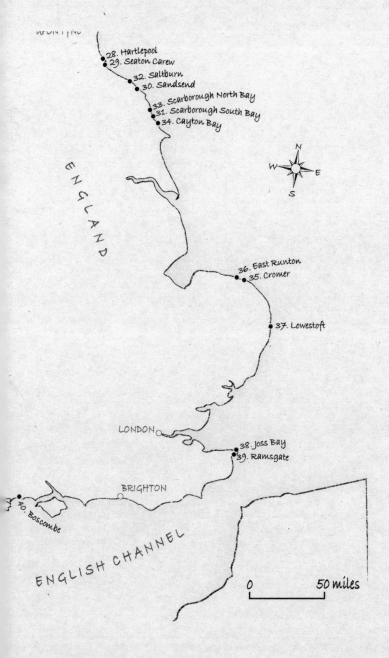

Contents

Prologue

'You can have this one if you want it,' Stevie said casually. I looked up to see an ugly wall of water snarling as it raced towards us.

It was vile out there, cold and bleak, with a howling wind churning up the Atlantic, making the waves rough and impossible to predict. The smaller ones were well above head high, the larger ones double that. A strong cross-shore rip was running, and we had to paddle constantly just to hold our position, tossed like corks among the chaos. Everything about the place was unfriendly, especially the water: shark-skin grey, shark-skin rough. Shark-eye menacing.

Everything except Stevie. As far as he was concerned, we were in it together. I found out later he was one of the best surfers in Scotland. For the moment, all I knew was that he was the best surfer in the water. But then there were only two of us good enough (Stevie) or stupid enough (me) to be out on a day like today.

Stevie was taking off on some outrageous waves. Waves that defied the laws of physics. Waves that seemed to drop away beneath his board as he stood. He was taking off on them with ease, gliding down the face and disappearing behind a churning wall of white-water as the wave powered him towards the rocky shore.

Occasionally I caught a glimpse of him as he rode this seething mass. Sometimes he flashed up on the lip for a second before dropping out of sight again in a burst of spray. Mostly all I saw was the end of the ride a hundred metres away, as he catapulted over the breaking foam before it engulfed him. He paddled back with a smile, then did it again. And again. And again. I, on the other hand, was catching nothing.

I didn't know he was one of the best surfers in Scotland, but I knew he was in a different league. And when a surfer in a different league calls you into a wave, pride, honour and self-respect dictate that you try your damnedest to catch it. He glanced up at the wave.

'You can have this one if you want it.'

I turned and paddled as if my life depended on it.

One

The Western Isles

Ever since I can remember, I've wanted to surf. When I was six or seven, I spent a summer spluttering around the shallows on a short plank made of plywood and grazes, captivated by the mysterious figures gliding across the sunset. A few years later, my first big art project was a clay surfer on a huge tube, copied, I imagine, from a photograph in a magazine. It was early evidence of a magnetic fascination with the sea, and I was devastated when my sculpture, along with several others, exploded in the kiln in a calamitous wipeout.

These days, surfing is tediously ubiquitous, hijacked to sell everything from cars to mortgages. There's nothing radical about surfing, and very little that's cool. Especially when it's surfers like me lurching towards the shoreline. You can sign up for lessons from Aberdeen to Aberystwyth, and pretty much everyone has. Back then it was a mysterious cult, guarded by jealous initiates. If you hadn't been born by the sea, preferably with webbed feet, you might as well forget it.

So forget it I did. I moved to Barcelona, not a city renowned for its surf. On winter days, when Homeric storms whipped the Mediterranean into action, a small band of self-conscious renegades would emerge like damp rats and put on a display of optimistic ineptitude that seemed to confirm the view that there's nothing worth surfing on the Med. I envied their efforts, if not their achievement. But I knew I was too old to learn.

Eventually the urge to give it a try anyway became too great. I assembled a group of friends, contacted a phantom surf school in northern Spain and spent a frustrating week with a doped-out chancer who taught us, badly, on boards dangerously ill-suited to our level. By the end of the week I had stood on my board once. For about a second. I was hooked. Just being in the water, waiting, was fun enough.

I returned home with a broken rib, fewer friends and the beginnings of what I would happily call a life-long passion if I hadn't already been halfway through my allotted span.

I immediately went out and bought a second-hand board, and joined the inept optimists surfing the Med whenever Neptune was displeased. Nothing he saw would have mitigated his displeasure.

As I improved, the limitations of Barcelona as a surfing destination became increasingly apparent, and anyway I had been away long enough. So I moved to Cardiff, which has great waves, then London, which doesn't. Barcelona might be flat most of the time; London is flat all of the time. It was definitely a step in the wrong direction.

If I wanted to surf more, I would have to do something radical: set up a surf shack, move to Hawaii, buy a donkey and offer rides... Anything that would get me closer to the sea. I couldn't justify blowing what little money I had on an extended trip abroad; I didn't want to move to Godawful-on-Sea on my own; and whenever I have taught friends to surf, I've found it boring beyond belief. So I decided to surf round Britain.

The idea was simple: surf a beach, camp, move on to the next beach, repeat. If everything went to plan, I would eventually find myself back where I started, write a best-selling book, and live happily ever after, preferably on or near a beach. That was the theory, anyway.

I had no idea how long the whole trip was going to take, or how many beaches I would surf along the way. Six months seemed reasonable (it wasn't). After that, real life would start to reassert itself (it did). And 80 waves was a rough estimate, given resonance by Jules Verne. It was just a guess, based, like most of my preparations, on blissful ignorance.

So I had a plan. Now I needed a van. Without one, I was going nowhere.

Inevitably I turned to the internet and spent hours surfing, though not the kind I was interested in. The internet is the worst place to buy a van but eventually I stumbled across one I quite liked, at a price I could just afford: a blue 1986 VW Caravelle with Devon conversion. No, that wouldn't have meant anything to me either. Basically not the classic VW campervan everyone imagines when they think of campervans, but the slightly later, square-looking model. It was exactly what I wanted. More to the point, it was just within my budget.

A few days later, in a caravan park above Hastings, I counted out two and a half thousand pounds in used twenties. It felt like a drugs deal. Was it worth it? It was the best decision of my life!

Driving to the sea front in Hastings was like steering a spaceship through a submarine dream. I floated in the cushioned stupor of a brave new world. In an instant, I felt like a different type of surfer. Not more committed. Certainly not more authentic. More versatile, perhaps. More able to drop everything and head to the coast. And definitely more likely to go surfing round the coast of Britain for a year.

The next seventeen days disappeared in a frenzy of preparation. At the end of it, I would like to report that my van was spotless, my inventory faultless and my departure blameless. This would be a lie. The reality was breathless, panic-stricken and full of doubts. But my deadline was upon me, and I was off. As I crossed the Thames on a sunny afternoon in late August, the tide was high, glittering with sunlight, freedom and bright anticipation. Battersea power station glowered, Parliament shone gold and not one of the twelve million people in the capital could have felt happier than I did. Finally, I was under way.

Rather inconveniently, I had recently acquired a shiny new girlfriend, Karen. To keep me company, she generously offered to join me for the long drive north. It seemed a little unfair just to abandon her, so we camped out at Crosby for a couple of days, to wander around Anthony Gormley's fabulous installation *Another Place*. A hundred iron figures stare out to sea, ravaged by wind, rain and water, waiting. Inadvertently, it's a sculpture about surfing. As good a place as any to start my trip. I dropped Karen off at the station and continued up to Oban, full of apprehension and delight.

WAVE 1 : Balevullin, Tiree

I had no idea what to expect in the Outer Hebrides. I knew you could surf there, but that was about it. I filled the van with enough food and petrol for an extended stay on a desert island and slept on the quayside, ready for the dawn ferry. Oban dock at five in the morning is a bleak place to start any adventure, but as we cast off and pushed through silent waters, I was ecstatic.

6

My first stop was Tiree, a convenient stepping stone on the way to the Western Isles which often features on weather maps as the windiest place in Britain. Clanking up the ramp from the ferry was like emerging onto a new planet, bare and featureless, with just a small wooden hut for a ferry terminal. After that, nothing but desolate moorland.

Inexcusably, I had failed to buy a decent map of the island. All I had was a large-scale road atlas, which was almost useless. Luckily, it's a small island, so you can more or less cover it all by trial and error.

I was aiming for the north-west edge of the island, where I thought there was the best chance of finding some waves, and soon came to a scattering of houses strewn higgledy-piggledy over the grassy hillside like sheep. It was as if a child had started to lay out a toy village and got bored before doing roads or shops or people. Beyond was a small, grass-edged scimitar of ivory sand framing an emerald bay, empty and beautiful. But the waves were rather small, and breaking close to shore. Not what you want to see when you've driven 600 miles to get there.

Everywhere seemed deserted, but on a grassy patch overlooking the sea were two vans, one with a wetsuit draped over the wing-mirror and a hand painted board: "Suds Surf School". Inside, Suds and his mate Adam were drinking tea. I introduced myself and asked if they had been in. They hadn't.

'It might get better as the tide drops,' Suds suggested, almost apologetically. Ten minutes later, the tide hadn't dropped appreciably, so I was surprised to see them heading down to the beach. 'Are you going in?' I asked casually. As if it wasn't obvious. 'Yeah, it's dropping off. It's not going to get any better.' 'If you're going in, I'm going in!' I told them. It wasn't the last time on the trip I would use these words. Or at least think them.

From down on the beach, the waves looked a lot better. As I warmed up, I watched Suds catch a couple of nice left-handers. Tall and slim, he had the effortless insouciance of an athlete in his element, catching waves with ease and finding enough time to fit his crouched form into their fast, curving walls before riding up and over the back as they crumbled below him. 'This is it,' I thought as I paddled out. 'My surf trip starts here!'

With a brisk off-shore breeze blowing, the bay was a smooth surface on which to etch my hopes for the coming months. Neat lines of swell were pushing in with an insistent but relaxed rhythm, rising gradually to about chest high before breaking suddenly and powerfully in water about the same depth. Under a grey sky, the dull green water was fabulously clear, and not as icily cold as I had feared.

Ahead of me, the sea started to rise in a smooth line, as a pulse of energy slid towards the beach. I let it glide beneath me, marvelling at its energy and beauty. Behind it, a bigger line was rising more sharply. This was my wave. The first wave of the day. Of the trip. Of the book. It had better be a good one. I swivelled the nose of the board round to face the beach and started to paddle.

The last time I had surfed had been four months earlier – seven frustrating days in Portugal with a damaged shoulder, staying with Sarah and Aldo at Arrifana Surf Lodge. The previous time had been three months before that, when I had inexplicably wrecked the shoulder in some ugly shore dump in Barcelona. Several physios had inflicted excruciating pain on me in various ingenious ways to little effect, until an ultra-sound revealed no serious damage and my shoulder decided to recover. In other words, I was unfit. Fit enough for a few lengths of Brockwell Lido before breakfast but that's all.

8

As the wave got closer, I paddled more vigorously, gaining speed to match the speed of the wave, so it would pick me up, rather than slip away beneath me.

It slipped away beneath me. No matter. There would be another. It was a nice day, I was in the water, it felt like a holiday. Let's face it, so far it was a holiday. Another set of lines started to peak up as they approached. I turned and started to paddle. The wave got closer, chest high and clean. I paddled harder. Nothing. The wave slipped beneath me and headed towards the beach, breaking with a rumble several metres inshore. I was clearly in the wrong place. Further along, Suds was catching everything that moved. Even his portly friend Adam was catching a few. I wasn't at the best spot on the beach, but it wasn't markedly worse than anywhere else. Just a bit worse. Perhaps that crucial bit worse. But I didn't feel ready to share their peak.

A wave came. I wasn't going to let it escape. I was in a better position and paddled hard. I felt the subtle lift as it picked me up. I pushed myself up, ready to jump to my feet. For a brief instant, I felt exquisite uncertainty and anticipation, not knowing what was about to happen, but hoping and expecting to be on my feet.

Without warning, I was pitched into a flailing vortex of water and surprise. In the time it had taken my slow reactions to register that I had caught a wave, the wave had caught me – and thrown me aside without a backward glance.

The closer it got to low tide, the worse the problem became. The waves broke more and more abruptly, making timing more and more critical. Too early and you don't catch the wave. Too late, and you're pitched into a surging whirlpool of whitewash. One moment you're on flat water, the next you're staring at a vertical drop, and the next, you're no longer staring at it, you're falling down it, head first.

The only solution is speed: paddle hard, get up early, get to your feet as quickly as possible. This is what I told myself as I paddled out. This is what I told myself as I sat on my board waiting for another wave. This is what I told myself as I wondered if the whole trip wasn't a huge and costly mistake.

Again and again I tried. Nothing. On some waves, I pulled back. On other waves, I was swept over the falls. On others I skated on one foot, or worse, one knee. I did everything except surf.

Finally I'd had enough. But as I paddled for shore, I came across a small wave that had somehow sneaked through and was beckoning seductively. I paddled, desperate for any small consolation. This time, somehow, the wave failed to pitch me off. I found myself standing! Actually standing! On a wave! I was surfing! The shock was too much. I fell off.

Three days to get here, two hours in the water, one second on a wave. Not a great ratio. I staggered up the beach, extremely dejected.

WAVE 2 : Balephuil Bay, Tiree

From Tiree, my plan was to continue to the Outer Hebrides. There was only one onward ferry a week and it departed the day after I arrived, so I had a choice: stay for a day or a week. There are worse places to be stranded for a week, but I was afraid of the knock-on effect. An extra week in Tiree could mean a colder week in Cromer several months later. I opted for the single night. Though as it turned out, Cromer couldn't have been any colder.

With thirty hours to surf as much of Tiree as possible, three beaches seemed a reasonable target. I'd just surfed one, I could surf a second later that afternoon, and a third the following morning. Unfortunately, I hadn't reckoned with The Maze.

If any break is well named, it's The Maze. I soon found myself lost in a labyrinth of dunes and grass. Parts were boggy, parts thistly, parts hummocky and parts bullocky. Parts were all four at the same time. Luckily the bullocks were more bemused than belligerent. But all of it stood between me and the beach. For three-quarters of an hour I wandered the grassy moonscape, hitting peaks and troughs, both literally and emotionally. I skirted round hillocks that seemed too high and clumps of bullocks that seemed too dense. Apart from that I went straight, through bogs, thistles and thinly-spaced bullocks.

Eventually, disorientated and dispirited, I reached the last line of hummocks. Beyond it, I could hear waves crashing onto the sand. I could smell the sea. One final push, and there it was, the Atlantic, laid out at my feet, immense, majestic.... and flat. The crashing waves were an abrupt flutter of maritime exhilaration a metre or two from dry land. Certainly nothing to surf. And it still took me thirty minutes to find my way back to the van.

I consulted my unsuitable road atlas and decided to try Balephuil, where a narrow lane leads to a row of smart cottages at the end of another beautiful curving bay of white sand and turquoise water. A lush meadow runs down to the beach, and beyond, moorland stretches to a long, low hill a mile or two away. If anywhere made you want to surf, it was here. But by now, dusk was upon me and the waves were unconvincing. After a long day that might have been better spent chasing wild geese, I had run out of time.

11

The following morning, the swell looked sporadic and noncommittal. Even so, I was determined to surf. My ferry was leaving in under three hours and I intended to catch it with salt in my hair and sand between my toes.

The water was cool and crystal clear, with occasional strands of seaweed floating in the shallows and pristine sand below, tinted green. Small waves peeled gently, then crumbled into a benign froth that tumbled innocently towards the beach with all the power and menace of champagne fizz. If the sea had been actual champagne, I couldn't have been happier. With not a soul to be seen, I felt desperately privileged just to be there.

I paddled for my first wave and felt the weightless lift, the hidden hand that picks you up and offers you a ride. It's the cue to jump to your feet. Decent surfers do it in a single, graceful movement, with the agility of a cat. I'm more of an indecent surfer. I generally lumber to my feet with the agility of a lame rhinoceros trying to balance on a tea tray. By the time I found myself standing, the wave was breaking around me. But at least I was standing on a wave. OK, so it was white-water. It's what beginners surf. But after six months out of the water with a shoulder injury, for now I was happy enough to surf the white-water. I needed to reacquaint the soles of my feet with the top of my board. Never on great terms, recently they had started to drift apart.

The champagne fizz fizzled out and I fell back into the water's cool embrace. As I paddled back, I caught a glimpse of a fisherman's buoy. Or possibly a grey beach ball, floating in the water. The undulating waves hid it from view until I was barely ten metres away. It was grey, alright. It was wrinkled. And it was staring at me intently with black, shining eyes. For a moment, I thought it was an old man out for his morning swim.

But in the instant before it slipped beneath the water, I realised it was a seal, sitting in the line-up, intrigued by the intruder.

Up to then, my surfing had been confined to long, mainly urban, distinctly populated beaches. Not the type frequented by seals, or wildlife of any kind beyond the occasional gull or disorientated jellyfish. This was the first time I had seen a seal in the line-up. I couldn't have been more excited. The seal was somewhat less impressed. It slipped beneath the surface, popped its head up a minute or two later, glared and vanished. I didn't see it again, but for the rest of the session, I couldn't escape the feeling I was being watched.

I paddled out and waited for another wave, luxuriating in the serene pleasure of sitting on a surfboard thirty metres from the shore of a small island. I was adrift on the Atlantic, with no-one in sight and no worries except when to catch the next wave.

The pulses of energy grew sharper and steeper as a set arrived. I turned and paddled. This time I was in the right place. The wave picked me up and when I lumbered to my feet I found I was just ahead of the crumbling curl. Without knowing how or why, I was gliding easily along the face of a low, clean wall of green water. Nothing flash. Nothing dramatic. But at least I was balanced and in control, my feet firmly on the board.

The wave seemed to go on and on, unfolding slowly as it eased its way towards the shore. It wasn't fast, it wasn't big. What it was, was pure pleasure! With the weight on my front foot, I kept the momentum of the board flowing at the speed of the wave, careful not to outpace it, careful not to let it race ahead, keeping an eye on the low green wall that unrolled beside me. It was a blissful ride, calm and controlled. And a real relief after

13

yesterday's disappointment. The surfing had properly started! I couldn't think of a more beautiful place to begin.

WAVE 3 : Vatersay

Unused to island roads, I almost missed the ferry. Fortunately it was an hour late, so I went to explore and almost missed it twice. We nosed through the narrow sound separating Tiree from Coll and headed for the high seas, ploughing through a rolling swell, buffeted by a strong wind that made any excursion out on deck brisk and brief. I scanned the white-flecked seas for a glimpse of dolphins, a whale, even a rumoured pod of orcas. Not so much as a sprat.

Eventually a line of dark humps appeared, strung out along a pin-sharp horizon. As we approached, they gleamed silver grey against the glancing sunlight, and started to resolve themselves into a clustered string of islands with attendant islets and outcrops. The Western Isles! The name itself is evocative, redolent of myth and mystery, of far-off lands shrouded in mist and legend. Today, though, they were bathed in gold.

A rainbow heralded our arrival, arching over the small castle that sits in the middle of the bay at Castlebay, the main settlement on Barra. A few dozen houses lie scattered almost at random around the foot of a rocky peak that looms above the bay, giving the town a temporary feel against its immutable environment.

At the tourist office, I picked up a map and an eccentric hitch-hiker from Canada in search of her roots. We headed to Vatersay, a separate island no more than a few miles across, linked to Barra by a short man-made causeway. At the far end, two beautiful, curving beaches face in opposite directions, separated by a narrow isthmus. The law of probability suggested I would find waves on at least one of them.

I also found Frank, a tall, granite-jawed American from Edinburgh who had just surfed his way down the Hebrides from north to south. On Lewis, he had consulted a local, who had told him all the places to surf from Eoropie down to Vatersay, and he had duly gone and surfed them. Now he told me all the places to surf, from Vatersay up to Eoropie, and I would do the same. This is how surf culture should work. Not the protective withholding of information that seems to pervade most regions, and which I was to stumble across more than once on my travels.

Together we yomped eagerly over the machair to take a look at the waves. The bay to the east was an aqua marine mill pond, the beach swept smooth, not a footprint to disturb its wind-etched perfection. To the west, on the exposed side of the isthmus, the dunes fell away steeply to a beach strewn with small rocks and flotsam. Lines of swell were rolling in, slightly perturbed by a brisk wind which frizzed the surface of the sea.

It wasn't great, but it was Frank's last day and he was going in. And if Frank was going in, I was going in. Not yet surf-fit, I was tired from my two sessions on Tiree, but I was already sensing that if you're a lone surfer in the Hebrides, opportunities to surf in company are few and far between. If someone is going in, it would be rude not to join them.

The waves were about chest high, but the interval was low and the peaks all over the place. If you did manage to catch anything, it would turn out to be a crumbling Wensleydale of a wave, white and insipid and not worth the effort; or an oozing Brie of a wave, squat and shape-less. I caught a handful but they weren't going anywhere. Worse, if you stayed on the white-water too long, you paid the price for those few seconds of mediocre ride with a double dose of pummelling to get back.

This didn't seem to deter Frank, whose long board was far better suited to the shapeless conditions, and who was catching some reasonable rides. I would look up from yet another failed attempt to catch some slush and see Frank's upper half whizzing along in front of me. My chagrin was tempered by the knowledge that I had weeks ahead of me to catch better waves, and couldn't begrudge Frank these few crumbs on his final day. In the end I left him to it.

After a long search for somewhere to camp, the best I could find was a patch of grass by an unused jetty, just off the road back to Barra. I was pacing my temporary demesne when I heard a voice from the road. It was Frank. We had made a loose date to go for a drink, but I already knew I wasn't likely to make it. I hadn't left civilisation so long ago to be missing it. Instead I invited Frank to dinner.

'Have you eaten? I'm cooking sausages.' 'I'm a vegetarian.' I didn't mention the vegetable curry living in the bottom of my so-called fridge. I had cooked it some time in the summer and discovered it lying in suspended animation before I left. It had already thawed out, been refrozen, thawed out again and spent several days in the van, in a fridge that was marginally less efficient than a cardboard box. It probably hadn't tasted that good in the first place. Even so I was saving it for another day. Today was sausages. I needed to eat them before they turned green.

When I dug them out, they were already green. They

too had spent several days in a fridge that was marginally less efficient than a cardboard box. Fortunately it was getting late and the light was going, so I couldn't tell how green. Anyway, by the time I had burned them in the gloom, they were no longer green, at least on the outside. They tasted fine. So too did the vegetable curry when I finally ate it two days later, after scraping away a thick forest of furry mould. At least a cardboard box doesn't pretend it's trying to keep your food fresh.

I left Vatersay the following morning and headed back to Barra. Crossing the causeway, the sea was still a game of two halves. To the east, calm and serene. To the west, windswept and choppy. It was the same all over Barra. I know, because I travelled the length and breadth of the island in search of a wave. Where it was exposed to the wind, it was too rough. Where it was sheltered, too flat.

Determined to leave no beach unchecked, I headed up to the narrow peninsula that stretches out to the north of the island. Not another isthmus, more a spit with aspirations. Halfway along, another large bay stretched gently round in a wide curve, facing east. The beach barely shelved, and as the tide was low, it revealed an immense expanse of flat sand, where a couple of men were digging for shellfish. Unusually for a beach, this one had windsocks at regular intervals. As I approached, a large plane swooped down at my shoulder and touched down on the sand. Welcome to Barra airport. It's the perfect place for impatient holidaymakers: you emerge from your plane straight onto the beach! The drawback is that flight schedules are dictated by the tide. By mid-tide, the runway is covered in water and you would need a seaplane to get anywhere.

WAVE 4 : Tangasdale Beach, Barra

My lightning tour of the island confirmed that every-where was either hellishly choppy or fiendishly flat. But I had noticed something that looked suspiciously like a reef, in the bay behind the Isle of Barra hotel.

A reef is a submerged stretch of rock and for surfers – unlike for 18th century mariners – they are a good thing. They throw up clean, powerful, well-shaped waves with impressive regularity, and at a fixed point. The downside is that the waves are fast and furious, with little room for mistakes. The other downside, is that they are indeed reefs. What's creating the waves are rocks below the surface. So when you fall off, that's what you bounce along: rocks below the surface.

My experience of reefs was limited. To be precise, I had surfed just one. But one that will be seared on my neurones forever. Lagide in Portugal. A short right, but a long, long left breaking over shallow, urchin-incrusted rocks. When I had finally managed to catch a left, uninterrupted and sufficiently stable to survive the drop, I had glimpsed eternity. It was by far the longest, most satisfying, most exhilarating ride, the most endless wave, of my brief surfing life to date.

Crucially, I had been with a surf instructor, Billy, whose reassurance, encouragement and knowledge had been invaluable. On Barra I was on my own. No one to tell me when to go. No one to tell me when not to go. No one to tell me when to stay in my van and not be so utterly stupid.

Even with my limited experience, this reef looked pretty horrible. A gash of white-water marked the spot where it lurked, and every so often, as the infrequent sets came

18

in, a vicious wall of water rose abruptly up and abruptly hurled itself down again. It certainly didn't have a lovely, long shoulder to surf along. More of a dismissive shrug.

To waste time before making any rash decisions, I sat in the hotel car park and texted one of my sisters, who had a friend on Barra. It turned out that the friend ran the hotel and was no more than fifty metres away. She was on the phone trying to get to Rotterdam to see her boyfriend and clearly had little interest in the dashing surfer cluttering up her lobby.

Her young receptionist Juliet was more welcoming. It's in the job description. She told me that some guests had surfed the reef the previous week. I didn't think I was good enough, I admitted. Not on my own. I didn't want to drown alone and unmourned. 'I'll come with you, if you like,' Juliet offered. It seemed too good to be true. I stammered and stuttered and made noises about not wanting to impose. But I was delighted. I returned to the van to wait for her to come off her shift, and to watch the reef, as I vacillated between 'Yes, we can!' and 'Are you insane?'

Eventually Juliet appeared, full of apologies and potatoes. She was holding a plate of food, which at first I thought was for me. It wasn't. She wolfed it down, standing in the car park, and explained that she hadn't had any lunch. Not the ideal preparation for surfing. She too was having doubts, it seemed. Very gamely, though, she offered to keep an eye on me in case I got dashed onto the rocks or swept out to sea.

Together we clambered down the rocks looking for a suitable jump-off point. The incoming tide was swirling around with impressive force, and the distance between the top of the peaks and the bottom of the troughs was considerable. With every snarl of swell, the rocks revealed their ragged, rapacious teeth, hungry for a bite of surfer or surfboard. The wind that had blown all day showed no sign of abating, the sky was grey, and in the middle of the bay, the wave was heaving and crashing over the reef like a chained beast.

Did I really want to go ahead with this? Even if I timed my jump from the rocks to avoid being stranded by the backwash or pounded by the next wave, even if I was able to battle out to the reef against wind and tide, even if I was in the right place at the right time, I wasn't convinced I had the skill or nerve to catch one of the steep, plunging waves that hurled themselves down with frightening regularity. In short, I was terrified.

It was Juliet who threw me a lifeline. She was probably bored of watching me prevaricate. 'Why don't you just surf the bay?'

The bay! I had almost forgotten about the bay. Curving round on the other side of the rocks, it hadn't looked great earlier on. But now, with the tide coming in, evening approaching and my nerve failing, it looked a lot more appealing. 'I usually jump off the rocks because I can't be bothered to paddle out from the beach,' she added. The jump-off point was on the same outcrop of rock, but dropped straight into clear, deep water. With Juliet watching, I picked my way to the edge and stood, waiting for my moment.

My moment came. I missed it. Instead, another wave came rushing over the rocks, wrapped itself around my knees and tackled me to the ground. I sprawled inelegantly, one hand grappling to stop myself falling backwards, the other desperately trying to keep my board clear of the sharp-edged rock. I struggled to my feet and instinctively dived straight in, board first, onto the back of the wave that had just sent me sprawling. I listened for the crunch of fibreglass on granite, certain I would catch the tail.

Nothing. With relief, I realised I was out in calm water, leaving the land, and ignominy, behind me.

True to her word, Juliet perched on the rocks like a mermaid. I floundered around in the sea like a hippo. My timing was still all over the place, but the fat waves, toppled by the on-shore wind, ignored my ineptitude. I was very late for the first wave, a decent-sized right, about shoulder high, which was already starting to break as I paddled. I carried on regardless. If I hadn't, there was every likelihood it was going to steamroll over my attempts at a rethink and then steamroll over me. With the water crumbling around me, I fumbled to my feet, still early enough to have to ride out a sizeable drop, but then landing in white-water.

I still had a fairly ambivalent attitude to white-water. The ambitious side of me dismissed it as a waste of time and effort that won't get you anywhere except back to the beach. But my inner slacker was still happy to ride white-water, provided it had angle and attitude and enough power to propel you along at a decent whack. For an intermediate surfer, it's all about time on the board. Plus there's always a chance the broken wave will take you back onto the green face, either because you manage to catch up with it or because the wave reforms as it approaches the beach.

It didn't. But I was out in front, with the wave frothing behind me like a rabid dog. I was heading left, but the wall of water was already white ahead of me so I switched right, hoping to throw the hound off my tracks. It kept on after me. The right started to drop off, so I switched left again. But it was too late. I fell back into the hound's slavering maw, and let it slobber all over me.

The next wave was better. The same battle with timing. The same alarming drop, and an exquisite moment of doubt - was I going to bury the nose in the wave and get catapulted off the front? Somehow I managed to point the board just far enough to the right, and for a split second, I was on the face, the green wall ahead of me. But the shock of the drop and the abrupt shift of weight to save the nose meant my balance had gone overboard. I went after it, falling into the wave as it unfurled ahead of me.

I paddled out again, determined to get it right. This time, I was early. I felt the gentle lift as the wave picked me up, and I struggled to my feet. With the extra millisecond or two from catching the wave early, I had the time to angle the board as I took the drop, avoiding another nose dive. I was ahead of the curl, out on the face. The wave was fantastic! Shoulder high, with plenty of power, and a clean wall ahead.

But I was teetering like a tightrope walker. And the more unbalanced I felt, the worse it got so I found myself stretching and extending as I overcompensated one way, then had to teeter back the other, overcompensating again. It was the Laurel and Hardy school of surfing.

Somehow I managed to stay upright, catching fleeting glimpses of something more decorous, feeling the power of the wave behind me as I sped towards the beach. Too far towards the beach. I narrowly escaped a brusque encounter with the sand.

Rather than paddle out against the waves, I decided to walk along the sand and ride the current out beside the rocks where Juliet, to my surprise, was still sitting. 'I'm going in now,' she said, and did. I like to think she had realised I didn't need a lifeguard. I suspect she was just very unimpressed. None of the waves I caught after that would have impressed her further.

By morning, drizzle had set in and wisps of mist were drifting up the valley like ghosts. The tide was going

22

out so I went to see if I could lure Juliet out later. I was fully aware that I was now that saddest of specimens: a middle-aged man flirting with a woman – a girl, even – half his age. She didn't treat me with the scorn I richly deserved, though I detected a more professional *froideur* in her manner today. And no, she didn't want to come surfing with me, you sad old git. I made a dignified exit ('Oh please come surfing, please, please') and headed into Castlebay.

At the Community Hall, the annual island show had assembled an impressive cornucopia of cakes, jams, swollen vegetables, home-made biscuits, flowers, bread, pickles, knots, knitwear, prawns, duck eggs, crabs and even painted stones. I missed the prize-giving, so I'll never know who snatched first prize for One Knot or Three Shellfish, but I returned later for the auction. Produce had been divided between a dozen or so boxes, each containing bread, cake, jam, vegetables, various herbs and something from the non-edible categories. It was like harvest festival at a particularly generous parish, except it was all up for sale.

When the bidding started, islanders enacted long-standing jealousies, wreathed in laughter, to push the price of each box to around ten pounds – a bargain, even if you had no interest in knots or knitwear. All I was interested in was cake, and they all had cake. I watched for seven or eight lots, then decided to join in.

'Do I hear five pounds?' 'Yes,' I announced, and raised my hand. The room fell silent. All eyes turned on the impertinent outsider. There was an uncomfortable pause. 'Do I hear six pounds?' He didn't, and neither did I. I looked around, willing someone to make a counter-bid. None came. Tense silence gripped the room. 'Gone!' I was mortified. With all eyes watching, I handed over my five pounds, feeling as if I might be run out of town. In a bitterly-contested duel, the next box went for £12, which made me feel even more guilty.

Afterwards, I was talking to local teacher Robert Ross when his nine-year-old daughter bounced up, proudly showing off her certificate: second place for A Painted Stone. She was struggling under the weight of a rough stone block, 8cm across, painted white with black spots. It was like something a giant would use to play Snakes and Ladders.

'Do you want it?' she asked her father. He didn't. 'Do you want it?' she asked his colleague, Tunde. He didn't either. 'Do *you* want it?'

Before I could say anything, she handed it to me and skipped off to join her friends. When she returned, I tried to give it back but she shook her head. So instead I gave her the random non-edible item from my box: a purse made from butcher's string. Like synchronised swimming, it was impressive but virtually useless, and she almost certainly ditched it at the first opportunity.

I, on the other hand, still have the painted stone on my dashboard, as a rugged mascot and memento of my journey, an ironic Hebridean nod towards furry dice. I saw several cars in the Hebrides with genuine furry dice, which only added to my pleasure.

Beside it I placed a plastic cup with the herbs from my box, and when these wilted, a pot of parsley from the supermarket, as a token garden for my temporary home. Remarkably, the parsley flourished. Later I added a Taj Mahal snow shaker Karen sent me from India. The three items brightened up the van and were a welcome distraction in slow traffic or slow waves.

WAVE 5 : Traigh Stir, North Uist

After three days on the island, Barra felt like home. It had everything. Waves, scenery, Juliet. Stick it in the Mediterranean and it would be ruined instantly by unscrupulous developers and vomiting Englishmen.

South Uist, in contrast, was bleak, with dark cloud sucking what little colour there was from a colourless landscape. The single-lane main road plods north between a knuckle of unfriendly hills to the east, and to the west, peaty wetlands that ooze out towards the sea. A scattering of dismal farms and houses lurked down unsigned roads, muttering darkly among themselves.

The sea was flat, so I continued on, over the moss-green stepping stone of Benbecula, where I have since surfed the picturesque horseshoe bay at Culla, and on to North Uist, where Frank had marked two beaches worth trying.

Traigh Stir is a small bay a few hundred metres across between two low rocky points. On the horizon, Haskeir Island and its attendant skerries float like a passing armada. The tide was low, leaving a semi-circular arena of white sand streaming with rivulets. Infrequent waves pushed into the bay, but when they came, they were a decent size – easily head high, thick and powerful. Most of them backed off just as you thought they should break, but the ones that broke had a long, gentle face, and plenty of time to get to your feet. It was hard work, though, despite the lulls. A strong current pushed you gently but constantly out of position, and I was wary of the low menacing rocks at each end of the bay.

I was entirely alone – and happy to be so – but it was a disquieting sensation, surfing on an unknown beach, with no one around, no one even in view, and not so much as a derelict bothy overlooking the bay. For the first time I felt the trembling thrill of anxiety. I had surfed alone before, but on familiar beaches where I knew what was out there – and under there – and usually there had been people on the shore. The feeling of being so isolated was unnerving, a teasing disquiet. Not fear, but a tingling nervousness. Or maybe just a healthy awareness of where I was and what I was doing, an adrenaline edge to keep me alert. I couldn't ignore it, so I did my best to enjoy it.

I caught a few average rides, and a couple of times missed a wave I should have caught – a moment of inattention, a last minute lapse, a slight complacency. I was determined to catch a decent wave and saw one starting to rise up. I turned towards the beach, ready to paddle. When I looked back, the wave had changed from a benign pulse into a snarling monster, an aggressive left that had doubled in height. I was still determined to get it, and paddled hard, stumbling to my feet the instant I felt it pick me up.

To my amazement, I found myself standing high up on the face. It was an entirely new sensation, like being halfway up a ladder against a sea-green wall: there's more to climb, but you're still a long way up. It was a moment of magnificent thrill. I didn't have to do anything – just enjoy the moment and not fall off. As I marvelled, I caught a glimpse of the rocks. They looked a lot closer than they should have been. And they were speeding towards me. I panicked and lurched into an abrupt turn, desperate to get away. Hopeless. Rather than the graceful carving arc I should have etched into the dark green face, I must have caught a rail. The board came to an abrupt halt and bucked me off, mid-turn. I went flying, flat on my back, into the pit of the wave. I was winded with the sudden shock and jarring disappointment. So much for the magnificent thrill.

I paddled out, determined to try again, finding it harder and harder to hold my position with tiring arms. A wave came. Another left. I turned and paddled, a little late. I took off just behind the peak as it broke, struggling to keep my balance in the breaking whitewash, and surfed down the face amid the jostling foam. I managed to get through it, still balanced and with plenty of momentum to drive me on.

Without thinking about what I was doing, I was somehow in the right place, in the right position, knees flexed for a bottom turn. I looked up and was greeted by the most spectacular sight of my surfing life so far: a perfect, dark green wall of water stretched out ahead of me, its lip somewhere above my line of sight. Clean, crisp and powerful. It was the first time I had found myself in control on a clean wave as high as this and it was an exhilarating sight, impressive, almost majestic, with all its power and force bearing down on me.

This time I wasn't going to be distracted by distant rocks or dismal balance. I surfed along it, almost overawed by the situation, full of reverence for the majesty of the wave but alive with ecstasy and glee. Even when it crumbled and collapsed, I didn't want to let go. This had been my wave. My shoulders ached and I knew I wasn't going to get another, so I held on to the whitewash, surfing all the way to shore, exhilarated and very happy. Even when I got there, I was half-tempted to go back for more. But I knew this wave had been special. I didn't want to ruin it. I waded out and up the beach in a cloud of sheer delight.

As I returned to the van, a local surfer was just leaving. He was suitably dour and not impressed to find a foreigner surfing his patch. 'I haven't seen anything worth surfing,' he said with a scowl, and drove off. I didn't tell him I had just had the wave of my life.

By now I was following *The Shipping Forecast* religiously. With gale-force winds forecast, I drove to Lochmaddy, to meet up with two intrepid friends, Becca and Anne, who were cycling up the Hebrides. Their idea of a rest day was hiking out to the beach at Sollas in a 50mph wind, and as surfing was out of the question, I felt obliged to join them.

Driving rain drenched us as we walked, paused long enough for the screaming wind to dry us out, then drenched us again on the way back. Violent waves with crests trailing like comets flashed against the storm-dark sky and crashed onto the wide, white moonscape of the beach. Banshees howled and snakes of sand slithered at our ankles, while wind-dried flotsam bowled and cart-wheeled headlong past. It was hellish and exhilarating, and certainly no day for surfing.

By morning, the wind had dropped. I had a ferry to catch, but first I wanted to see the stone circle at Beinn Langais. Not to be missed, apparently. Although neither was the ferry.

I've always had a thing for standing stones. I vividly remember visiting Stonehenge as a child, in the days when you were still allowed to touch them – and as a five-year-old, clamber over them. Later I spent an idyllic teenage summer working on a campsite in Brittany, cleaning tents by day, and by night spending angst-filled hours alone among the menhirs. I could feel their energy as I watched for shooting stars against the glittering sky, and forlornly missed the then love of my life with the pain only a teen-ager can feel who has just mislaid his first girlfriend.

Driving up South Uist a few days earlier I had hiked up to the single stone above Staionebrig. It was overlooked by a phone mast and surrounded by discarded building material, which compromised its majesty. But when I put my ear to its weathered face, shaggy with lichen, I could have sworn I heard a distant battle cry. A passing seabird, perhaps, its call carried on the wind. But the effect was electric.

The stones at Beinn Langais are small and rough, almost indistinguishable from the rocks lying nearby. It's their alignment that marks them out, their unspoilt location that makes them special. Having misread the map, I approached from above, striding breathlessly across wild moorland in the sunshine to find the stones garlanded in bright heather, with the loch shining below, deep blue. I walked around them, savouring the calm and beauty of the place, enjoying the grass beneath my feet and the wind on my face, trying to take in the magnitude of their existence. Their age makes a mockery of human endeavour, their endurance underlines our transience. Whoever put them there, whatever their beliefs and struggles, their happiness and pain, they're gone, leaving no trace but this. Just as we'll be gone, our existence similarly unmarked against the immensity of time.

I reached out and touched the main stone, and felt its power. It was strangely reassuring. Almost like receiving the blessing of the island and being granted permission to continue with the trip. In the long run, it's all pointless anyway, so go ahead and pursue your little project, if it means so much to you. It's worth no more or less than anything else, so why not? I left feeling reassured, empowered, calm. As if I had just glimpsed the infinite and not been overwhelmed. Taking their blessing for the road ahead.

WAVE 6 : Scarasta, Harris

As if cycling up the Hebrides wasn't exercise enough, Becca also wanted to get a surf in. I had two boards and two wetsuits, and when we got off the ferry, the beach at Scarasta, a few miles beyond Leverburgh, seemed the ideal opportunity. What I didn't have, I now discovered, was a spare leash. While Becca happily floundered in the shallows catching plenty of broken waves, I headed further out, full of confidence and swagger after my triumph at Traigh Stir. My swagger was short-lived.

Surfing without a leash is an interesting experience. In the early days of surfing, you had no option, so you were always at risk of losing your board. Even today, lots of people surf without a leash in certain conditions. I'm not one of those people. Without a leash, you're constantly worried what's going to happen to your board if you fall off, so you only go for waves you think you can catch and ride safely. You become tense and wary, and your surfing suffers.

Even so, the waves seemed reasonable: shoulder high, fairly powerful, but buffeted by a strong wind that was sneaking round the hill to the south. And there was the small matter of several lines of white-water to negotiate. I got through the first thirty metres reasonably quickly, but after that, progress was impossible. No matter how hard I tried, there were always several more lines of crashing foam between me and the open sea. I paddled and duck-dived and recovered and paddled and duck-dived and still I was no further out. My optimism soon turned to despair.

Eventually I called a temporary truce. Was it my imagination or were the waves easier further down the beach?

30

I caught a miserable rag of whitewash back to the shore, collected Becca, who was doing fine in the shallows, and we walked down the beach.

Immediately things changed. This often happens. If you're trying and failing, instead of wasting energy in a struggle you're not going to win, it's better to get out, have a rest and take a good look at what the waves are doing. Now at least I was able to get through the white-water to where the waves were breaking.

The problem was what happened next. My smaller board felt as insubstantial as a nail file and without a leash, I couldn't commit. I just didn't want to let go of the board, because I knew it would end up in the shallows without me and I would be faced with a demoralising slog to get back out again.

Finally I admitted defeat. Becca had got out and was sitting on the beach. It was time to reclaim the larger board. The difference was instant. If nothing else, I had no excuses. I had to go for it. But the tide had dropped, and the waves were steep and hollow. Once again I found myself staring down the abyss of a gaping beach break. I duly went over the falls a few times – though at least now my board wasn't hauled away and hurled onto the beach. Eventually, with despair and exhaustion struggling for control over my now-battered body, I made one final attempt to actually surf. I put my remaining energy into one last paddle. I caught the wave. Leapt to my feet. I did it - I was up! The wave hollowed out and I plunged straight down the face, no time to turn. The nose dived deep into the water and I was catapulted off. Enough. I could paddle no more, and disconsolately called it a day.

WAVE 7 : Clach Steinigidh, Harris

After this debacle, I needed to regain my confidence. It was the start of a pattern I would come to recognise and repeat with depressing regularity: a great surf followed by a crushingly terrible surf, followed by the determination to erase the disappointment and grab at least an average surf, even if it meant going back to basics.

Between Scarasta and Seilebost were four or five tiny beaches nestling between the rocks. One looked promising, below a standing stone guarded by four doe-eyed highland cows. Waves were breaking about twenty metres out, opening up just enough for a quick ride, while in the shallows the storm had brought in a bank of kelp and seaweed, which was being churned around like dirty washing.

My arms were tired after the previous day's fruitless battle, but at least here it was easy enough to get out – you could wade most of the way, then paddle a few strokes into the line-up. When it came to catching the waves, though, either I didn't have the speed or they didn't have the power. Eventually we met halfway, on a chest-high wave with a clean face. It was going right, not too hollow, but not flat and formless either. I angled my board, paddled hard and caught it before it could get away. It was a decent drop down the face, but this time, with the slight angle, I was able to make it comfortably without plunging to the sea bed. I kept low, instinctively grabbing my rail and tucking into the curve of the wave. The shore was close, and the ride only lasted a few seconds. But a ride it was. A couple more followed, almost identical to the first: the weightless bliss of the drop, part hope, part fear, followed by the fleeting instant of electricity and awareness as you align yourself with the ocean; then the early, uncontrollable end as the wave explodes into a million droplets of water, each hurling themselves at the shore. Brief but blissful, an addictive injection of adrenaline, infinitely satisfying, yet immediately leaving you wanting another.

Exhausted but with honour restored, I drove up the barren east side of Harris, a bleak, beautiful, rock-strewn landscape punctuated by tiny coves; then on to Lewis, where I picked up a hitch-hiker at a bus-stop. Lennie was a retired fencer with hair as wild as heather and a face as weathered as the surrounding hills. English was his second language after Gaelic, and his sonorous voice, full of peat and whisky, was pure delight. As we drove, he pointed to a hotel just off the main road.

'Can you stop here?' he instructed. 'I have to cash a cheque.' I waited as Lennie hobbled into the hotel. A few minutes later he hobbled back. 'They wouldn't cash my cheque,' he grumbled. 'They've already cashed two today.'

A mile down the road, I noticed him taking surreptitious glances at me. 'Do you mind if I have a dram?' he eventually asked. He pulled out a hipflask and took a discreet nip. A few miles further on, he got it out again. 'Would you like a dram?' he offered. I was expecting some hellish firewater, but it was decent whisky, and we drove on in companionable silence.

The following morning, I met Lennie again. He had flagged a car down and was asking for a lift. The instant he saw me, he abruptly abandoned negotiations and shuffled over. My passenger door didn't unlock from the inside, so I had to get out and open it for him. I felt more like his chauffeur than a passing stranger. It was early, and this time his hip-flask didn't appear. Or maybe he had drunk it dry and was going to Stornoway for a refill.

WAVE 8 : Bru, Lewis

Up to now, every beach had been sandy and picturesque. Bru was different. Bru wasn't sandy and it certainly wasnt picturesque: a grey band of rocks and boulders strewn with fisherman's jetsam, below a scrubby fringe of harsh grass. Low clouds threatened violence against a bleak sky. At the water's edge, the stones rumbled ominously in the undertow and as I dived in, I heard the ugly grind of fins scraping on stone. It was an eerie, uncomfortable place, with a sense of danger lurking nearby. The sea was shark-skin grey, shark-skin rough. Beneath me, everything was shark-eye black.

I surfed below my best, catching just one clean, powerful left with a good drop and a brief, shoulder-high wall. But fear and foreboding tugged at my feet or tipped me over, and as time went on, I got colder and less confident. Miserable, almost.

Even getting out was tricky. Strong breakers lashed round the large boulders that skulked in the shallows, slippery with seaweed. I stumbled and slipped and scrabbled, trying to protect my board from the stones that stubbed my toes. They rumbled vague threats as I fumbled around, until eventually I managed to escape, bruised and dissatisfied.

I returned the next day, determined to do better. Conditions were worse. Much worse. It looked decidedly ugly, with a big swell, strong wind and huge, swirling waves. After a good long look I decided I had to go in anyway. Honour demanded it. I had to put the beach's demons to rest.

As I walked back to get my board, I was relieved to see a van appear. I wouldn't have to surf the monster alone.

34

Stevie, a rugged Daniel Craig lookalike, wound down his window. 'It's the best you'll find today,' he said, with a rueful smile. We changed and I followed him into the water, trying to take the same line through the shallows and out into the howling mess.

It was atrocious out there, a dark, heaving maelstrom splashed with white, as huge waves thundered down on us from out of a darkened sky. I'm not sure I would have managed it alone, but Stevie seemed relaxed and confident, and his presence calmed me slightly.

The sky darkened further. A squall of rain swept through. The roiling ocean pounded and pummelled us, bouncing us around like ants on a blanket, and we had to paddle constantly against the wind.

Stevie was catching outrageous waves with nonchalance and ease, taking off late, right under the lip, as the wave started to curl over his head. He would fly down the impossibly steep face into a dramatic bottom turn, then carve expertly along a violent, thundering wall of water that propelled him towards the shore, hidden from my sight by the exploding chaos. I was sitting further down the line, perfectly positioned to see the size of these monsters as he caught them. I would guess Stevie is around 5'8". When he stood, the waves were twice as tall as he was.

Overawed – and frankly terrified – by my surroundings, I couldn't catch a thing. I paddled too early, or stood up too soon or pulled back just in time, or baled out as I went over the falls. Classic mistakes of the unconfident. Or incompetent. Or plain cowardly. A couple of times I got caught beneath a large wave and held down in the cold black depths for what seemed like forever. As the waves continued to pound down on us, I grew increasingly frustrated and annoyed by my cowardice, my inability to launch myself into certain disaster.

Stevie didn't seem to mind. When we weren't paddling against wind and current, we chatted like old friends. It was rough, he acknowledged, and the wave was breaking all over the place. But you just need time in the water, he advised. It didn't make me feel any better, though I appreciated the surfer solidarity. He could have just ignored me. I was careful to stay out of his way, though, knowing I wasn't likely to get anything anyway, and not wanting to prevent him catching anything. If I thought he might go for a wave, I didn't even paddle.

He probably sensed this. Or perhaps he was throwing me a lifeline. Either way, I am immensely grateful. As we sat, a wave started to bear down on us. Alone, I would have certainly ignored it, and more probably paddled towards it, to get through it before it broke.

'You can have this one if you want it,' he said casually. I looked up to see an ugly wall of water snarling as it raced towards us. He was offering me a wave. I couldn't turn it down. Without thinking twice, I turned and paddled as hard as I could.

At first, nothing seemed to happen. I paddled even harder. This time I felt the gentle lift as the wave took hold of me, and I scrabbled to my feet, barely aware what I was doing. Barely time to register fear. Nothing else mattered, I just had to surf this wave.

I seemed to be on a high plateau of rough water, with a sharp drop somewhere ahead. There was a slight push as the wave started to propel me. I pressed down on my front foot, bringing my weight forward to seize its momentum. With a sudden burst of exhilarating acceleration, suddenly weightless, I was off, riding down the rough face of an immense wall of water, heading left. Spray was flying everywhere, shooting from the rails of my board. I was desperate to keep my balance on the choppy surface, aware of the struggle but somehow in control. I seemed to drop forever, speeding down an endless slope of seething water. There was a sudden bump and I felt the board take to the air, landing with a jolt a second later and continuing to speed on. Somehow, it failed to buck me off, and I held my balance.

The wave powered forward, taking me with it. I was on my forehand, face towards the wave, desperate to cling on as it thundered and rolled. It towered above me, well overhead as it surged on. It was utterly exhilarating, enthralling, amazing, a thrilling explosion of adrenaline and fear and elation rolled into a violent, unfurling vortex of water. I could barely believe I was surfing it, so different was it to anything I had ever surfed before. Or even experienced before.

Ahead of me, the wall started to break. I powered on and managed to get round the collapsing wall, back on to the rough green face, still immense as it sped towards the shore. I was hanging on desperately, thrilled and exhilarated and elated, unable to take it all in, instinctively and unconsciously calling on every ounce of experience I could possibly muster to stay upright and in control. It was sublime and astonishing, and it went on forever.

Ahead of me, the wall started to close down, falling more steeply away before exploding with a final crash of energy. I was concerned I would be caught under it and swept closer to shore, where the rocks lurked beneath the surface. Just before it collapsed, still tall and powerful, I made a desperate dive up and over the low wall, aware it was about to take me out in a mass of crashing foam. I landed in black water and came up, elated, electricity coursing through my body. A hundred metres away, Stevie was watching. He saw me reappear, and gave me the raised fist, the surfers salute. I had done it!

WAVE 9 : Eoropie, Lewis

Saturday night in Stornoway is a great place for a whisky crawl. Every bar has live music and a selection of single malts, and Becca, Anne and I celebrated our Hebridean adventure like locals. Sunday is a different matter. They take their Sabbath seriously on Lewis. Nothing is open, nothing moves. As I drove the deserted road out to Eoropie, I passed church after sombre church humming with hymns, but not a soul in sight.

I was exhausted, my body limp and relaxed, with the luxurious looseness that comes with long, tiring sessions in the water. It was my last day on Lewis; I barely had the energy for a final session but I really wanted to surf the northern tip of the Hebrides.

On the way, I had a quick look at Bru, just in case. Fortunately it wasn't breaking. Neither was Barvas, a reef on the far side of the bay. Instead, Eoropie was perfect. It's a long, wide, gently-shelving beach surrounded by rolling dunes and lush meadows leaping with rabbits. The storm had passed, leaving chest-high waves that rolled lazily to shore in the late afternoon sunshine. Perfect for an exhausted surfer's elegiac final session.

After the drama and violence of Bru, this was paradise. Almost immediately I caught a fabulous right that opened slowly, allowing me to follow the curl in a controlled crouch, feeling the unhurried power of the ocean as it pushed onwards, clean and smooth. The contrast to the panic and nerves of the last few days was vast. This was bliss. I made a fat cut-back and stuck to the pocket as the wave unfurled, rolling on and on, not like the speeding express train at Bru; more like a free-wheeling bicycle. It felt like a bigger, longer, more powerful bookend to the first wave I had caught, back on Tiree: the same insouciant ease, the same relaxed power and slow, steady advance, the same pleasure and surprise.

Eventually I dragged myself up the beach and went to investigate the very tip of the island. Gannets wheeled and plunged into the clear water like darts, emerging a few seconds later like broken umbrellas struggling to reassemble themselves, before flapping off to try again.

As I drove back to Stornoway, the churches were still humming in the gathering dusk, their windows bright with God and electricity. I felt like a heretic. But a happy one.

The following morning I caught the early ferry back to the mainland. Ullapool was resplendent. A row of white houses lined the quayside to greet us, gleaming in the bright sunshine. I couldn't bring myself to leave, and spent a melancholy hour wandering the foreshore, where huge jellyfish, stranded by the tide, oozed like iridescent dinner plates.

A few hundred metres out of town I came to a T-junction with a stark choice: north or south. I desperately wanted to continue north. That's where my journey lay. But there were two things I had to do first, both important, both to the south. It was too soon to be interrupting my journey, but I had no choice. Reluctantly, I turned right. South.

Two

The North Coast of Scotland

I left the van at Tarbert station and caught the train to London clutching a barbecue to jettison, my sheets to wash and several empty cartons to recycle. I felt like a Martian on shore-leave.

A week later, I was back, with sheets freshly laundered and Karen at my side. I should have been heading straight up to the north coast, but first I had to make a brief detour to Kintyre. Karen had been invited to her fabulous friend Moira's amazing birthday weekend at Saddell Castle, and I was her 'plus one'. It was the first time we had appeared in public and we duly played the cute/cloying new couple: whispering in corners, smooching on the dance-floor... and sneaking off for a surreptitious surf.

WAVE 10 : Westport, Kintyre

While the rest of the party went for a walk, we drove to Westport, at the top of a featureless beach that stretches all the way down to Machrihanish. A brisk westerly wind had banished the clouds and bright sunshine glanced off the sea as if it were armour. In the car park, a local surfer was sitting on the fence. 'How is it?' I asked. 'Pisch.'

He wasn't wrong. The wind was kicking up choppy, chaotic swell and only the local surf school were out, struggling with wind as much as tide. But I hadn't surfed for a week. Pisch or not, I was going in.

Sure enough, it was pisch. A strong current swept you towards a patch of boulders, or sucked you into a deep lagoon where the waves weren't breaking but you couldn't escape. Where they were breaking was all over the place, left, right, never where you expected and mostly round your ears. With the wind howling and the spray flying and whitewash coming at you from all angles, it was a constant struggle just to stay on your board, let alone make any kind of progress. If the sun hadn't been shining, it would have been miserable. Instead it was glorious! Not classic conditions, and something of a challenge. On the other hand, a wind-blown battle is good for your fitness, good for your stamina, even good for predicting where and when an approaching lump is going to break. I persevered. But first I got out to have another look. I had learned my lesson from Scarasta.

The most consistent wave was breaking on a reform, so that's where I headed, staying well clear of the rip, the rocks and the whirlpool. I caught a few: a quick catch, a brief fling, an abrupt end. Only one opened up, heading right, not even waist high. Scant reward for the effort, but reward no less.

Surfing over, we rejoined the party to continue a glorious weekend of warmth and friendship.

We returned recently in less happy circumstances, for Moira's funeral. A wonderful, generous soul, she was killed by a truck on Lambeth Bridge as she cycled to work. Words cannot express how senseless, avoidable and tragic her untimely death was, or how sad it makes me to remember that glittering weekend and its glittering

41

hostess. In the words of the minister, may she rest in peace and rise in glory.

WAVE 11 : Machrihanish, Kintyre

The party ended and everyone else went home. On a grey, drizzly Monday, Machrihanish was as dour and dreich as anywhere in Scotland. Still, I had a job to do. From the car park, I walked along the main street in my wetsuit and down a track through the links, where three golfers were just teeing off into the drizzle. A fourth was playing his ball from the five-mile bunker that is the beach.

A powerful swell was rolling in, about shoulder high, and at the southern end of the beach, where it curves gracefully round to meet the village, the wind was just offshore enough to clean up the faces of the waves. As I paddled out, I caught a glimpse of something floating in the water. An old spar, perhaps, blackened and weathered with age. My initial concern was that it might be a rock. Where there's one, there may be others. Whatever it was kept disappearing from sight as the peaks and troughs rolled under me, so I was almost upon it when I realised it wasn't a spar, but a seal. It was asleep, dreaming of fish, its nose out of the water to breathe as it floated. When I was no more than ten metres away, it woke with a start. Noiselessly, it closed its wide nostrils and slipped beneath the surface without a ripple. One moment it was there, the next gone. It reappeared a little further away, took a look at me, then disappeared for good.

The sea was an unrelenting grey, the sky a symphony of greys and blacks. Only the brilliant white of the breaking waves interrupted the monotone, and on land, the strip of dull green stretched out behind the strand of even duller yellow. The waves were a decent size, slow-moving, almost majestic, until they were toppled by a revolutionary rabble of whitewash, a good seventy metres from shore.

Getting out was easy enough but now the waves seemed to be breaking with renewed violence. Several times, as I attempted to duck-dive through an onslaught of crashing whitewash, I was taken aback, literally and figuratively, by the force of the water. As soon as I could, I picked out a wave and turned to paddle. A sizeable left was breaking, offering a nice shoulder with a clean, smooth face, brushed smooth by the sweep of the wind. I took off and pushed myself up. Too much messing around in mediocre conditions had made me lazy. Or if not lazy, imprecise. My feet were a little far back, and as I planed down the face of the wave, I danced around, unable to catch my balance long enough to establish a stable base. Ahead, the wave crumbled, and though I tried to stay upright on the desperate whitewash, I couldn't.

I paddled back, further out this time, beyond the clutches of the late-breaking waves, to wait for something bigger and better. Eventually it came, a luscious wall of water, again breaking left. I set off, planing down the huge expanse of the shoulder, feet facing the wave, properly balanced this time and in control. Not a combination I was too familiar with. So unfamiliar, in fact, that I didn't really know what to do next – except keep going. So I did, and found myself way ahead of the curl, on what felt like a tall, green wall of water. Not steep, perhaps, but far from flat.

Unnervingly, everything seemed to fall silent. The roar of the wave had disappeared and for a moment I was discon-nected from space and time, frozen in a sublime snapshot of eternity, my senses alive but unable to understand what was happening. It felt like nothing I had experienced before, a disjunction between the thrill of movement and the silence around me. My eyes and feet and every pore of my skin were alive to the exhilaration of the situation; my ears were somehow in a separate universe.

In my silent reverie, I was in danger of outrunning the wave. I came round in a careful cut-back, looking for the curl. Then back, cheek to the wave for a final short run before it closed down, rocks still on my mind as I dived off into the crashing foam.

* * *

I dropped Karen in Oban and continued north, back towards Ullapool. Along the way was the most westerly point on the British mainland, at the end of the Ardnamurchan Peninsula. It looked like a minor detour, with the chance of a surf before the long drive north. I thought I should take a look.

It turned out to be a slow, single-lane slog through thick pines, with occasional glimpses of beautiful bays but enough traffic to halt momentum at every turn. At the end of it, Sanna Bay was gloomy and unwelcoming. A small group of unfriendly houses lurked below a blasted heath, and the few souls in evidence glowered from dark doorways, shunning drizzle and strangers alike. And, of course, the sea was flat.

I can see how, in a better mood, in better weather, if you're a better person and there are better waves, Sanna is nice enough. But I was rather disappointed. Somewhat demoralised, I spent the night in the lee of a ruined house, then continued to Ullapool, where blustery autumn had blown away the sunshine. I slept on the quayside and left early the next morning, destination north.

WAVE 12 : Melvich

By the time I finally reached the north coast, I was desperate to surf. The wind was buffeting in from the east, and the beaches around Durness were rough and unsurfable. I kept going, driven on by implacable wind and howling impatience. Further west, the map showed a handful of deep bays protected by jutting headlands. Farr Bay, Strathy, Melvich – names that meant nothing to me then but are now etched on my memory. They promised shelter from the worst of the wind, and on the map didn't look too far. Perhaps forty miles as the curlew flies, with a couple of sea lochs to wiggle around on the way. I had been driving for two days straight. What was another hour?

Except it was another three hours. What looked like a quick squiggle round a loch was a forty-minute trek, urged on by wind down one side, pushed back vigorously up the other. Twice. With a lot of moorland in between. Devastatingly beautiful, but my tired mind was on other things.

When I finally got to the first sheltered beach, Farr Bay, I couldn't believe my eyes. Surfers! Three surf vans drawn up like a wagon train in hostile territory. I parked badly and jogged down to the beach, crossing paths with a local farmer. From his expression, hostile territory was exactly where I was. Four surfers were in the water, but no one seemed to be catching anything in swirling conditions. On the beach, a fifth surfer suggested Strathy, 15 minutes along the road. I had come this far, what was another 15 minutes? I left them to it.

I was to run into this motley group several times over the next two weeks, and would soon regret not joining them on that first afternoon. Or at least not making the effort to get to know them. Surfers were few and far between, so it was worth making friends with people who knew the area and had a weather eye out for the waves. This I realised with hindsight. For now, I just wanted to surf. I continued eastwards, hoping to find somewhere before it got dark.

At Strathy, two surfers were just getting out. Try Melvich, they suggested? It was beginning to look as if I had missed my chance.

Melvich greeted me with near-perfect conditions. The sea was as smooth and bright as the slow river flowing down to meet it. Elegant lines pushed sedately into the bay, rising up to head height, sharp as knives, before cascading over in a photogenic curl that peeled its way smoothly along the full length of the wave. The wind had dropped entirely and all was quiet, apart from the regular crash of the surf. As dusk approached, I grabbed my board and headed into the water, revelling in the solitude and tingling with anticipation.

Given such sublime conditions, I would like to report that I rode the waves like a surfer possessed. It wasn't quite like that. The curl might have been photogenic but it was intent on hurling me over. Several times it sent me flying over the falls into the gaping abyss, a horrible, plunging descent of flailing arms and stubborn fibreglass, with the uncertainty of how you and your board are likely to interact when you land.

I realised I had to be a bit more circumspect about which waves I chose to paddle for. They all looked perfect. They weren't all perfect for me. Eventually, rather than the thundering, hollow stallions that raced by, casting me aside as they went, I spotted a smaller, slower beast which tolerated my tiring efforts and let me clamber onto its broad back. Not a great wave, but a relief to be on it. And it gave me a boost of confidence. Not every wave was impossible.

I went for several more, arms tiring with each one. I realised I needed to go back to basics. Paddle hard. Catch it early. Otherwise I would be spending the evening – maybe the trip – being hurled over the falls or shaken off the shoulder.

Darkness was approaching and I was tiring. Too much falling off waves. Too much paddling back into position. Too much going for the wrong wave. So I waited for the right wave. Obvious, really. And when it came – or one that looked like it – I paddled as hard as I could. It caught me, earlier this time, and I got to my feet, staying low, heading down the face on my backhand, my outside arm not quite grabbing the rail, but hovering close, keeping me in position. I flew down the face of the wave, balanced and with enough control for a rudimentary bottom turn to keep me in the pocket. Ahead of me, the wave was closing down. I had no more energy left, so I surfed out the white-water, still powerful as it gushed over flat, dark shallows shining with the reflection of the reddening sky.

The following morning, the swell had dropped slightly and the sun was out, startling the landscape into a display of shocked brilliance. Relaxed and happy, I was able to take a better look at my surroundings. From the road, a rough track clatters down the hill, over a cattle grid, past cows grazing the long grass and into a small, sloping parking area. Dunes covered in thick marram grass obscure the shore, below a deep blue strip of open sea framed by steep headlands. In the valley bottom down to the right, the slow-moving mirror of the river takes a final languorous curl before flowing into the sea. A lone fisherman often stands at its edge, casting a fly onto the unruffled surface, barely troubling the reflection of an elegant grey mansion on the far bank.

WAVE 13: Balnakeil

I could have stayed at Melvich for weeks, but I had a trial to attend. Yes, m'lud, a dog trial. I thought it would be a good way to meet some locals and gather material I could use if I ever got round to writing a book about the trip. I was right on both counts, and for a while imagined attending idiosyncratic events the length of the British coastline in order to pack my narrative with colourful characters and amusing anecdotes. Fortunately for both of us, patient reader, it was my last conscious attempt at conjuring up material. After this, it's just surfing, more or less. But that morning, I was still hoping to be Bruce Chatwin or Paul Theroux, so I turned away from the waves and set off on the long trek back to Durness.

My knowledge of sheepdog trials was limited. I was expecting a garrulous group of farmers, farmers' wives, weathered farmhands and buxom milkmaids, milling around a cosy farmhouse kitchen, where an immense table groaned with freshly-baked cake. I was disappointed. Whether it was the wind or a natural proclivity for solitude, the farmers and their wives stayed in their cars, parked in two neat lines facing a large sloping field. For refreshment, an urn was propped on straw bales in a draughty barn. As for buxom milkmaids, I guess there's not much call for them on a sheep farm.

The competitors were, to a man, clear-eyed, lusty

farmers with bad knees and an average age of 137. To a dog, they were sleek, keen and vulpine. The farmer would stand at the bottom of the field as four sheep were bundled through a gate at the top, a quarter of a mile away, where they wandered around, bewildered. At a word from the farmer, the dog would tear up the hill in a long arc, then swoop down on them. Like a wolf on the fold, in fact. Whereupon the sheep panicked and ran, while the dog tried to usher them down the hill.

It was basically a drive-in for farmers showing the same short film (*"Sheep in a Field"*) on an endless loop. After an hour I knew the plot and most of the subtext. Anyway, I wasn't here to watch sheepdogs; I was here to surf. The wind was still howling but the tide should have turned. It was time to take a break between reels.

Sango Bay was flat so I headed to Balnakeil, a mile west of Durness. While the sheepdog trials just over the hill were wreathed in cloud, Balnakeil was bathed in beautiful sunshine. A small swell was running, mostly wind chop, weak and shapeless and scoured by the rasping gale. Only the waves at the western end, sheltered by a churchyard on a low headland, had any kind of shape. Here a slight rip weaved around the scattering of rocks, luring surfers in with the promise of an easy ride and the risk of a bite taken out of their boards to pay for it.

But no sooner had you left the sanctuary of the rocks than you were blown into the maelstrom, where waves became a lottery. The only solution was to stick close to the cliffs and catch whatever came your way. A few of them opened up enough for a brief ride, but then you were left exposed, forced to wade back to the rocks or struggle out against the wind. The water was crystal clear, though, and apart from one slightly longer left, the highlight of the session was not the surfing, but striding through shallows speckled like a minestrone soup with weed and the deceptive fleeting flashes of fleeing fish.

WAVE 14: Strathy

The weather didn't look like improving, so again I headed for shelter. For the third time in three days I found myself trundling along the northern edge of Britain, this time in fierce rain and a gusting south-westerly gale. I had surfed Melvich. It was time to try Strathy.

As I rounded the bumpy hillside, I was amazed to find the car park beside the graveyard buzzing with surfers in various states of undress, shrugging off the persistent Scottish drizzle. One unfortunate had driven from Aberdeen, five hours away, only to wrench his ankle on the steep hill down to the beach. He was still in his wetsuit, disconsolately showing off an ankle the size of a grapefruit.

The line-up was busy without being too crowded, and the atmosphere was relaxed and friendly. The wind had cleaned up the bay, leaving a smooth expanse of water undulating with powerful pulses that slipped in like serpents before exploding onto the beach. The waves were well overhead and mirror smooth, and there were some very good surfers, catching some very impressive rides. I wasn't going to get a look in on the main peak so instead I chose a side peak, and sat on the shoulder, waiting for the right wave. Conditions were excellent, and even the side peak would have stood comparison with a good day at a lot of beaches.

It was here that I first saw Achilles. He had just got up on a fabulous wave, a little over head high. He took it perfectly, just as it was about to break, with a long, peeling wall of water stretching generously ahead of him – so far ahead, unfortunately, that someone else decided to paddle into it too. Not out of malice, I suspect, but inexperience – either he hadn't seen Achilles, or didn't realise he was about to get in his way. But according to the unwritten rules of surfing – and to common sense – if someone is already riding a wave, they have priority on that wave, and everyone else has to pull back and stay out of the way.

From my vantage point further down the line, it was like watching a slow-motion car crash. I knew what was about to happen, but I could do nothing to prevent it. The novice caught the wave and struggled to his feet, bringing that beautiful wall tumbling down. Behind him, Achilles kept surfing, and would probably have charged into him if the novice hadn't fallen off just as the wave, now a chaos of disruption, gave a final harrumph and crashed itself into oblivion, obliterating them both.

The novice spluttered to the surface in a tangle of leash and limbs. As he looked around to get his bearings, the first thing he saw was his nemesis, giving him a glare that would freeze a wave mid-curl. From his expression and body language, I thought Achilles was about to paddle over and punch him. Instead, he made sure the unfortunate novice was locked into his laser-like stare, then jabbed two fingers towards his own eyes in the universal sign for 'Look where you're going!' Message delivered, he turned and paddled for shore, tired of the errors of fools. I don't know how the novice felt, but I was a disinterested onlooker and it had put the fear of God in me.

When I got out an hour later, the car park was wet and sullen. The mood had changed from happy anticipation to bristling introspection, unusual for a surfers' car park. The rain didn't help, dampening clothes and moods, driving everyone into their vans as soon as they had peeled off their wetsuits. As I dragged myself back to the van, I spotted Achilles' board, a distinctive, brightly-coloured short board, fat and almost fish-like, with plenty of volume to catch waves easily. It lay fins up in the rain, beside a menacing van with blacked out windows that had parked high up on the grass overlooking the beach and to hell with anyone else. I scurried past in case Achilles should emerge, fiery eyes blazing.

I saw him a little later, walking his black dog. He was unmistakeable: tall and muscular, with granite features, like an Easter Island statue, but less likely to break into a smile. He carried himself with the easy self-assurance of an athlete, powerful and composed. He was like a warrior-king of classical mythology. I am Achilles. The ground itself quaked as he passed.

* * *

On a wet Sunday afternoon, with the swell dropping and the rain picking up, the car park beside the graveyard was no place to sit around in a damp van. It was time to venture into Thurso.

I had heard a lot about Thurso. What surfer hasn't? It's Britain's most famous reef break, a glorious slab of Scottish flagstone that throws up powerful, reeling waves into a chilly river mouth. That was Thurso the wave. Thurso the town, on that wet afternoon, was crashingly underwhelming. It squatted in a crease in the hills like a scorpion guarding its lair, a dark stain against the vibrant green of the surrounding countryside. Grey stone build-ings closed in around you, damp and indifferent. Even the sky, so wide and generous out on the moors, weighed heavily on the town, menacing the streets with rain and demolition.

The only place open was a bar called the Y-Not, a name that invited a catalogue of answers including (but not restricted to): the loud music, gloomy modern decor, soulless atmosphere and immoderate prices for unpleasant beers and disgusting wines. On the plus side, it had a plug and a wifi signal, and for the next two hours, I made it my home.

I was about to leave when Achilles walked in with a group of acolytes. My instinct was to slide down in my seat, finish what I was doing and slink away. I'm not in the habit of approaching strange men in bars, surfers or otherwise, and particularly not thugs like Achilles. On the other hand, they almost certainly knew more than I did about surfing in Scotland – which was not difficult, as I knew nothing – so I went over to say hello. And they were charming, of course. Or as charming as a gang of dour, semi-feral builders from Leeds and Scarborough are likely to be when the fat kid (or in this case, the old kid) turns up and asks them – more or less directly – if he can be their friend.

Achilles himself sat slightly apart, aloof. I told him what I was doing, and he nodded his approval, watching over his court while the jesters competed for his attention. When they left, he invited me to join them in the farmyard at Thurso East. But after the mayhem at Strathy, I didn't fancy another muddy circus, camping in a bleak, manure-streaked, rain-runnelled farmyard. I wasn't planning on surfing Thurso, still less under the watchful eye of this band of seasoned surfers. I muttered something about Melvich, and headed in the opposite direction, regretting my decision with every dark mile.

The mud-streaked, rain-runnelled car park at Melvich

on a cold Monday morning was bleak enough, although at least I had it to myself. Spiky marram grass guarded the path to the beach, and every fruitless foray to check the waves was a damp and painful gauntlet of pricks and drips. Strathy was no better, Armadale worse. I returned to Melvich and postponement. The caravan of Yorkshire surfers rolled through on their way back towards Durness. I had driven that road three times in three days. I was in no hurry to do it again. They left me to my melancholy.

Finally, as the dark clouds grew yet darker with the threat of impending dusk, I reluctantly pulled on my damp wetsuit and trudged back towards the beach, alone. The water was like ale, brown and translucent from the peat that washed off the hills, with a light, foamy head where the waves swilled onto the beach. It was like surfing in beer, unusual but not unpleasant.

Immediately I caught three waves. Paddle hard. Catch early. Each was better than the one before, the third one a real gem. I wasn't exactly springing to my feet, but the fatter wave and earlier catch gave plenty of time to clamber to your feet and set your line. And where before the wave had closed down on me almost as soon as I was on it, this time it walled up ahead. It's a sight to lift the heart and quicken the pulse, the promise of speed and exhilaration, the lotus fruit that the surfer addict yearns to taste. I emerged revitalised, the dark dogs banished, my mood restored.

The weak October sun that broke through the following day was welcome relief, a chance to dry out damp towels, damp carpet, damp clothes, damp mood. I did the rounds of the local beaches. Still nothing. But as I sat and watched the waves at Farr Bay, I was joined by the least likely surfmobile I had seen: a maroon Mini – built in the days when mini really meant mini – with two long surfboards strapped to the roof, overhanging front and back to an alarming degree. Crammed inside were two large men, lanky Michael and his stocky co-pilot Roddy in sturdy tweed trousers and a thick Aran jumper. Together they looked like competitors in the Wacky Races, a surfing Sancho Panza attending his garrulous Don Quijote.

Later, I was surfing at Melvich when they reappeared. Michael rode a tall, skinny Rocinante of a board, while Roddy puffed along on a fat BIC donkey, paddling happily in the head high swell without actually catching anything. He told me it was only his second surf ever. After that, I kept out of his way.

The tide was filling in and the waves weren't great, but Michael was very philosophical about it. "We see too many photos in magazines and videos, and it's not always like that," he told me. It's a sentiment I like to remember whenever conditions aren't ideal, which is often. Or when my surfing fails to light up the waves, which is almost always.

* * *

In Thurso, I had scribbled the five-day wave forecast on a paper bag and from what I could decipher, now was a good time to head back west, to try Sango and Can of Beans. But did I really want to drive all that way again for the sake of a couple of beaches and the chance to see Cape Wrath? I had surfed Balnakeil, surely that was enough.

At issue was the essence of the trip. If I was going to try and surf all the way round the coast, I couldn't really justify missing two key beaches and a sizeable chunk of coastline. To do so would damage the integrity of the whole project. As for Cape Wrath, although not surfable, it's the furthermost corner of Britain. If I was going to start cutting corners, I might as well turn round and head straight for Newquay. Slightly reluctantly, I set off along the roof of Britain once again.

WAVE 15: Ceannabeinne

A couple of miles before Durness, the road sweeps past a small beach cut into the cliffs like a bite from a sponge cake. A steep path bounces down the hillside from hummock to grassy hillock, alongside a swirling, peaty burn. The map says Ceannabeinne and it took me a while to realise this was the renowned Can of Beans.

It's a pretty beach, the kind that makes you want to surf, and to surf well. I had driven past several times, and it had always looked small, clean and fast. Today it wasn't small and it certainly wasn't clean. And if it wasn't fast, it wasn't slow either. Did I really want to go in? Not really. I sat in the van watching.

Eventually a surfer appeared carrying a BIC board. I was interested to see how he would cope with the heavy conditions, and to find out just how big the waves were. Without someone surfing, it's often difficult to gauge. As soon as he paddled out, I could see they were considerably bigger than they had looked. What swung it, though, wasn't the size of the waves or the presence of a beginner on a BIC. It was a seal. A huge, ravaged male, staring with intent at the ungainly intruder. I grabbed my board and headed down to join them.

When I got there, the surfer was getting out and the seal had left. So much for surfing with seals. Or surfers.

His name was Jerry and he had the neat moustache and clipped accent of a World War I flying ace. I didn't establish whether he was actually a fighter pilot, but given the number of RAF personnel I encountered around the coast of Britain, it wouldn't surprise me.

The waves were pouring in thick and fast, with a low interval turning the shallows into a swirling mess. But at the east end of the beach, where low cliffs cut into the bay at an abrupt angle, a powerful rip whisked you past the rocks and out into the bay. To add to the excitement, the sharp angle of the cliff obscured the waves from view, so they seemed to appear from nowhere, stampeding round the corner in a frenzied chaos, like corralled cattle tripping over one another in wide-eyed panic.

I waded out beside the cliff and waited. Each time I thought the coast was clear, a rogue bull snorted with derision and charged round the corner. There was no way of predicting when; you just had to go. I entrusted myself to the speeding rip and immediately a raging beast bristled ahead, ready to charge. I paddled to meet it, pushed down on my board and managed to dive under the foaming lip. When I came up, I was being carried away from the rocks. A couple more strokes, angling out towards the bay, and I was sitting in the line-up, ready to surf.

Except the rip had other ideas. It wanted to sweep me into the middle of the bay, where a different peak was breaking, all chop and violence and unpredictable explosion. There was a choice: fight back against the rip in the hope of catching a peeling right-hander off the rocks; or let yourself drift and catch a heavy left-hander breaking into the bay. Not that it was really a choice. With no alternative, I tried for the left-hander. Big mistake. The wave caught me and tossed me down in a chaos of white-water, trampling all over me then leaving me floundering limply around the impact zone. I tried to battle back out against the breaking waves but it was hopeless. I had to wade back to shore, walk over to the corner, and risk the dangers of the rip again. At least the rip took you where you wanted to go, and with very little effort. I repeated the cycle several times, stopping once or twice to chat to Jerry, who had seen the rip in action and decided to have another go. It was a relief to share the frustrations of the session with another surfer, though it didn't help much. Neither of us wreathed ourselves in glory.

* * *

Cape Wrath is one of those places that attract you by name alone. It sounds dramatic and violent, a place of terrible storms and seething currents, a place to approach with trepidation and fear. It's not quite the most northerly point in Britain but it's more exposed, more dramatic and far more isolated than any of our island's other extremities. And a lot harder to reach. Sticking out at the topmost corner of Britain, it feels like the very end of the world.

To get there, a ramshackle ferry chugs across the Kyle of Durness, with room for a dozen tightly-packed tourists, a dog and a Yorkshireman, who cranks up an ancient minibus waiting at the far side and jolts you across ten miles of rugged moorland to the lighthouse at the end of the world. Beyond that, nothing.

Standing at the corner of Britain is an exhilarating feeling. Wrath comes from the Viking word for turning point, and it doesn't take a great leap to see longships in the heaving waters below, turning their prows southwards as they round the cape, heading for pillages new. Nowhere else can you look down one side of the country, turn your head and look along another. To the south are undulating cliffs, with a yellow gash in the distance that marks Sandwood Bay. To the east, a solid line of cliffs stretches as far as the eye can see. Look north and there is nothing until you get to the North Pole. There is nowhere in Britain like it.

Just east of the cape, you can see Kervaig, a narrow bay with golden sand, overshadowed by Clo Mor, the tallest sea cliffs in Britain. A few hundred metres out, twin stacks emerge from the water like the façade of a great Gothic cathedral, immense, yet dwarfed by the huge cliffs beside them. A great place to surf, I thought, before dismissing the idea as impractical, inadvisable, even impossible.

Back at the ferry, an SAS officer was waiting. He was controlling civilian movements in advance of a major NATO exercise in the area, and had the affable self-assurance of someone who knows he could kill a surfer with his bare hands. It's difficult to know what to talk about with a trained killer, so we talked about the weather. 'It's due to close in by nineteen hundred,' he warned, with admirable precision. I rushed off to catch a surf at Sango Bay, and sure enough, by nineteen hundred it had.

WAVE 16: Sango Bay

There are many beautiful beaches around Britain. Sango Bay is one of the most beautiful. It's just a few hundred metres across, and most of it disappears at high tide. What makes it so pretty are the rocks, a scattering of low stacks that huddle on the sand like fishwives waiting for the boats to return. A couple of lone rocks stand further out, either right in the line-up or just where you fear the waves might throw you. Even at mid-tide they lurk in the back of your mind, especially if you're new to the beach and unfamiliar with where they are and what else might be lurking.

With a storm on the way, the sky was black, giving the rocks an ominous air. Occasional squally showers were driving through, but the wind was off-shore and the sea smooth, with a long, long interval between waves, so there was very little disturbance once you got beyond the single line of heavy shore dump pounding the shallows.

This was harder than it looked. A few metres from the beach, a thick, head-high wave abruptly and violently folded over itself, churning up sand from the sea bed and sweeping away anything in its path. The first time I tried to get through, the wave sent me flailing to the bottom. The second time, it caught me as I was paddling out. I felt it pick me up and hurl me down on my back, like a karate black belt, sending me over the falls backwards. Not the most decorous start to a session.

On the far side of the shore dump, the sea was deceptively calm. Sinuous pulses undulated past majestically, almost mysteriously. None broke before it reached that violent wall of havoc closer in.

I waited, keeping a wary eye on the tips of two rocks that broke the surface out towards the back of the line-out. A local body-boarder in his fifties paddled out and we chatted. Eventually, a promising wave appeared. It was larger than I had been expecting, and I knew immediately I had to go for it or it was going to mug me. I was on my shorter board, and worried I wouldn't find my balance, but it was too late. I turned and paddled, my reflexes kicked in and suddenly I found I was on my feet, standing on my board, high up on the clean, dark green face, heading left.

I stayed high, keeping one eye on the lip, the other on the rock stack that was wading out to wrap me in its mussel-bound arms. It was a glorious feeling! For once, I was poised and controlled as I shot along the face, so high up, marvelling at the sensation, delighted and surprised to find myself up there, master of all I surveyed. It was a moment that seemed to extend and unwind and last. This was the magic of wave time, so different to real time.

And then, too soon, the lip began to break along its length. I didn't want to mess with the rocks, and was just working out what to do next when the wave wrestled the decision from me. The lip took me out, knocking me sideways and sending me down into the foam. But I came up grinning and delighted, very happy to have caught the wave, especially on my shorter board.

WAVE 17: Thurso East

Of all the waves in Britain, Thurso has always seemed the most iconic. It's the wave every surfer has heard of, a touchstone by which all others are measured. Not quite spoken of in hushed tones, but certainly with awe and respect. I had no intention of surfing there.

In the howling cauldron at Bru, Stevie had asked if I was heading to Thurso and I had shaken my head sheepishly. No, Thurso wasn't for me. It was out of my league. Way out. One day, perhaps, but not yet. I had a vague idea of completing my journey round Britain then returning to give it a shot, when I was more competent, more experienced. For the moment, I wasn't anywhere near good enough.

As I talked to other surfers on the north coast, though, my feelings about the wave changed. I slowly realised Thurso wasn't a mythical wave, mentioned in fear and awe. It crept into the conversation alongside Melvich and Strathy, another break to surf while you're up there. In a different league, maybe, but not a different world. Other surfers I met had surfed there and they weren't super-human or super-reckless. Or super-drowned. They mentioned it casually, not conspiratorially, and I began to dream I might be able to go in there.

When surfers talk about surfing Thurso, they mean the reef on the far side of the river, just beyond the unlovely suburb of Thurso East. I had read accounts of it; of the aura and atmosphere of the break, in the shadow of a ruined castle; of the picturesque farm track to get there; of the thunderous explosion of waves hurling themselves onto the flagstone shelf that makes the wave so particular. I was expecting great things.

But the first time I drove past the row of pretty cottages and into the shabby, mud-filled farmyard, it all seemed rather lacking in ceremony and circumstance. "Is that it?" I wondered. Even the castle was relatively modest, very different to the rambling medieval fortress I had imagined. Like many of Scotland's castles, it's more of a fortified mansion, boasting just enough turrets to raise its status from country house. It's certainly not the kind of place you would envisage Macbeth. Sadly, it's in a parlous condition. Even the rooks and brambles might need alternative accommodation soon.

Like the castle, at first glance the wave too seemed to lack majesty. It broke some way off, beyond a barbed-wire fence fluttering with trapped scraps of plastic, and across a wide expanse of grey rocks and lurid green rock pools. It's only when you see someone take off on a wave that the majesty truly returns. Then the scale of the scene before you suddenly makes sense, and you start to realise why Thurso enjoys such a proud reputation. Thurso takes its name from Thor, the Norse god of war, and for good reason. It is indeed powerful and thundering.

I wasn't going to surf there though. I wasn't even going to sleep there. I headed back to town, and slept in the lee of a shipping container beside the river, rocked and storm-tossed by the violent wind that had blown me in from Cape Wrath. By morning, the wind had abated slightly so I decided to check out the breaks further east, nerves gnawing at my stomach. Whatever happened, I didn't want to surf at Thurso.

Murkle, Dunnet, Ham: nothing. Gills: nothing. Round Duncansby Head to Skirza and Freswick: still nothing. On the way back, I passed through the tragi-comic outburst that is John O'Groats, and felt sorry for the cyclists who make it their goal. It's possibly the ugliest place in Britain, its lack of charm matched only by a similar travesty at Land's End.

On the quayside at Gills Bay, I recognised Achilles' van and hesitantly went to say hello. We got talking and somehow made a joint decision to check out Strathy. But as I passed the castle gates at Thurso East, I decided to have a look anyway. It still looked pretty hairy. And even though I wasn't going in, the tremulous dread that had gripped me all day renewed its hold. Perhaps my body knew something I didn't.

On to Strathy, twenty miles away. Achilles was already there, but it was deserted, and for good reason. It was a huge, heaving mess. So too was Melvich. By now the strong winds were dropping, the squally showers had passed and it was turning into a clear, sunny Sunday afternoon. Melvich was at its most beautiful and serene. I wanted to stay. Not to surf, just to enjoy the scenery and be still.

But something was drawing me back to Thurso. With a feeling of dread, I left the sanctuary of Melvich and headed east again. Finally, around late afternoon, after a hundred interesting but surf-free miles, I was back where I had started. As I approached Thurso again, the tremulous fear intensified.

By the time I got there, the wind had dropped completely. It still looked choppy, but it was starting to look manageable. Three Irish lads were just getting out, leaving three surfers still in the water. The nerves and foreboding that had been gnawing at my stomach all day grew stronger. If I *was* going to do it, now was the time. Surely I had to at least try. If not, I was sure to regret it. Achilles had been in earlier, and was quietly encouraging, in his understated Yorkshire way. 'If you want to do it, just go for it,' he said softly. Excellent advice. For surfing, for life generally.

I really didn't want to do it, though. But at the same time, I didn't want not to do it. Or rather, I didn't want not to have done it. If I didn't give it a shot, I knew I was in for a night of regret followed by a repeat of this same moment of fear and doubt – possibly in worsening conditions – every day until either I finally went in or abandoned the whole sorry enterprise.

Excited and terrified in equal measure, I struggled into my wetsuit and slid down the bank to the edge of the rocks to warm up. I had watched several surfers pick their way through the rock pools, so I knew where to go. But I took my time, partly because it felt like a momentous occasion; partly to avoid the ignominy of slipping and falling over. I made it to the water's edge and eased my way in, close to the channel carved out by the river as it flows into the bay. The water was cold, and black as coal. I waded deeper, racked by apprehension, feeling my way carefully until I was clear to paddle.

My knowledge of reefs was limited, based on the few things I had read and some snippets of conversation, which mostly focused on how great they were, occasionally how tricky they were, but never what you had to do to navigate them safely. My only option was to observe and learn, and preferably not the hard way. But I was still tremulous and hesitant with nerves. Not what you want for a successful surf.

The waves were coming in at a couple of feet above the heads of the surfers catching them, with plenty of power and volume. Terrified and exhilarated, I paddled closer, staying well behind where the wave was breaking, and out of the way of the three surfers. They were Norwegian, it turned out, and all surfing pretty well. I felt like the useless learner who's going to ruin the waves for everyone, himself included.

From time to time a bigger wave swept in, and I found myself punching through a steep, almost vertical wall to reach the safety of the other side. It was yet another new experience and a strange sensation – in an instant what you think you know about the laws of physics is swept aside in the sensory overload of unusual angles and improbable perspectives.

I was wary of the rogue wave that would hurl me to the sea bed, but with each successful duck-dive, my nerves were quelled slightly. Not that I was anywhere near the take-off zone. I wasn't ready for that just yet. I watched and waited and paddled to stay out of the way. Eventually the Norwegians each caught a wave and disappeared off towards the shore. I was left alone, free to make my own mistakes until they paddled back. This time it really was now or never. I was terrified.

A wave came. I paddled. But at the last minute it peaked up and dropped away below me. I pulled back desperately. I knew I would have been heading straight to the bottom of the sea. I also knew it was all in the mind. I just had to do it. If I had learned anything, (apart from paddle hard, catch early) it was not to look down. Look along the wave, at where you want to go. Not down, where you fear you'll end up. Easy – until you're on the top of a wave, staring at a vertical drop, and afraid it's going to send you to the deep. And all the time, you can't quite ignore the feeling that this is all madness.

I waited. I was still upbeat. Quivering with nerves but still happy – ecstatic, even – to be there. The three Norwegians paddled back to the line-up. I waited. My wave would come. We all waited. Waves came, each a possible ride, a possible danger. Eventually the three Norwegians caught three more waves. My turn. I tried again. Same thing. A terrifying precipice and a cowardly retreat. It wasn't looking good.

The Norwegians returned. By now the light was starting to fade. Two of them caught waves and got out. The third one caught a wave. I tried again. This time I paddled but somehow got caught up in the wave as it was breaking, missed my footing and fell. But at least I fell into white-water. It was powerful but it didn't suck me down or drag me into the impact zone. Only slightly panicked, I flailed back onto my board and paddled desperately back out to safe water.

The remaining Norwegian got one last wave and got out too. This was a mixed blessing. On the one hand, there was no one to witness my shame, incompetence and fear. On the other, there was no one marking my place in the water. For all I knew, I could be drifting off the peak, aiming for waves I could never catch.

I probably shouldn't have stayed out on my own. It's inadvisable anywhere. On an unknown reef it's doubly inadvisable. At dusk, even more so. But I couldn't face going in without catching something. The ignominy and damage to my confidence would have made it worse than not paddling out there at all. Who knows when I would have this chance again? I had to catch something.

My nerves had eased slightly as I grew more comfortable with the size and power of the waves – and with the reality of the benign conditions over the reputation of the famous reef. But with the fading light and growing sense of solitude, those nerves returned. Nothing about my situation was comfortable, and I was getting colder and more tired by the minute. Gripped by conflicting emotions, I waited.

Eventually a more manageable wave came through. It was starting to break, but I went for it anyway. I had paddled for too many, too soon, to think I was going to get an early catch; and I had stared down the chasm of too many others to know what a late catch would look like. In my current state, a breaking wave was fine. I went, almost overwhelmed by the whitewash. But somehow I managed to struggle to my feet, while the whole of the North Atlantic hammered on my back. I was way behind the pocket, chasing the green face, with as much chance of catching it as I was of doing a loop-the-loop. But I was up and riding at Thurso! I could hardly believe it.

It didn't last long. I didn't know the reef or how shallow it got or what was lurking under there, and I didn't want to find out the hard way. I let myself fall back into the white-water's soft embrace.

By now night was almost upon me. The castle was a dark and brooding presence. Across the bay, the lights of Thurso and Scrabster sparkled in the twilight. They offered distant comfort. I could have been safe and warm in a nice pub with people and laughter around me. Instead I was cold and alone and exposed and exhausted. I was miserable. But still not ready to come in. I had caught the semblance of a wave. I needed to catch the real thing. Even if I had to stay out all night.

As I paddled back out, the moon broke free of the farm above the reef. A big, bright harvest moon, not quite full but not far off. It encouraged me to stay out a little longer, holding back the darkness while I tried once more. Eventually a wave came, similar to the first, starting to break. With all that was left of my energy, I paddled, and scrabbled to my feet amidst the torrential gush. Again I was behind the green face, but closer this time. I could sense it just ahead of me, so I was better positioned to harness the force of the wave as it unfurled. Harness? I mean hang on desperately as it powered towards the shore. So hang on I did. Not a huge wave. Not a great wave. But a wave. As I waded in over the rocky shelf towards the dark and lonely shore and the sanctuary of my van, my frustration was tempered by happiness and relief. All I had caught were two breaking waves. But I still felt as if I had passed some kind of milestone. I was delighted.

It wasn't enough, though. Not by a long way. I had been in and escaped unscathed, but the experience had only whetted my appetite. Now I was hungry for the real thing. I wanted to catch a proper wave. I was still nervous of surfing at Thurso, but at least I had overcome my outright fear of going in. Things could only get better.

The next day was bright and calm. I woke up on Thurso sea front, and from the comfort of my bed looked over at the reef. A few people were out, but it looked quite small – an optical illusion, I now realise – and the tide almost at high. I was exhausted from the night before so I went off to the library for an hour or two, trying to ignore the Siren call of the wave.

It was hopeless, of course. By mid-day I couldn't stop myself heading back to the farmyard to have a look. And it looked fabulous. Four people out, a long, long interval and not a breath of wind. Conditions you dream about. The waves were coming in at around one and a half times the height of the surfers on them, with some of them twice as high. But it was as clean and clear as a mountain lake. This was my opportunity.

I paddled out in bright sunshine and sat on the shoulder, admiring the power and beauty of the wave. I had never seen such fantastic waves. With such a long interval they seemed to slide in out of nowhere, pushing sinuously up against the mirror-smooth surface of the sea before suddenly doubling, tripling in size, rising into an abrupt peak, rearing up like a bear, toppling over in an explosive curl of force and momentum, a perfect parabola of energy that went spinning and churning along the reef.

As I watched, I began to get a feel for the wave: which one to take, where it was peaking. After staying out of the way of the other surfers for a good ten to fifteen minutes – partly courtesy, partly fear – I realised it was time to try and join the party.

Again I waited for all four of them to catch a wave and hare off into the distance, surfing it all the way to the end. It's a long paddle back, so their absence left me alone for a while. As soon as the last one went, I paddled into position.

The session the night before might have boosted my confidence, but it had done nothing to quell my nerves. If anything, the perfect conditions were making me more nervous. The waves were cleaner, but they were bigger.

And I felt that there was more at stake. It was one thing to mess up choppy waves in the gathering gloom of dusk, Quite another to mess up perfect waves in beautiful sunshine, before an audience of my fellow surfers both in the water and, for all I knew, on the shore.

A wave slipped sinuously towards me. I turned and paddled. Nothing. It slipped off without me. Damn. Must paddle harder. There was a lull. The first of the four surfers was returning. Not good news. I didn't want to miss my slot. Another wave approached, growing alarmingly as it got closer. But I couldn't back down now. I had to go for it. And I had to catch it. I paddled harder this time. As hard as I could, just as the tip of the wave was starting to feather. An immense, sheer slide dropped away before me as the wave started to slip past. But it wasn't an impossible chasm. It was steep, but it wasn't threatening to swallow me up. And crucially, I was paddling hard enough for the wave to pick me up and take me with it.

I'm not sure what happened next. It wasn't instinct, or reflex. It certainly wasn't conscious action. But somewhere along the road from Tiree to Bru to Sango to Melvich, my feet had learned what to do, and when. One moment I was paddling, terrified of what might happen. The next I was standing on my board, flying down a steep expanse of burnished steel, body crouched for balance, mind racing, every nerve, every sinew caught up in survival mode, alert to what was happening.

The screaming slide seemed to plunge at an improbable angle, threatening to pitch me off way before I got to the bottom. Somehow it didn't. I held on, weight on my back foot, until my board had plummeted as far as it would go. Somehow it knew how to steer round into a bottom turn. An instant of unbalance, a moment of teetering, but miraculously I held it together and now I was speeding along the open face, being chased by a gnashing monster hell-bent on engulfing me in its foaming jaws.

I was on my backhand, back to the wave, head turned to see what was going on behind my shoulder. The sensation of the sea's energy impelling me on was utterly unique. The wave snarled and foamed and tried to outpace me, but its eager aggression pushed me onwards, just in the pocket, holding a straight line, surfing as fast as I could, just fast enough to hold my lead as we both, the wave and I, raced along the shoreline. It was exhilarating and nerve-racking and entirely new. Pretty much every other wave I had been on unfurled its energy early on, so its strength decreased as it rolled towards the beach. Here, not only did it not decrease, it seemed to redouble, powering on insistently, with no sign of relinquishing its hold, no question of fading. It was sublime. An awe-inspiring show of nature's power, seen in thundering close-up. I sped along, clinging to my precarious, privileged position in the monster's wake, as insignificant and overshadowed as a butterfly on a rhino's back.

Eventually the beast flicked its tail and pitched me over into the dark water, rolling me around in the gurgling maelstrom, caught up in the swirling vortex of energy, spinning over and over, no idea which way was up or down, or how long I would be spinning. One arm instinctively went up to protect my head and face, the other stretched out as counterbalance, and to ward off rocks. It duly grazed the rough rock of the reef, a harsh reminder of what lay beneath. The wave rolled on, leaving me to splutter to my feet, waist deep in water, a long way from where I had started. And with a big smile that even the long paddle back couldn't banish. It had finally happened. I could not have been happier.

Back at the peak, I sat and waited for the right wave

to come along again. No hurry. It was a fabulous day. Sunny, completely still, and with sinuous pulses of energy pushing in at a languorous interval beneath a mirror-smooth sea. Again, the four youths – art students from Falmouth – caught waves and disappeared. Again my moment came. Again, that blur of action, as somehow I caught the wave and found myself surfing. Not so big or powerful, this time. But I was more in control. More balanced. More able to take in my surroundings as they flew past, particularly the fabulous, snarling mouth of the wave, so brown, so smooth, so clean, burnished by the sun into a cauldron of dark shining bronze. All too soon, the wave ended.

A third followed. More precarious this time. I struggled to stand even as I slid down the face. But once up, the same voracious power, the same endless reeling of energy and beauty, the same sensation of standing on the rampant flank of raw nature, unnoticed and insignificant. And this time I held my balance as the wave rolled on, following it to the very end, until it dissipated its final throes beneath my feet, with just enough energy left to catapult my board over its dying back, letting me drop onto my stomach to gather the remaining momentum and head towards the peak. Three waves. Maybe thirty minutes. A lifetime.

After that, nothing. I missed a few, I let a few go, I gave way to other surfers. The sun went in, the swell dropped off, I got cold. I even went over the falls, a headlong dive that mirrored what had happened to my surfing. I was relieved not to hit anything on the way down. I got colder and colder, more and more dispirited until finally I knew I had to call it a day. But I had surfed Thurso! Even if I hadn't really surfed it well, those three waves had been sublime. I will remember them forever.

And now I felt as if I had joined some sort of unspoken fraternity. I could hang around watching the reef without feeling like a fraud. Over the next few days I chatted to other surfers, comparing notes, swapping stories, sharing triumphs and failures or just an assessment of conditions. I gradually got to know Achilles a little. He had the soul of a poet and lived the life of a van vagabond. I brewed him coffee and we discussed waves, nature, beauty, life.

On my third morning, I shared a brief, wind-blown session with two surfers from Cornwall, Tup and Billy, who were about my age and full of useful tips when we met up for a drink later on. 'You've got to really want a wave,' Tup told me. 'Otherwise you won't catch it.' It's advice I remember whenever I'm missing waves I'm too scared to catch.

The Norwegians too I saw a few times, either out in the water or at one of Thurso's deserted pubs. They were hilarious, like a cartoon gang or parody boy band, all comic outfits and odd haircuts. 'It's just water,' one of them told me, when I confided my fear of the reef. This too I try to remember whenever my nerve fails.

Two days later, conditions changed again. The wind dropped and moved to off-shore, the swell grew from head high to double that. The early morning sun glanced off perfect waves. As soon as word spread, the masses would rally. I decided to get in while the going was good.

Too good, as it turned out. Way beyond my ability. But it was another beautiful spectacle best seen from the water, a stunning display of the power of the sea. Huge, perfect waves groomed clean by the wind curled and crashed in beautiful arcs of energy. I tried to catch them, but these were monsters, and intolerant of my puny efforts. A couple of times, the monster's tail whipped me from behind as I tried to paddle, and sent me sprawling.

73

A couple of times it mugged me – and others – as we tried to punch through an immense wall of water. A couple of times it tolerated my attempts and let me ride – though never in its full majestic beauty. But still the thrill was worth the effort and discomfort, the ecstatic fear. This was Thurso on a different scale. A timely reminder of my own modest powers. I retired, overawed and exhausted.

By afternoon, the waves were smaller and the hordes had arrived. It was a choppy, crowded surf, picking off leftovers and fighting the kelp that clutches at unwary surfers around low tide. It was fine, but nothing to compare with the burnished perfection I had stumbled across a few days earlier.

The atmosphere, too, was different. Less generous, less celebratory. The worst culprit was not a local at all, but a bald, English homunculus posted to Thurso to count fish. In the water he was unpleasant and selfish, trying hard to ingratiate himself with the locals and irritating everyone else. He went for every wave, no matter who was outside him, and when he realised he wouldn't make it, yelled 'Go!' to anyone inside, as if this late call excused hogging the wave. Single-handedly he poisoned the atmosphere, and though I managed to snag a few waves despite his efforts, when I left the water I was spitting.

Happily, it didn't take long for this despicable character to receive divine retribution or whatever you want to call it when unfortunate things happen to unpleasant people. As the sun went down, a lonely figure could be seen racing up and down the shoreline. The homunculus had lost his board! It couldn't have happened to a less nice person. A couple of us watched with exquisite schadenfreude as the sun set on the idiot's increasingly frantic search, hopping from rock to rock like the Gollum he so closely resembled.

No one deserves to lose their board for good, though, no matter how unpleasant they are. After twenty minutes of comic searching, he found it, relatively unscathed, washed up by the same wave that had ripped it from him in the first place. Thor had made his point.

* * *

To say I was sorry to leave Thurso would be an under-statement. The following morning, I was filled with melancholy. If I could have gone in again, I would have done, but the wind was on-shore and the waves small and messy, and anyway my arms had no energy left at all. The farmyard was full of vans, each with a surfer or two patiently waiting for conditions to improve, and I chatted idly to a few, putting off my departure as long as possible. Mostly I regretted all the waves I was going to miss, and the radical improvement in my surfing that wouldn't now be happening.

Two friends of Achilles had just arrived, and sympa-thised with my reluctance to leave. They migrated north for several months each year, and had surfed everywhere, even Shetland. 'Anywhere else you go, you can't help comparing it with that,' Chris, the older brother, warned me, stabbing a finger towards the reef. Sadly, he proved to be right.

Finally I took my leave of Achilles. He had drawn me a surf map of his local area, Scarborough and Cayton: where to surf, where to avoid, who to talk to. It felt like a benediction to help me on my way. It didn't soften my melancholy, but it tinged it with hope. Enough to send me on the next stage full of optimism. And somehow I knew I would see Achilles again.

Three

The East Coast of Scotland

The further south I drove, the sadder I was to have left Thurso. From what I could tell, it was flat all the way to Dover. Nothing at Nairn. Nothing at Burghead. At Lossiemouth, knee-high slop, and Hercules aircraft droning in low over the beach like bumblebees. At Cullen, skink, and more slop. I was beginning to despair.

WAVE 18: Sandend

At Sandend, things started to look up. The weather was closing in but the wind was off-shore, and as the tide pushed in, a clean wave was rolling into the wide, sandy bay. A row of pretty stone cottages huddled above the rocks like anxious fishermen. Below them, a powerful rip traced a nerve-racking slalom between submerged teeth, then out to the wind-whipped peak beyond.

The waves were shoulder high, but strong and shapely, groomed by the brisk wind. A month ago, I might have found them challenging. Now I found them a relief. For the past week, I had been way out of my depth, struggling against nerves in conditions that were at the edge of my ability, and with the knowledge of an unforgiving reef in the dark water somewhere below. Now I was back on a beach break, in more benign surf, finding waves where I had expected nothing. It was fantastic! Beautiful drops into clear, clean faces, mostly left onto my forehand, so the full beauty of the wave presented itself as I swooped down the face into the waiting wall. After the trembling fear of Thurso, and the worry there would be no waves down the North Sea, it was a delicious surprise.

I camped on the cliffs above the village, in the lee of a derelict farm. The night was pitch black, not a light to be seen, and I was troubled by haunting dreams. In the morning, I went to investigate a curious stone dovecote that stood like a sentinel at the cliff edge. Below it were the ruined remains of a castle that had once perched precariously on its steep outcrop but now seemed to be melting back into the rock like chocolate. All from different eras, the three abandoned edifices – castle, dovecote, farm – represented cycles of hope and despair, success and failure, the dramas of the past undocumented, their protagonists unremembered, their homes ruined. No less than stone circles and cairns, they spoke of forgotten lives. Of endeavour come to nothing. I found them both troubling and reassuring. They suggested that the only solution is optimistic nihilism. It all comes to nothing; you still have to try.

Banff was flat. Gardenstown was flat. Cullen was still flat. Three hours, 90 miles and one steak pie later, I returned to Sandend. It was a lot smaller and slower than the day before, but it was still fun. Clean, waist-high waves on an incoming tide offered shortish rides, but what they lacked in quality, they made up for in quantity. If the ruined castle and derelict farmhouse suggested anything, it was Carpe Diem. Or Carpe Undam. I seized the waves. I didn't know when I would be back.

The following day, I should have been heading to Fraserburgh. But instead, I had a date in Aberdeen. Karen, a daughter in exile of that great, grey city, was coming up on the train to see me. The least I could do was be there to meet her. I followed signs to the station and found myself funnelled into the multi-storey car park.

I parked without problems, but as I went to put money in the machine, I realised there was a short-stay waiting zone where you could park for free. I returned to the van, reversed out of my space and drove down the ramp to. . . CRUNCH. A scraping, crunching bang above my head. I stamped on the brake. A lightning bolt of panic shot through me. I had just decapitated my beloved van! That was it. My trip was over.

I delicately, excruciatingly, eased the van backwards up the ramp and jumped out to inspect the damage, fearing the worst. The roof itself was fine, but I had managed to destroy the skylight in the middle. My van now had a gaping hole in the roof where there should have been a window. Not ideal in rainy Scotland. My initial prognosis was correct. I was finished.

For the moment there was nothing I could do. I had a girlfriend to catch. I rushed to the platform, pretended nothing was wrong and greeted Karen as if I hadn't seen her for a month. It wasn't very convincing, apparently. She later said I had seemed distracted. Distracted doesn't come close. My van had a hole in it. I was distraught.

I patched the hole with a scrap of plastic and searched for a more permanent solution while I explored the coastline north of Aberdeen, taking Karen with me to translate.

WAVE 19: Fraserburgh

After the isolated wilderness of the north coast, Fraserburgh was a jolt: a town beach, a seafront promenade and even a greasy café. I felt like Robinson Crusoe returning to civilisation, impressed and repelled in equal measure. It was a flat, wet October Tuesday. Not a great day for surfing. But the water was clean and clear, and young gannets were diving for fish on new wings, just out of reach. As we watched, a surfer got in. If he was in, I was in.

The waves were waist-high at best, breaking close to shore: a short wade out, a quick paddle and up. I was happy to lose count of how many I caught. Wave after wave, short and simple, remembering the basics. Even my last wave took me six waves before I could tear myself away, and when I finally emerged, it was because I could surf no more.

A few days later, I kissed Karen goodbye at the station, staying well clear of any low beams, and continued south. A week getting fat on fresh duck eggs was fine, but I was behind schedule.

WAVE 20: Gullane

Aberdeen was flat. Stonehaven was flat. St Andrews was dark, Dickensian and flat. When I reached Edinburgh, I had to leave the van for a couple of days for a flying visit to Barcelona. Admin, not amusement. There were waves but I was unable to surf them. By the time I reached North Berwick, yet again I was desperate.

North Berwick is an elegant town of stone houses and antique wharves, punctuated by a couple of church steeples that add to its prettiness. Twin beaches arc out from a small stone harbour like angels' wings, the western beach scattered with patches of rock and green-bearded boulders, the eastern beach with more prominent rocks and tidal reefs, plus a sea-water paddling pool for small children and lazy seagulls.

The sun shone but a strong easterly wind was blowing, so the sea was wild and untamed. I periodically checked the distant waves through binoculars, until I realised that to the young mothers at the paddling pool I looked like a ragged man in a dodgy campervan leering at their kids. Not wanting to get lynched, I hurriedly put down the binoculars and went to check the surf on foot.

What had looked rough at low tide, by mid-tide was barbarous, so I decided to head not east, towards the open sea, but west, deeper into the Firth of Forth.

At Dirleton, a long trudge over unlovely dunes led to a small, rocky beach. I stared intently at the heaving mess, trying to see surfable waves in the snarling maelstrom. There were none so I trudged back.

Gullane, even further west, looked better sheltered against the violence coming in from the east. The question was, how sheltered? Was there enough swell to get round the small headland, or was it absorbing everything the storm could throw at it? With no expectation of finding anything, I went to have a look.

To my amazement, the car park above the break was packed. A dozen surfers were pulling off wet wetsuits, while several others trudged up the path from the beach. Don't tell me I've missed the party, I thought.

I wasn't the only one. Two other surfer-come-latelies were scanning the waves from the cliff-top car park, one with binoculars. Even without binoculars, I could tell what I had missed. The brief curlicue of the bay was calm, but occasional smooth sets were reeling round the point in elegant, gently unfurling curls. At the foot of the cliff, the waves seemed a little bigger, but the beach was hidden from view, so you couldn't tell where they were breaking. My fellow scouts articulated what the dripping wetsuits around us implied: it was all over.

I explained what I had seen over at Dirleton. Despite my pessimistic description, they decided to head over there. I declined to join them. Instead, I grabbed my board and jogged down through the woods, to see if there was anything to salvage from the day. On the path, I ran into yet more surfers coming the other way. Their expressions said everything, a familiar combination of scorn, sympathy and smugness.

When I got to the beach, I realised why. Chest-high, glassy waves were peeling into the bay in clean, sharp lines. But they broke no more than a dozen metres out before hurling themselves onto the steeply-shelving sand. With dusk falling, I was facing a desperate shore dump.

I really didn't want to snap my board in the shallows, but it was far too late to go anywhere else, and it might be my last shot at this beach, tucked so far along the Firth of Forth. Either I resigned myself to waves – and a session – that promised to be nasty, brutish and short, or I trudged back, clammy and dispirited, and wrote the beach off.

On the other hand, one of the most satisfying rides I can remember came from conditions that were just as unpromising, and far more challenging. On a surf camp in Portugal some years ago, I teamed up with a fellow Brit called Bart to search for something more interesting than the knee-high sausage rolls we were being offered one afternoon. We drove for miles down dusty, sun-scorched tracks, checking out a handful of breaks which we foolishly rejected, certain there was something better just around the corner. By the time we had exhausted our thirst for adventure, it was late and low tide. We had reached a beautiful, deserted beach, but the waves were a thundering close-out, pummelling the shore with sudden, awful violence.

Bart decided to vent his frustration by running laps of the beach. Much as I like running, I was there to surf. Conditions were impossible, but I went in anyway, on a surf school NSP Fish, a short, fat, plastic board that was more likely to survive the inevitable pounding than either me or my fibreglass 6'10". Wave after wave guillotined the sand, full of violence and power. Several caught me and guillotined me down with them. Others let me pull back unscathed. None seemed even vaguely surfable. Even so, I stayed out there, waiting and watching, trying to find a chink in the ocean's liquid armour, fighting the current to hold my position, constantly scanning the most likely location for a lapse in the ocean's ferocious concentration.

Eventually, an opportunity came. A wave that offered a hint of green face and a shoulder to fly on. I went for it, with little expectation of success. But even as the edifice came crashing down around me, I managed to stand. I held on, surfing the chaos in a brief burst of adrenaline and excitement, until the explosion subsided and left me knee-deep on the shore. One fleeting wave for an hour of grinding effort. But I had caught it, and surfed it, against all expectation. And it gave me greater pleasure and satisfaction than a hundred easy, unchallenging, accessible rides.

Here at Gullane, the waves were short and fast, jacking up quickly and reeling onto the shore, with a beautiful, smooth face reflecting a glimpse of what might have been.

I missed a good number of them, pulling out of certain headlong drops, wary of dry land just a few metres away. Or I was swept over the falls. Or once, catapulted like an Olympic diver as I jumped to my feet, using my surfboard as a springboard to plunge headfirst into the unknown. In the ten days since Fraserburgh, the water had cooled by several degrees, and each tumble was a skull-piercing shock.

But when I caught a wave, it was sublime. The clean, smooth face rewarded the effort of an early catch, and the few seconds before the wave closed down flashed past in a rush of perfection.

Each wave I surfed was a minor triumph of will and co-ordination, resisting the challenge of the wave and the threat of the beach, and surfing along the face for a few metres, to squeeze the most out of every pulse. For a surfer of my modest ability, just managing to be up and poised, no matter how fleetingly, is the elixir of surf. In a sport of sensations, it's that first hit that lights you up, the sudden moment of control and speed as all the variables combine to make everything possible. It doesn't matter that it lasts so short a time. In your mind, those moments extend forever, each memory crystallised in a glorious image, a single flash that encapsulates all the fleeting sensations that flash past along the way.

Dusk deepened and the sun sank towards the horizon, falling in a direct line with the rolling furl of the wave, so I was surfing into the sunset. As the sky exploded into tropical orange, the water was burnished a fiery bronze. Each wave as it curled was lit like a liquid kaleidoscope, reflecting the apocalyptic sun along every inch of its mirrored, moving curve, a gleaming half-tube of rolling energy. I caught a final wave along this unfurling curl of fire, and emerged from the glittering water with rubies dripping from my board, delighted.

WAVE 21: North Berwick

Gullane was flat again the following day so I returned to North Berwick. Some places you want to surf just because you like the location. The swell was dropping but the east beach still looked quite promising, with a decent wave sneaking between the expanses of low rock that bookend the near half of the beach.

After the exercise in precision timing at Gullane the night before, I started well on my 6'5", catching a decent chest-high wave that had a good wall. I dropped into it easily, but must have got over-excited, because the next thing I knew I had caught a rail and was catapulted into the water. After a long wait, the next one just petered out beneath my feet. I stoically went down with my ship, balancing on my board as it sank, until the water was up to my knees.

The swell was fading fast and I was tempted to quit. Instead, eager to surf North Berwick properly, I went for my larger board. Immediately I caught several nice lefts, but the looming rocks menaced the end of the wave, bringing each ride to an early finish. As the tide dropped, though, the waves started to reform nicely on the inside, jacking up into a steep wall that gave each ride a final thrill. This last section became increasingly abrupt and powerful, little more than a shore dump, with the bottom falling out of the wave an instant before the whole thing came crashing down in a final gasp of energy. But that final burst made it worth holding on to whatever momentum you could muster. It wasn't a classic session, by any means. Nor is it a classic beach, troubled as it is by all those rocks. But once again, I was glad to have surfed there, cementing my affection for the town.

Later, I wandered the streets, browsing idly for pies and books. At the old-fashioned junk shop, among the antique golf clubs, unmatched crockery and obsolete camera equipment, I found a delicate glass, not much larger than a thimble. Perfect for sipping whisky in moderate quantities once the nights started to close in. It felt ancient even if it wasn't, and for a mere 50p improved my quality of life beyond recognition. A duvet and sheets, a decent coffee-maker, proper mugs, Radio 4, and now a whisky glass: living in a van for long periods, it's little things that make life more comfortable.

WAVE 22: Pease Bay

If North Berwick is an elegant Victorian matron showing a smart façade and just a glimpse of lace petticoats, Pease Bay is a supermarket check-out girl whose indifference and cheap make-up can't quite conceal her natural beauty. In a pretty green fold of the coastline, rows of caravans creep up the hillside like a pixellated rash. And not just a few, a phalanx. A wet Sunday afternoon didn't improve the prospect, and after so many empty Scottish beaches, my initial reaction was dismay. But at least there were waves. Clean, sharp lines pushing nicely into the bay – a little too close together, perhaps, but reassuringly regular. With trepidation, I rolled on down the hill.

The muddy car park was full of taciturn surfers getting out of their wetsuits. Had I missed the boat again? I got undressed in the light Scottish drizzle, picked my way barefoot down the tarmac road, and jogged through the caravan park. It was like a village, complete with a size-able supermarket and its own pub, which bristled with signs saying No Wetsuits. Several smokers bristled with similar antipathy. They seemed like a different species, viewing the idea of surfing on a wet Sunday in October as inadvisable, possibly even inconceivable, like giraffes contemplating the concept of flying.

From the water, it was easier to ignore the lines of caravans. Most of the time you're looking out to sea anyway. The waves were around chest high, but lacking real power, and once again I made the mistake of taking the wrong board. Yes, I know what you're thinking. As I hobbled back to get my larger board, the smokers outside the clubhouse were thinking the same thing.

It was worth it, though. The first thirty minutes had been a litany of frustration and missed waves. The next hour or so was a fanfare of rides. The drizzle stopped, the sun came out, and although the waves were fat and soft, they were big enough and long enough to be fun, if not particularly memorable or exciting. By now there were only a few of us out, two on a different peak, while I shared the main peak with a surfer on a BIC. We chatted, but every time we had to duck through a wave, he would get pushed back several metres, and I found myself talking to the sea. If nothing else, I was getting better at duck-diving.

Eventually, the heavy rain that had fallen all morning started to gush off the surrounding hills. It brought with it the distinct smell of human sewage washed down from the campsite. Life's too short for diphtheria, so I got out. But it's a tribute to the good work done by Surfers Against Sewage that this kind of experience is now exceptional rather than commonplace.

WAVE 23: Coldingham Bay

Two days later, Coldingham Bay was everything Pease Bay wasn't. Its few houses and ramshackle hotel blend in more easily than rows of identical caravans. Most of the hillside had been reclaimed by brambles, which lit the bay in a blaze of autumnal reds and golds, fiery in the bright sunshine.

The water was cleaner and crisper than any I had seen since leaving the north coast, a beautiful, limpid blue, similar to Sango Bay. The swell had dropped to around waist height, though, and the waves were weak. A long-boarder was out, catching nothing – three strokes are never going to get you into a weak wave, no matter how long your board. He didn't stay long.

I caught a few close-outs, getting up in time for a metre or two of green face before the whitewash won, and then a better wave – except my front foot was too far back, so the board pivoted and I slammed face first into the low green wall. After that, I made a conscious effort to think about my feet, and now I was up ahead of the curl, high on the wave. What a difference! You have so much time to look around, so much control, so much space to make decisions, work out what you're doing and where you want to go. I stayed high, riding the top, literally on the crest of a wave. Once again I exhilarated as the wave went on and on and everything came together. It only lasted a few seconds, I imagine, but those seconds seemed to stretch to minutes. As the wave closed down, I even managed the rudiments of a floater. Too little and too late, but the intention was there.

Clear water, a pretty bay, sunshine. Not the greatest of sessions, but a satisfying end to my Scottish odyssey – an odyssey that had started so unpromisingly back on Tiree, picked up at Hosta and Bru, reached a roaring crescendo at Thurso then faded in a gradual diminuendo down the east coast. Now faced with a flat spell, I spent a few days striding the cliffs above St Abbs, or sitting in my van writing. Finally, as I was about to move on, I discovered a public shower beside the small stone harbour there. My first. At least I left Scotland clean.

Four

Northumberland

England welcomes you back with a fast food van. No band, no banner, just a bloke selling burgers. After two months in Scotland, I was underwhelmed. I drove on, past Conundrum Farm, which raises questions, through Berwick-on-Tweed and on to Scremerston.

Beside the railway line, a quiet road bumps over dusty scrub, attracting the usual parade of nocturnal miscreants in hilarious cars, looking for privacy or trouble. I bumped on, and rolled to a halt on a patch of low, scrappy dune overlooking a narrow, scrappy beach. After the splendid isolation of St Abbs Head, it was wretched. But dusk was falling. It would have to do.

WAVE 24: Scremerston

The following morning, things looked a little brighter. The crimson sunrise was stunning, though the beach was still more shabby than beautiful, edged with harsh waste-land and scattered with pebbles. Every hundred metres, narrow staves of rock stretched towards the water like ribs, each speckled with limpets and lank seaweed, and runnelled by a regular grid, as if they had been paved with rock-effect floor tiles. Beyond, there were waves. I felt I ought to go in.

I was determined to make it into November without boots, but as I paddled out each time, I had to press my feet together, trying to minimise the windchill. Low interval, waist-high waves were kicking up a lot of white-water, making it very unsatisfying, and it was very cold! I caught a few, making the most of the face, working on my bottom turn, doing what I could. But it was a struggle, and after forty minutes I realised I wasn't really enjoying being out there. It wasn't the cold, or the mediocre waves. It just didn't feel right. I caught a wave and rode the white-water in.

As I picked up my board to wade into shore, I realised why. One of the fins had been pushed inwards and, instead of snapping, which is what fins are supposed to do under pressure, had wrenched its two mountings out of place, gashing the fibreglass and making the board unrideable. Welcome to England. I drove south, cursing. It wasn't the most penitent attitude to bring to Holy Island.

A true pilgrim would have made more of an effort to surf on Holy Island. Surfing is as close as you can get to walking on water, so this was the place to do it. If Jesus was a surfer – and there's someone at every crowded break who thinks he is, with his blonde beard, benign gaze and bothersome long board – I'm sure he would have tried harder to catch some waves there. Being a weak mortal, I took one look at the car park, did a U-turn (physical, not spiritual) and left, stopping only to admire a flock of curlews poking tentatively at the mud beside the causeway.

I continued on to Bamburgh, and found what seemed, in the twilight, to be a convenient parking place overlooking the beach. Overnight, this humble lay-by transformed itself into the most stunning spot imaginable: the tide was out, and a wide strand of empty beach stretched off into the distance; a thick autumn mist hung in the air, tinged red by the rising sun; and above it, Bamburgh Castle's majestic battlements stood in forbidding silhouette against the watery sky. It was outrageously picturesque. So picturesque, I later discovered, that Turner had painted this same view two hundred years earlier.

What the view lacked, though, for me if not for Turner, were waves. The tide was too far out, the sand too featureless. It was a beautiful morning so I decided to explore. Bamburgh, Seahouses, Beadnell Bay – all flat or flat enough. Eventually I reached Embleton, where I tramped across the golf course and over the dunes to have a look. There was a bit of a wave, but by now lethargy had seized me. I tramped back and sat and waited and watched the half-term hordes tramp in my footsteps with kites and spades and kids and dogs. Eventually I gathered just enough energy to achieve escape velocity and have another look. Sure enough, it had picked up. I couldn't reasonably refuse to go in, though I was feeling fairly ambivalent about the idea.

Wave 25: Embleton

Waist- to chest-high waves. Bright sunshine. I had a blast! For an hour I didn't stop, catching wave after wave after wave. At the far end of the bay, the imposing ruins of Dunstanburgh Castle clinging to its headland like a derelict's teeth added a frisson of drama. Short of an extra metre of swell and an off-shore wind, things couldn't have been better. The moral is clear. Always Go In. It never fails.

But as I dragged myself back up the beach, exhausted and content, I was tapped on the shoulder by a childhood memory that filled me with bitter-sweet melancholy for lost time. It was triggered by the ruined castle up on the headland, which I remembered from a family holiday, camping nearby when I was eight or nine. I still remember the icy chill of the sea that sun-drenched summer, and strolling among the castle ruins at dusk, as swallows soared and wheeled among the ruined towers.

The memory that caused the wash of nostalgia was from earlier, though, and the opposite end of the country, Devon, or possibly Cornwall. We had a new frisbee – new that day, even – and when we grew tired of dropping it, we decided to bury it in the sand, my sisters and I, and play Find-the-Treasure. Except once we had buried it, we couldn't find it again. With growing panic, we ploughed the sand in ever larger circles, growing sandier and more desperate, until we barely knew even which beach we had buried it in. We spent childhood hours and childhood aeons searching for it, trapped forever like children in a fairytale, afraid what our wicked stepmother would do when she found out (though for the record, she's our actual mother, and she isn't wicked).

Finally, after hours, maybe years, searching, we were forced to accept defeat and confess our foolishness. And hey presto! My father, omniscient as always, stuck one foot in the sand, asked us what the reward was, and dug it out, all within a few seconds. We almost wept with gratitude and surprise.

The memory had remained buried for thirty years, but as I emerged from the surf, something about the sand, ploughed up by the tramping hordes, and the memories, ploughed up by the ruined castle, reminded me of that childhood beach. I was filled with longing for the security and certainty of childhood, when the worst tragedy in the world – a lost frisbee – is resolved by the omnipotent intervention of an all-seeing father. I returned to the van, infused with exquisite melancholy.

Twice I set off to revisit the ruined castle, once along the sand and later along the golf course. Both times, we turned back, my exhausted body and I. It just wasn't interested. It knew what it wanted, and it wasn't a five-mile walk to see a pile of stones, no matter how pictur-esque or significant. What it wanted was to sit in the van and drink coffee and read the paper. I was forced to let it have its way. Which is probably how it should be. If you have the energy to go for a walk when you get out of the water, you haven't been surfing hard enough.

I drove back to Bamburgh along narrow country lanes, the low autumn sun shining brightly through the trees, casting a flickering semaphore of light and dark across my retina, like an incipient migraine. Suddenly I came across a pheasant lying in the middle of the road, dead but resplendent in the sunshine.

I have no explanation for what I did next. I had done nothing like it before. But for some reason I stopped and walked back to inspect the bird. Sure enough it was dead. But it seemed neatly dead. And more importantly, recently dead. I felt its breast feathers. It was still warm.

There was something about being in the van, self-contained, self-sufficient and not quite living by standard rules, that must have sparked a subconscious thought-process. Or perhaps it was my fast-approaching destitu-tion. Or the desire for a change from pasta with vegetable mush. Whatever the reason, I took a furtive glance to check no one was watching, picked the bird up by the feet and took it back to the van. I had just found dinner.

Having a dead animal hanging in your vehicle is quite

unnerving. Having one hanging in your bedroom is odder still, but that's essentially what your van becomes every night. By morning I had named him Felix, and we were the best of friends.

But what a filthy morning! The happy sunshine was gone, blasted away by howling wind and violent rain that lashed against the van like waves against a harbour wall. The sea was a churning mess of white, while Bamburgh Castle glowered with menace beneath a low canopy of storm clouds. It was the First of November. All Hallows. It felt as if wailing spirits filled the air in a soaking *danse macabre*.

Driven to the verge of insanity by the screaming wind rocking the van, and then by the clock-ticking silence of the local coffee-house, I decided to get my broken board sorted out. Felix would enjoy the ride.

WAVE 26: Tynemouth

Tynemouth was a terrifying hour south. The gusting wind fought a constant battle to wrest control of the van, trying relentlessly to barge me sideways into the fast lane, regardless of what might be coming past. Only as I approached Tynemouth did the wind finally pause. It was a brief lull, but when it picked up again, it had changed direction. Instead of a howling on-shore mess, what greeted me as I parked outside the surf shop was off-shore perfection: big, clean, beautifully-groomed rollers pummelling in from the east.

It was so unexpected, and the waves breaking so far out, that at first I didn't take it in. It was only when I saw someone on a wave that the magnitude of it all struck home. Not only were the waves clean, they were huge, barrelling smoothly off the point at the south end of the beach and reeling into the bay, while the late afternoon sun peeked through the storm clouds to add a glowering intensity to the sea, polarising the light into thunderous blacks and blues.

The view from the beach was even more impressive. Huge sets were booming in, and there were just three other surfers on this peak, while a dozen or more competed for waves closer to the point, quarter of a mile away. More by luck than judgement, I located a narrow channel and managed to get out comparatively easily, ducking beneath six or seven incoming waves and feeling their devastating power as they scourged my back. The internet is awash with serene underwater shots of surfers slipping effortlessly beneath powerful vortices of water with the grace and elegance of mermaids. This has never been my experience. It always feels to me as if I'm being raked over with a thousand-pronged plough.

Within a few minutes I was out beyond the peak, to where the rolling waves throw up steep walls that slip beneath you, taking you up in a crescendo of water and plunging you down the other side. It's an exhilarating and terrifying place to be. You're safe from the pummelling but a long way from the beach, and part of you wants to stay there, in the comparative security out back, rather than risk your safety amidst the hurling mess closer to shore.

The water was cold, though, and the driving wind added an extra chill that quickly wrapped its tight fingers around your skull. It's often called an ice-cream headache, but headache isn't the right word. It's not an ache, it's a sharp, clamping pain, skin deep, that feels as if your scalp is being stretched tight around your skull

95

and pricked with a thousand needles. Worse still was the spray, which blew off each crest and scoured your eyes like sand.

The atmosphere in the water, though, was fantastic. One guy was actually jiggling up and down on his board with glee as he sat waiting for the next set to arrive. 'I'm so excited!' he told the world in general 'This is unbelievable'.

They were the biggest waves I had come across since Thurso, and like Thurso, they filled me with dread. I had to keep telling myself 'It's just water'. At least it was sand rather than rock down there, where it stopped being just water. The wind kept blowing me backwards as I paddled into waves, or once, when I was sure I was on the wave, it blew me back as I got to my feet, a fraction too early. Or I pulled out, certain I was heading for a nasty tumble down a sheer face. The demons of self-doubt that had plagued me at Thurso started whispering in my ears, conspiring with the banshee-wail of the wind to make me question my ability. Once again I was suffering from that fatal surfing flaw, lack of confidence.

At Thurso I had realised this can go one of two ways. Either you suffer a morale-sapping downward spiral, missing wave after wave until finally you couldn't catch a rumble of whitewash on a beginner's board. Or you force yourself into an act of reckless, suicidal disregard and hope you come out standing. For want of any better ideas, this was what I did.

A set was coming. Everyone else was either paddling back out or was too far along the beach. If I wanted it, it was mine. The low hump of smooth water grew and steepened, rising smoothly as it drew closer. I turned and started paddling, fighting to get enough speed against the driving wind. The wave loomed above me as it reached my feet. I felt its power take over from my puny paddling. As it started to pick me up, it didn't feel as if I was quite on it, but I knew this was a misapprehension. If I didn't get up now, it would be too late, and I would be tumbling down the front in a chaos of flailing limbs and bruising fibreglass. I scrambled to my feet in that fleeting window of opportunity, barely registering what I was doing, just relying on an automatic trigger between my neurones and my muscles.

Before I knew it, I was standing on my board as it plummeted down the steep, long face. It was an early catch, before the wave had started to break, but now it did, crumbling and growing into a crashing roar somewhere behind me. The steep plunge was an infinite ecstasy of fear and thrill, over in the beat of a racing heart, but seeming to draw itself out for long seconds. This was surf time. Wave time. Like the act of surfing itself, it seemed to defy laws of physics that apply everywhere else in the universe.

Not that I was in control. I was screaming down a steep wall of water on a narrow length of fibreglass. It felt precarious, borrowed, temporary. I managed to hold my balance as my feet somehow guided the board round into a bottom turn, redirecting the nose to run along the wave as it unfurled and rolled on, parallel to the beach that lay somewhere off in the distance. Glancing over my shoulder I glimpsed the wave, a tall, brown monster that towered over me, chasing the pathetic human who dared to run before its powerful magnificence. I was on an exquisite knife-edge, not quite in control, not quite losing my balance, as the wave roared and growled and crashed down behind me. It was sublime, the essence of surfing, full of life and energy and flashing transience that gives it all meaning. The evanescent elixir of a surfer's life.

And all too soon it ended. I ran out of wave. I found myself caught between the seething mass chasing behind me and a crashing wall of water rushing to greet me. The wave closed down in an all-engulfing explosion of energy and random power. I was caught in the sudden unleashing of chaos, swallowed up by the darkness, my board sent flying, my senses disrupted as I swirled around in its embrace, rolled around unseeing and upside down. I floated around in the blind confusion of the breaking water, waiting for the wave to calm. As I did, down in the watery darkness I felt a grin spread across my face, a big smile of immense satisfaction. It was as if an itch that had been bothering me since Thurso had finally been scratched. As if somehow I had conquered my demons.

Demons don't stay conquered for long, though. No matter how satisfying a wave, there's always another one behind. Another opportunity to get it wrong, miss the wave, catch a rail, fall down the face. Surfing is a series of never-ending challenges, each wave taking you back to square one. You get better. You just don't get better than the wave.

Too soon, darkness fell. I stayed out, catching what I could, trying to replicate the wonder of that one wave. The longer I stayed out, the more tiredness slowed my reactions and dulled my limbs. But even though I caught fewer and fewer waves, and none to match that one burst of brilliance, I couldn't drag myself away.

As the light faded and the street above the beach glowed orange, the moon rose, full and bright. It was Nature telling us to stay out and make the most of the waves. So that's what we did. The atmosphere was electric, the child-like enthusiasm of earlier replaced by a different thrill, a recognition of something special, shared wordlessly between the small handful of surfers still out. To left and right, everything was pitch black. Only the incoming swell, lit by the moon, was visible, a dark shadow as a line approached, then breaking bright and luminescent. Even when you caught one, you had to surf it virtually blind, feeling your way in the dark.

By now my arms burned with absolute exhaustion. Reluctantly I headed in, surfing out the white-water towards the deserted beach, where streetlights appeared like haloes to my salt-scoured irises.

WAVE 27: Alnmouth

I trundled back up the coast in glorious November sunshine, checking various beaches until eventually I reached Alnmouth, sitting primly on a hill above its river mouth. Tiny waves, no more than thigh high, peeled cleanly onto the narrow strand. There was nothing else around, so I went in a couple of times, messing around in the water in bright sunshine.

Having spent years surfing in Barcelona, I was used to the idea that you can have fun even when the waves aren't very big. Once you resign yourself to focussing on technique rather than catching the wave of your life – and can overcome your self-consciousness about surfing in such minimal conditions – everything else is a bonus.

I used each session to work on my fitness and technique, playing with my weight and centre of gravity at the point of take-off to see what would happen. Small waves are less forgiving than big ones. They don't do any of the work for you, and if you don't get to your feet immediately, at exactly the right moment, you don't have a wave to surf. But also there is no fear factor. Nowhere to fall. Nothing to worry about. Just paddle, pop up, stand, repeat, with a few seconds of green face as an incentive, and pleasure as a reward. It was a lot more fun than it had looked.

Alnmouth was charming, but I was horrified by the amount of rubbish that washed up onto its narrow ribbon of sand. All beaches have a certain amount of jetsam littering the high tide mark, but at Alnmouth it was intolerable: drinks bottles, plastic bags, shoes, a punctured football, empty oil canisters, crisp packets – it was impossible to take three steps without walking over a single-use bottle or a wisp of plastic.

Most of the time I did what everybody else did, and ignored it. Occasionally it was too much to ignore. I would pick up a particularly large or offensive piece of plastic. Then another. Before long, I would have both hands full. So I would pick up a storm-tossed fertiliser sack or shipwrecked shopping bag and decant everything into that. But then I would have spare capacity, so I kept on filling. When that sack filled up, there was always another. By the time I was back at the van, I was struggling to juggle two huge sacks stuffed to bursting with plastic detritus. Until we end our ridiculous and unnecessary indulgence in plastic bags and plastic bottles, the situation can only get worse. But if everyone picked up three pieces of plastic each time they went to the beach, the beaches would be cleaner and they might think twice about using a disposable bag at the supermarket, or a plastic bottle next time they're thirsty.

There was also the small matter of what to do about Felix. He had been tagging along for four days now, without a word of complaint, just hanging in his foot-well, keeping a low profile. He was like a very undemanding pet. Even so, it was time to do something with him. And that meant plucking.

The problem was where to pluck a pheasant without attracting unwelcome attention. The car park was too randomly busy, and I certainly wasn't going to do it in the van – I would be breathing in feathers for weeks. So I put him in a bag and we strolled up the beach, Felix and I, to where the bleached hulk of a dead tree could conceal a furtive pheasant-plucker from public view.

It was a lot easier than I had feared, though far more fiddly, and it took a good twenty minutes to reduce Felix from plump beauty to skinny wretch. I saved the worst for last, hacking through the neck with an ancient Swiss Army knife, and pulling out the guts in a single congealed handful. Almost immediately a large black Labrador came barrelling up and before I could intervene had wolfed the innards in two gulps, heart, lungs, stomach and all. She was gazing at the rest with doleful eyes when her owner appeared. I made my excuses and hurried back to the van to cook pheasant stew with mushrooms and red wine. It was delicious.

I left Alnmouth and spent Guy Fawkes Night with friends in a pretty village just outside Newcastle. Jane and Toby live in domestic bliss, in a lovely house, with lovely kids, and steady, respectable, well-paid jobs. The contrast with my own situation couldn't have been more stark. But who needs those things when you've got a van and a surfboard and a plan to surf round Britain? Except when you wake up screaming at five in the morning and fear for your future, as I did rather too frequently.

After several weeks on the road, to sleep in a warm bed in a warm house, freshly showered, was sublime. It certainly made a change from waking up alone in a damp van surrounded by disapproving dog-walkers. I left glowing, and went for an invigorating second surf at Tynemouth in smaller, cleaner waves. Then I picked Karen up at the station and we headed back to Bamburgh, a dark hour away. If she was exchanging a centrally-heated flat for a cramped campervan in November, the least I could do was surprise and impress her with the best view in the region. The following morning she was duly surprised and impressed.

On the Sunday morning we went for a walk along the beach beneath the castle, a wide strand dotted with rashes of rock and seaweed. We had been walking for about an hour when we came across a seabird staring mournfully out to sea. From a distance it looked like a penguin, but turned out to be a stranded guillemot covered in patches of oil. It had attracted the attention of a group of dog-walkers and particularly their dog, which cannoned up to the strange creature and bowled exuberantly over it, taking the bewildered bird bowling over as it went. Things didn't look good for the guillemot so I whipped off my T-shirt from under my jumper, wrapped the bird in it, tucked it under my arm and we headed back to the van. Gary – as we inevitably named our guillemot – took it in his webbed stride, poking out from my T-shirt and staring around with interest.

For the second time in a week, I found myself in possession of a strange bird. After the delicious pheasant ragout, I briefly wondered about guillemot goulash. But instead we tracked down the Swan and Wildlife Trust in Berwick, about an hour north. There had been a glut of oily guillemots, and they treated Gary as you might treat an oil-stained shirt: a good scrub with strong detergent, a decent rinse, then leave to dry in a warm place (under a halogen lamp, not draped over a radiator).

Freshly scrubbed, they placed him in a small pen with a bowl of fish and three guillemots they had prepared earlier. All three sulked and stared at the walls, harrumphing grumpily at the indignity of it, for all the world like flustered members of a gentleman's club wearing ill-fitting dinner jackets, feathers ruffled by some breach of etiquette. I called a few days later, to see how he was. They thought that among the dozen recent guillemots, Gary was one of the few to have survived. But they probably say that to all the gulls.

* * *

After two nights with Karen in the van and another night with my Newcastle friends, it was tough getting back on the road, despite a beautiful afternoon that shimmered gold and bronze through autumn leaves. My spirits weren't improved by a fruitless detour via the centre of Newcastle to pick up my board. They had told me it was being delivered that afternoon, but when I got there, it hadn't arrived. Worse still, it wouldn't be ready for another week.

As dusk fell, I drove south, but the further I went, the less chance there seemed of finding somewhere to sleep. Every car park was flooded in the nuclear glow of relentless street-lighting and bristled with forbidding barriers and stern threats. After the glorious expanse of Northumberland, with its empty hills and dark castles, the apocalyptic sprawl of Tyne and Wear was wretched.

Before I knew it, I was being sucked towards Hartlepool, tired, desperate and miserable. I was on the verge of despair when fate threw me a lifeline: a small parking area at Blackhall Rocks, and the only spot on the entire coastline not swamped by the piercing yellow of electric street light. In the dark, I couldn't tell what it was like, but the black expanse ahead could only be sea. I was still tired and miserable, but at least I had somewhere to sleep.

Dawn arrived in a magnificent explosion of reds and purples. I made a cup of tea and wandered to the edge of the cliff. Below, lines of swell broke onto a rocky beach at the foot of rough, uneven cliffs lit pink by the rising sun. Somehow, in the dark, I had stumbled on a surf spot.

I didn't surf it, I regret to say. Not then, not ever. The waves were quite small – though that has never stopped me. But I couldn't see a clear peak and didn't want to sit there for six hours waiting for one, if indeed there was one. Anyway, I had my sights on Hartlepool.

WAVE 28: Hartlepool Headland

Hartlepool Headland is an odd beach, post-industrial and haunted by its past. A row of unlovely semi-detached houses line the road along the sea front, incongruous and seemingly oblivious to their privileged location. At the end of the street a featureless park marks the site of Hartlepool's vanished industry, with the skeleton of a warehouse looming like the ghost of a factory beside the cemetery. A ruined pier runs out to sea, unused and unusable except by fishermen. It was still useful for surfing, though, anchoring down the sand that would otherwise swirl through, to create sandbanks which would throw up waves.

Apart from the occasional dog-walker and a small crew of tremulous oyster-catchers, as I walked down to the water with my board, I had the wide expanse to myself. For such an urban beach, it was remarkably empty. The waves were bigger than they had looked from up on the seafront, about chest high and very cold. As I feared, it was breaking all over the place, messed up by an onshore wind, though not enough to smudge the lines entirely.

They were fast and short-lived, and I found myself going over the falls more often than I really wanted. So again I decided to treat it as a training session, catch and drop, staccato bursts of adrenaline, and bail out before the whitewash whisked you to shore. It was too cold, and too much effort, and the white-water too relentless to stray too far inshore. The rides were short but exciting, with just enough size and power to make them a challenge and a thrill. You had to make snap decisions, turn and paddle and hope it offered enough face to make a decent bottom turn, get into the pocket and hold on for the second or two before it closed down completely.

When I had had enough, I caught what turned out to be best wave of the day, a powerful, shoulder-high burst of energy that came out of nowhere. On tired feet, I almost missed it, landing too far back on my board, threatening to stall. But remarkably I just had time to jump forward as I flew down the face, somehow managing to balance enough to get into position for a bottom turn, enjoying a final scoop of green face before the wave crumbled and I surfed on the white foam towards the beach, smiling at my lucky escape. Not a classic session, but not bad for the unpromising conditions.

WAVE 29: Seaton Carew

If Hartlepool felt post-industrial, Seaton Carew, just across the bay, is resolutely industrial. It was by far the ugliest beach I had surfed so far, and definitely a candidate for ugliest beach in Britain. Ugly, but perversely not unattractive, at least on a sunny November morning. Anyway, there were waves breaking, which was the key thing, especially as it turned out that the beach seemed less ugly when you were in the water. Though it was still pretty ugly.

The car park is a scrap of uneven wasteground trapped between warehouses and commercial compounds, and even at high tide the waterline is several hundred metres away, across a rubble-strewn wilderness shimmering with shattered glass. The white-water fizzes as it seethes and swirls, a real chemical fizz, so you half fear it will melt your wetsuit – or your eyeballs. It's like a beach from a J.G.Ballard story, struck by some man-made tragedy that has wiped out most of society and left the landscape raw and uninhabitable.

On the far side of the bay, to the north, Hartlepool headland was sunlit and seductive, its boarded-up pubs and mean terraces hidden behind a more picturesque version of the town. But what really makes the beach unique and monumental are the huge steelworks to the south. In the sunshine they glinted a burnished silver, spouting vast plumes of silvery-grey smoke that challenged the clouds for supremacy of the skyline.

The waves were about chest high, and some of them opened nicely. A light off-shore breeze kept them clean and shapely, and they were fast. After the sessions at Alnmouth and Hartlepool, my timing was improving. The downside was that my arms still ached from the previous afternoon. It was a case of gritting your teeth and going for it. There was a nice strong shoulder, so even if you weren't right on the peak, you could feel the powerful lift as the wave picked you up. After racing to beat closeouts for two sessions, it felt luxurious; as if I had hours to make the catch.

I caught a few brief rights, then switched to the lefts, on my fore-hand. Almost immediately I spotted a fabulous wave that was starting to wall up well. I paddled hard, made the drop, managed a good bottom turn and was off, shooting along the face of the wave as it tried to gallop away, off towards the steelworks. I hung onto its mane as it galloped, then threw my board up onto its back in a near-floater as it collapsed.

Eventually, starting to tire, I wondered whether to call it a day. I had caught a fair few, and enjoyed the session, and it didn't look as if conditions were going to pick up. No shame in getting out now, certainly.

As I sat on my board considering my options, I realised that a decent wave was looming towards me, almost without warning, and I was in the perfect place to catch it. At the very last minute, I turned and paddled, not convinced I had given myself enough time. My frantic catch held, and I was up and turning into a beautiful clean face. It wasn't the longest wave of the day, but it was certainly the easiest and most unexpected. A good wave to end on. It's always nice to quit while you're ahead, though in practice, always difficult not to go back for another.

Five

Cleveland and Yorkshire

Two weeks after I had taken it in, my board was finally ready. I picked it up and went off to check out the Gare, at the mouth of the Tees. It was a sunny goose chase, bumping down rough tracks alongside the steelworks to a weed-strewn, water-filled no-man's land frequented only by fishermen, and probably gangsters. The wave only breaks a few times a year and inevitably it was flat, so it was just me and the fishermen, but it was still worth a detour on my road south.

Arriving in Saltburn, my spirits lifted. It felt like a surf town. The car park was filled with people struggling into and out of wetsuits, the water bobbed with surfers and everywhere you looked were boards. The only thing missing were waves. At the surf shop, a gnarled but friendly Yorkshireman tried to talk up the conditions but even a casual visitor could see it wasn't happening. I decided to wait. Perhaps it would pick up in the afternoon.

Seventeen days later, I was still waiting. Seventeen days looking out on a dead flat sea. Seventeen days staring at the horizon. Seventeen days trying to summon up waves from the deep. It was the longest seventeen days I could remember.

So this was the great flaw in my plan: the North Sea. I had known the surf would sometimes be inconsistent. I had known there would be occasional flat spells. I hadn't realised they would stretch almost to infinity. Or so it felt, as every day dawned clear and still, and as flat as a serene miller's untroubled dreams of a perfectly placid mill pond.

There are worse places to be stranded – as I would discover later in my journey – and anyway, I had no choice. This was the challenge I had set myself, to surf round Britain consecutively. If I had wanted to chase waves around the country, it would have been a different trip.

Fortunately, I found somewhere a stranded surfer could sit out an extended flat spell more or less undisturbed. Just south of Redcar an invisible line marks the point where everything stops being grim, depressing and industrial, and starts being charming and pretty. For several nights I slept on that line, on the stretch of no-man's land between harsh Redcar and genteel Saltburn, just outside the village of Marske.

Here, two rudimentary car parks loiter on the scrub that overlooks the sea. I preferred the one nearer to Marske. It was closer to civilisation, and less far to walk to the public toilets. This is an important consideration when you're living in a van.

In early November, both car parks were mostly deserted. Just a handful of dog-walkers, a few travelling sales-reps and the odd van crammed with sniggering labourers, who would scoff their chips then toss the wrappers out of the window. Why wouldn't they? It's the last unpolluted spot for 80 miles, so where better to throw their rubbish?

The two car parks – if that isn't too elegant a word for the asymmetric blotches of rough tarmac – were set back from the road and gave an illusion of privacy. By night one of the two was usually deserted, but the other – and which it was changed every night – regularly hosted a ballet of flashing headlights, revving motors and restless cars chasing one another around like sparrows. The first time I found myself caught up in it, I thought I had stumbled across a complex drug negotiation.

One night I returned after dark to find my preferred car park silent. I switched off the engine and sat, watching and listening in the darkness. Suddenly a pair of headlights cut through the black. An engine revved up and a bright red Mini burst across the tarmac. It pulled an abrupt hand-brake turn that sent gravel skittering into the darkness, and reversed briskly into the space beside me. In an empty car park this was no coincidence.

My window was open a few inches. So was the Mini's. I could see the tip of a cigarette glowing in the dark. In the silence, I could almost hear the unknown driver think. I was terrified. It was some kind of overture, but I didn't know what. Part of me was curious to find out. Part of me really wasn't. I sat, tense, feeling an electric bolt of unspoken contact between us. It left me paralysed. What if it was a scam? A con? An elaborate prelude to robbery?

A light went on in the Mini, and I realised it wasn't a con, it was a come-on. The driver lasciviously readjusted her rear-view mirror and applied a deliberate layer of crimson lipstick to full lips that were already glistening. Her actions were provocative and unmistakable. And she wasn't unattractive.

I didn't know how to react. Uncomplicated sex with an attractive stranger? Hell, yeah! No one would ever know, dear reader. I wouldn't tell anyone and I'm sure you wouldn't either. But alone I felt vulnerable. And clearly the invitation wasn't based on my winning personality. If she had seen me in daylight, unshaven and wearing an outsize charity shop anorak that made me look more like a candidate for care in the community than casual sex in a car park, she would have hit the accelerator. Also, I didn't know the etiquette. Should I hoot my horn? Introduce myself? Invite her in for a glass of wine? We were so close she could probably hear my pulse racing.

The light clicked off and we stayed there, me frozen with indecision, while she waited for a response. Her cigarette glowed invitingly. What did I have to lose? Still I did nothing. And no girl likes to be kept waiting. With a contemptuous flick, she tossed the glowing butt out of the window, turned on the ignition and accelerated away as abruptly as she had arrived.

I watched her go with a mixture of relief and regret. Was it a missed opportunity or a lucky escape? I felt slightly disappointed. With her. With myself. On the other hand, as I thought back, I saw more clearly that her jaw-line had been a little heavier than you might expect. And her thick rouge couldn't quite mask the hint of a five o'clock shadow. Sex with a stranger in a strange car park would have been an interesting new experience. But I was only ready for one new experience at a time.

After that, I was left alone. Word must have got out: don't bother with the blue camper van. He's not a proper dogger.

* * *

As I wasn't staying in campsites, a constant problem was finding water. The van came with a tank that held nearly thirty litres, and I supplemented it with a couple of five-litre bottles in case that ran out. I became an expert at spotting outside taps, standpipes or public toilets where I could refill them surreptitiously. Councils which had installed tap-free basins were a real drag. I learned to be as careful as a transatlantic sailor with my supplies, and was astonished by how little water you can get by on if you try. Doing the washing up was an exercise in frugality, as was my daily body wash. Even so, water was one of the trickier aspects of life on the road.

In Scotland I used to rinse my wetsuit, and often myself, in streams and rivers running down to the beach. In England there were fewer streams, and my wetsuit went unrinsed for weeks on end, though if it was raining I would leave it outside for a while. But I was always careful to hang it up to dry after every surf – not least so it would be dry when I put it on again. It didn't seem to suffer at all, so perhaps rinsing the salt away is less important than you might think.

Feeling like a becalmed mariner – which in some ways I was – I resigned myself to a routine of writing, strolling along the beach and gazing wistfully out to sea. On sunny days, it was a delight. On grey days, the hours dragged. For a change of scene, I would drive into Saltburn and gaze wistfully out to sea there instead.

Eventually I headed south, across the moors towards Whitby. I could come back when the waves returned. I had no clear idea where I was going. I just wanted to sit out the flat spell. The van wasn't running very well, and I clattered over the moors like a rattling sled on an ancient roller-coaster, flying down the downhill stretches, struggling up the up, until the road levelled out beside a four-mile beach and I rolled to a standstill. At the far end of the beach, just visible in the distance, was Whitby, famous for vampires and chips. At the near end, the appropriately-named village of Sandsend sheltered in the lee of low cliffs topped by woodland. It's a cute, hobbit-village of stone cottages nestling in a wooded glade, their

112

chimneys puffing smoke and contentment. Beside them, a row of uptight white mansions stare inscrutably out to sea.

Whenever I was on the move, I felt slightly anxious, not knowing if I would find somewhere to park for the night. The worst thing was arriving late, after a long drive, trying to find a suitable campsite based on nothing more than a map and a hunch. When I found somewhere, I would sit and watch for several minutes, trying to decide if it felt right. Often it wouldn't – too busy, too conspicuous, too intrusive – and I would try somewhere else. Often, if there was nowhere better, I would have to return.

Constantly moving from place to place was exhausting. I needed stability, and sometimes found myself staying in one place for several days in an attempt to create it. It helped when there were waves. Having a wetsuit draped over my wing mirror lent legitimacy to my presence. I was there to surf. In the absence of waves, I was just a bum in a van.

Beside the cliffs at Sandsend, slightly away from the village, was a small car park so close to the water that fishermen cast their lines from it at high tide. A row of wooden garages could easily double as beach huts, and at the end of the row were a couple of parking spaces where a shy van could shelter at night, like an elephant hiding behind a scrawny thorn tree, in the mistaken belief no one will notice. At the village pub, a ten-minute stroll away, the landlady was friendly and didn't mind a scruffy bum coming in late to plug in his laptop. Within a couple of days I felt like a local.

Before I had set out on this trip, I had imagined spending my evenings in an endless sequence of quaint local pubs, being entertained by an endless sequence of

113

quaint anecdotes from an endless parade of quaint locals. The truth didn't quite match my expectations.

One problem was distance. I was determined to sleep next to, near to or at the very least overlooking the sea every night. There seemed no good reason not to. That usually meant parking some way from towns and villages, where sleeping on the sea front is generally discouraged. And for the most part, towns and villages are where the pubs are. So only rarely was I within walking distance of one. Whenever I was, I made the most of it – even when it meant a twenty-minute death-defying stumble along a dark cliff-top, as it sometimes did.

When I did find a quaint and charming pub, it was usually filled with regulars who had long run out of interesting things to say to one another, but insisted on saying it anyway. Pubs are like children, I concluded. When they're your own, you love them. When they're not, the pleasure soon wears off. Sandsend was an exception.

The days passed and still the weather refused to change. Then one afternoon, I went for my daily walk along the beach, past the green-bearded stumps of a lost jetty. The sea was silvered like fish scales as it caught the last rays of sunshine before it dipped behind the hills. In the shallows a red setter splashed anxiously, desperate to pounce on an oblivious shag bobbing for fish just out of the dog's eager depth. But at the water's edge a slender ribbon of violence hurled itself onto the sand in frustration, time after time. Was this the harbinger of waves to come? After seventeen days, it seemed difficult to believe.

WAVE 30: Sandsend

The following morning, I was woken by the sound of surfers getting ready to surf. There's something unmistakeable about the slamming of doors, the silent struggling into wetsuits, the wordless anticipation. Sure enough, when I peered through the curtains, two surfers were getting their boards out. I got dressed and went to investigate.

There was a wave, but from the car park it didn't look particularly special, a slight ripple breaking way off beyond the exposed rock of the reef. It wasn't until one of the men had made his way painstakingly around the edge of the seaweed-covered flats and out into the water that I realised I had completely misjudged the size. What from a distance looked like knee-high dribble was at least head high. Clearly I still had a lot to learn.

I wolfed down a banana and followed them out, taking a long arc round the edge of the pebble-and-sand beach rather than slip-slide over the glistening pink stone, with its pitted rock pools and bright patches of fuzzy green seaweed.

I confess I was nervous. My experience on reefs was still very limited – just two: Lagide in Portugal and Thurso in Scotland. Both had served up the wave of my life – with a side-helping of fear and uncertainty. At Sandsend, once again, I didn't know what was out there. But it was a fine day for a surf. Overcast and cold, admittedly, but there wasn't a breath of wind. Smooth, clean lines of energy were pushing sinuously in, like a hand moving below a sheet of silk.

As always, I was wary of antagonising the locals. Too much so, perhaps. After saying hello, I held back, and for the first twenty minutes made sure I let plenty of waves go through if there was any chance either of them would take it – a decision I repeatedly regretted when they too let them go and the wait between sets made itself felt. I was still feeling my way round reef etiquette.

Eventually a wave came that I felt I should go for. I paddled, but I wasn't going to catch it, so I pulled back. Just as I did, it tried to pick me up and take me with it anyway. Another stroke and I would have had it. Or even if I hadn't pulled back. But now, in addition to missing a nice wave, I was out of position. The wise thing would have been to paddle back to the take-off point, but instead, I thought I could just catch the next wave as it started to break. It was already looming behind me. Panicked, I paddled for it. But it was too late. As the wave broke around me, I struggled to my feet, but was bogged down in white-water, and the clean face raced off without me. It was hopeless. I let the board fly ahead while I fell back into the foam. Today of all days I wasn't going to surf whitewash.

I paddled back to the take-off and waited, regretting my earlier deference and the waves that we had all missed. Another wave came my way. I paddled, and felt it catch me. Slowly – almost painfully – I hauled myself to my feet. By now I was half way down the face. I recovered, and found myself on a long, peeling left that seemed to stretch on and on. It was a fabulous wave, and I didn't want to mess it up. Instead I surfed it too hesitantly, looping shallow turns top and bottom, failing to make the most of it, taking care not to make any abrupt movements. As I went, I had one eye on the shore below the cliffs – the waves seemed to drive into the corner of the bay, threatening to trap an unsuspecting surfer there, plus I was unsure how deep the water was. I needn't have worried. When the wave finally ended, I was a long way from the cliff and still around waist deep.

I paddled back, glad to have made it to the end, but feeling I really hadn't made the most of the wave. It was a long paddle, time enough to watch my two companions perform far better. Pete, the older of the two, was on an outrageously long epoxy longboard, and was catching anything going. Jamie, in his mid-twenties, on a short board, was catching less, but surfing with skill.

It was cold in the water, and I was almost sorry to have left my gloves behind. I had pulled one on, then pulled it off again. I hate wearing gloves in the water. They slow you down and tire you out and if you can get away with leaving them behind, you should. But it was late November. The gloves would be coming on soon. I got back to the take-off point and waited, hands clamped under my arms for illusory warmth.

A wave came. I had priority, I think, but I thought I should pass this one up. I wasn't sure I would get it, and I had just had a pretty good wave.

'You take it,' I told Jamie, as the wave gathered itself up. 'There's a good one behind it as well,' he said, as he turned and paddled.

I hadn't seen it, but he was right. Not a good one. A great one! Much bigger and much cleaner. For once my deference had paid immediate dividends. I turned and paddled as hard as I could. Paddle hard. Paddle early.

I took the drop and suddenly I was on a powerful, peeling dream of a wave, just over head high and clean as lightning, a steady, unstoppable pulse of pure energy reeling in from the far north. It was fantastic.

This time I surfed it with more confidence, and a lot more skill. I made the most of every second. I looped together decent top turns, bold re-entries, and sharp bottom turns in a sinuous ribbon inscribed along the wave as it raced across the reef. Most of all, I was taking care to surf smoothly, no sudden movements or brusque changes of weight that would snag a rail and pitch me off. I was determined to surf the wave as it demanded to be surfed, taking my lead from its smooth, sinuous power, surfing with it, not just on it.

I was on my forehand, facing the wave, watching where I had to go, where I was aiming for, where the wave was unfurling. After what seemed like months of surfing on my backhand, it was a revelation to be on my forehand again. You can see exactly what's happening and react to it, staying close to the pocket – the powerful curl that will keep your momentum running and keep you surfing while the wave reels on beside you, smooth and relentless.

I could feel its power beneath me, propelling me onwards as I swept down its smooth face, gathering the momentum to turn at the base then rise again to the crest, followed by the dream-like weightlessness as I came off the top again, and then repeated the movement, swooping down to gather momentum once more.

All the frustrations and failures, all the half-waves and late waves and broken waves and missed waves, all the experience accrued over months and years of trying to improve as a surfer, all fed into this one moment. For that one wave I surfed like an angel, out of my skin, suddenly immortal. Past and future disappeared. All that mattered – all that existed – was the now, a glorious instant of perfection that lasted for eternity, hooked up to the electric intensity of that endless wave. I surfed better than I had ever surfed before, exhilarating in it, fully conscious of the power and precision beneath my feet, aware of every instant as it opened up before me.

118

After about a thousand years I surfed past Jamie as he was paddling back out. His expression confirmed what I could feel beneath my feet, that this wasn't just any wave. It was *the* wave. And it was showing no signs of coming to an end. I surfed on, exhilarated.

But I must have been distracted as I passed him, and got too far ahead of the wave. Suddenly I felt the power of the wave slip away. I had looped up into a top turn and the wave seemed to peter out, leaving me in danger of stalling or coming off the back or sinking or something that wasn't maintaining my momentum. Calamity!

I pressed forward, pushing down on my front foot, trying to recapture the vanishing momentum. And just when I thought it was too late, the wave caught up and took me back into its strong grip. I felt the exhilarating surge of re-entry as once again I made the drop, a full six feet from top to bottom, heading straight down the wave and into another bottom turn. I felt my stomach fly up, like going over a hump-back bridge. And once again I was off, eternity extending itself, unfurling endlessly, unwrapping and enveloping me in its eternal embrace.

The wave lasted forever, but it also jumped me back in time, connecting me seamlessly, timelessly, with that other eternal, everlasting wave I had had the good fortune to surf at Lagide, another left, another wave of a lifetime of similar size and power, similarly endless, which I had somehow managed to surf similarly well. I surfed on

Eventually eternity came to end. The endless moment was over. The cliffs loomed and ahead of me the wave was about to close down. As it exploded into white-water, I catapulted over the lip, aiming just to dive over the top. But my momentum threw me high into the air. I flew up, and came down with a splash. Even before I resumed the surface, a grin was stretching my face from ear to ear.

119

This was happiness! This was ecstasy! This was surfing! As I set out on the long paddle back to the take-off point, I couldn't have been happier.

I caught a few other waves, but none like that one. Too soon, the swell vanished. As the tide comes in, it starts to hit the base of the cliffs. The waves bounce back and cancel out the pulses undulating over the reef, so they lose shape and power. One minute the waves are perfect, the next they're gone. We had no choice. The session was over.

It was still early, so after a celebratory breakfast, I decided to go and look for Shhh...., the least secret "secret spot" in Britain. The whole issue of secret spots amuses me. They have the aura of the Holy Grail, spoken of in whispers and dark looks, fiercely protected by those in the know. On the other hand, armed with an Ordnance Survey map, a little understanding of how waves work, and the time, energy and inclination to tramp off the beaten track to hidden bays and distant headlands, most secrets can be unlocked.

Shhh... is different. No tramping involved. It's in a picturesque village, and visible from the road across the moors. It even features in one of my guidebooks. Nevertheless, the locals are well-drilled in protecting its identity. And not just the surfing locals.

'I'm not really allowed to talk about it,' the little old lady at the newsagent told me, with a glint of grand-motherly concern in her blue eyes, mixed with steely determination. Fortunately, the scandalous ladies at the sandwich shop down by the harbour were less reticent.

'Oh yes, it's just over there,' one of them said, pointing at the obvious wave just beyond the harbour wall, breaking over what was clearly a reef. But if it was so good, where was everyone? I watched for a while, trying to weigh up my state of warmth and contentment against the exhaustion, doubts and humiliation that would inevitably replace them if I went in. That morning I had had the surf of my life. I didn't want to ruin it retrospectively. I could always come back tomorrow.

I wandered up the hill through the village. It is ludicrously picturesque, a huddle of quaint, colourful fishermen's houses sprawling higgledy-piggledy down a cobbled lane towards the harbour. You'll have seen it in ads inviting you to Yorkshire. Though not inviting you to Yorkshire to surf, obviously. At least not to surf here.

Overnight the wind picked up, whipping the serene pond of the previous seventeen days into a screaming chaos. As dusk fell, I trundled over to Runswick Bay, hoping to find a sheltered corner to surf the following morning. A forlorn hope, as it turned out. To say Monday morning dawned rather overstates the case. Night softened to dark grey and the storm raged. By nine o'clock, there was just enough light to see it was utterly unsurfable. Looking at the map, the only place that might have any shelter was Scarborough.

WAVE 31: Scarborough South Bay

Like many seaside towns in winter, Scarborough felt semi-deserted, particularly the promenade, where tacky amusement arcades chirruped and pinged quietly to themselves. Nearby, the small harbour was unexpectedly pretty, full of reeking lobster pots, lazy shags and fishermen mending their nets, while up on the headland, the ruins of a medieval castle looked out over the town's twin bays.

121

The gale was howling from the north-east, so the North Bay was a screaming mess. I headed for the South Bay, hoping to find some shelter in the lee of the harbour. As I rolled down the hill, sitting at the traffic lights waiting to cross my path was a van that looked strangely familiar. I did a double take. Could it really be the same van? It should have been sitting in a certain farm yard up in Thurso. Or thundering over some Hebridean moorland in search of a hidden cove. But the blacked-out windows and uncompromising silhouette were unmistakeable. Achilles!

I hooted and waved and gestured that I was heading for the harbour car park just beyond the lights. Achilles looked startled. I parked badly and jogged back to the junction. No sign of him, or his ominous vehicle. I trudged back, and had pretty much given up hope of seeing him, when he appeared. I made him coffee and quizzed him eagerly for news of the north coast.

He sounded fairly despondent. The atmosphere had soured and he and his friends had come back earlier than planned. He muttered darkly about the locals, rolled a cigarette and stared moodily across the bay. I was disappointed. Perhaps I had been hoping for a vicarious thrill from his tales of Thurso. Out of the water, he was a gentle giant. But I had caught a glimpse of his flashing temper that first day in Strathy. He was a good surfer and knew his rights. I couldn't imagine him deferring to anyone, local or otherwise, at Thurso or anywhere else. His quiet determination to follow his own path was part of his charm, and he wasn't the kind of person to let others intimidate him. But he certainly wasn't a thug, and was far more sensitive than his appearance or lifestyle suggested. I was disappointed for him, and for what it says about surfers in general.

122

The sun was shining intermittently and the fierce wind was showing no sign of easing. But while the South Bay was certainly rough, it wasn't completely blown out. It was time to get in, before the tide got too high. With the wind coming in from the north east, the curve of the bay created a sliding scale of wave size and power. Tucked in beside the harbour, the wind was almost off-shore, but the waves were weak and inconsequential. On the far side of the curve, it was almost directly on-shore, blowing up waves that were huge and chaotic. The secret was to find the mid-point, a compromise between chaos and quality. Comparative quality. Wherever you were, the wind was fierce and the waves unruly.

I opted for about seven o'clock on the half-dial of the bay, roughly in front of the theatre and about thirty metres in, where the waves were just above head height and reasonably clean. Achilles, more confident, more adventurous, more willing to struggle with the elements, was further round and further out, where the waves towered over him. He had longer to wait between surfable waves, but when they came, they looked impressive: a vertiginous drop, a brief looming wall, then they were absorbed back into the undulations of the bay before reforming closer to shore, where mere mortals fed on their crumbs.

It was hard work picking the right spot, and even harder staying there, but the rewards were worthwhile, and I caught enough decent rides to compensate for the cold and the wind. In the lulls between waves, I watched Achilles with admiration. We saluted one another, two lunatics against the weather, and he indicated that I should join him further out. I declined. I knew my limits.

Slowly, cold and tiredness took hold, and despite the brief appearance of a rainbow over the harbour, I reluctantly got out, riding the whitewash in towards the rising tideline, and reaching my van just as a hailstorm hit. Achilles showed no sign of quitting. He was still out there long after I had washed and changed. I had some work to send off, and headed into town to plug in my laptop. When I returned, I was disappointed to discover he had gone. This time I wasn't so sure I would see him again.

WAVE 32: Saltburn

Somewhere along the road from Scotland I had got out of the habit of surfing twice on the same day. The days were getting shorter and by four o'clock it was dark, so it was harder to fit in two sessions, especially when the tide was against you. Worse, I was painfully aware of the toll each surf took on my body, particularly as the weather got colder. It was hard enough surfing three days in a row, with twenty-four hours to recover between dips. Three hours' recovery just wasn't enough, at least not on a regular basis. In your twenties, perhaps. But I was long past my twenties.

There was another reason I had got out of the habit: it was too damn cold. When your feet still ache from one session, it's hard to contemplate a second. Putting on a damp wetsuit is one thing. A dripping wet wetsuit is quite another. It was December. That morning I had woken to find a layer of ice on the inside of my windows. Warm it wasn't.

But I was heading south the next day, to see Karen before she went away for several months. I would be out of the water for at least a week. After a second, less memorable session at Sandsend, I decided to retrace my steps and check out Saltburn before I left.

Putting on a wet wetsuit in a damp van in winter is grotesque. Very cold, very clammy, very uncomfortable. It's an unpleasant sensation that gets gradually worse. The worst thing is that you can't get it over with quickly. It takes time to get into a wetsuit, wet or otherwise, especially a thick winter suit. It feels even longer when you're wincing and fighting the instinct to recoil. And the more of you that's in, the more horrible it feels. The real nadir comes as you zip it up and the damp pelt grips you tight. After that it's merely uncomfortable and a little chilly. Just what you need when you're about to plunge into a cold, turbulent sea. I have a fairly high tolerance for cold and discomfort, but even so, zipping myself into a wet wetsuit was something I never really got used to. The cold water? No problem. The numb fingers and aching feet? An unavoidable hazard. The post-surf chill? A temporary inconvenience that wears off in an hour or two. But pulling on a wet wetsuit twice in one day, before it's at least had a chance to drip a little dry? It was the single least pleasant aspect of the whole sorry venture.

The surf, though, was sublime. Smooth sets walled up at twice the height of the surfers riding them. There was just the small matter of seething white-water to get through first. The local surfnoscenti jump off the pier, despite the warning signs. I'm something of a coward when it comes to diving blind into unknown water, so I took the hard route, out through the breaking waves. It was utter Calvary.

My arms were already exhausted before I set foot in the water, and the swirling waves did nothing to relieve them. At first, my shoulders merely ached. Soon they burned. Wave after wave exploded just ahead, each one engulfing me in foaming chaos. Each time, I duck-dived and felt the chaos rake over me. Each time, I came up spluttering to see another wave looming over me. Each time, I groaned inwardly and dived again, my shoulders now molten agony. At one point, I was on the verge of turning back. It was quite simply overwhelming. I didn't have the power to push through.

But just as I thought it was hopeless, I hit a slight lull. Fighting the pain, I made an urgent push for safety, desperate to get beyond the impact zone. The next set held off, and when it came, I was relieved to feel it slip beneath me, throwing me up and letting me gently down like a parent playing with a child. I had made it.

I sat on my board, enjoying the tranquillity on the far side of the tumult. Six surfers were nicely spread, like a line of buoys stretching towards the pier. The wave was peaking all over the place. You just had to wait until one came your way.

With a hint of offshore wind, the waves were clean, and although big, the face of the wave was steep rather than vertiginous. Soon enough, one came my way. I paddled hard, got up fast and suddenly I was on it, high up on the face, heading left. I felt the sudden thrill of surprise, exhilaration and trepidation that bursts over you, almost too fast to register, as you focus on what you're doing, desperate not to mess it up. It's almost like experiencing it from the corner of your eye, something phenomenal and amazing that you don't dare look at directly in case distraction throws you off. You're torn between experiencing the sensation and maintaining the action that ensures it continues. The key, of course, is to do both.

I didn't dare attempt anything too radical. Instead I wiggled up and down the top of the face a bit. I'd like to think this was rail-to-rail surfing but I have my doubts. A couple of cutbacks kept me close to the curl, and again I had the divine sensation of losing momentum, thinking I had lost the wave, putting pressure on my front foot and swooping back down the face in a whooshing re-entry. And all this on my forehand, watching the wave thunder along beside me, well above my head.

The next wave was similar, but as I tried to stand, I fumbled and missed my footing. I was on the wave, but my back foot was trailing like a rudder as I struggled to get up. Somehow I reeled it in, found the foot pad and recovered. There was still plenty of time to surf the wave, and I managed to thread together a succession of continuous turns, top and bottom.

The paddle back wasn't getting any easier. I was cold and tired. The light started to fade into autumnal gloom, the tide turned and somewhere out there I mislaid my mojo. I paddled and missed wave after wave, fearful of being sent into the maelstrom again for no reward. A few huge sets came through that had me scrabbling for the horizon. Behind the clouds the moon rose. Everyone left. My shoulders ached. The dark thickened. After a positive start, soon I was close to despair, stuck out there on my own, failing to catch anything no matter how I tried.

In the end, I opted for a breaking wave. Never a great idea but it seemed like the only solution. It broke. I stuck with it, riding the white-water – that infernal white-water. I fell again. Some more whitewash. Then a long, long whoosh to the beach, lying on my board, smiling despite the frustration.

The following day I drove south, and spent the next week saying a protracted farewell to Karen, who was off to India for six months to explore her own mid-life crisis. We should probably have arranged to travel somewhere together, but I was determined to surf, and she was determined to follow in her grandmother's footsteps around the subcontinent. Whether our relationship would survive the separation, remained to be seen. Clearly it was a risk we were each prepared to take.

* * *

Ten days later, I was back on the road. Karen was now on a different continent; I could get on with the task in hand. And now I had a deadline: I had promised to join her in India in April. I had to complete the trip by then. At least that was the plan.

In theory, I had done Yorkshire. I had surfed Saltburn, Sandsend and Scarborough South. I would have liked to have surfed Shhh..., as well as Robin Hood's Bay and Runswick, but in each case conditions had been against me. I could continue my route without dishonour, breeze through Lincolnshire, tick off Norfolk and still be out of the North Sea by Christmas.

Unfortunately, something was calling me back. Whether it was the spirit of Achilles summoning me again to his home breaks, or a feeling of having not quite completed my mission, I felt I had to surf Scarborough's other bay, and more importantly Cayton, another emblematic bay a few miles further south. So no slinking straight to Norfolk for the next leg of the journey. Back to Scarborough it was.

It had been cold when I left. Now, in mid-December, it was freezing. I woke up on my first morning back to find a layer of frozen condensation on the inside of the windows and chunks of ice floating in my water bottle like miniature icebergs. After ten days of central heating, it was a shock. Still, I had a job to do.

WAVE 33: Scarborough North Bay

Unlike the South Bay with its ornate pavilion, chirping arcades and pretty harbour, the North Bay feels cut off from the town while still managing to be unremittingly urban. On a damp December morning, it was bleak and miserable. Waist-high chop muddled about in the shallows, along with three beginners. The tide was already filling in the bay, and even though I hadn't surfed for two weeks, it didn't look like a great prospect. I was just about to head off and check somewhere else when Morgan arrived.

I had met Morgan briefly at Sandsend and over the next few days we formed an unspoken team. He wasn't the world's best surfer, but then neither was I, and as the cold started to bite, it was reassuring to have a comrade in arms. If he was going in, I was going in.

By any objective criteria, it was a very average session: choppy, brutish and short. But after the enforced break, it felt great. It was cold but not mortally cold, and though the peak jumped around, if you could pin it down long enough to get some speed up, there were some reasonable rides around. Too soon, though, the tide started tickling the base of the sea wall and the waves stopped breaking. Wordlessly we each took the decision to catch a final wave and head towards the shore, striding through thigh-high water to get to the steps, and safety.

WAVE 34: Cayton Bay

It had been a short session, so I decided to check out Cayton Bay, a couple of miles further south. It's poorly signposted and unprepossessing, and only the fluttering flags of the surf shop tell you you're in the right place. From the cliff-top, clean sets seemed to be peeling nicely across the middle of the bay, just in front of the ruined pill-box that squats on the foreshore. A couple of surfers and a kayaker seemed to be getting on OK, though from above it was hard to tell how big the waves were.

Various surfers had told me that tomorrow was going to be bigger, so I was faced with the surfer's quandary – go in now or save your energy for later? But I was beginning to learn that it's better to catch a reasonable surf when you can, for tomorrow may come wind and wild water. I decided to go for it.

Further down the beach, a knot of young bucks were scrapping for a different peak. They were welcome to it. Better to surf a reasonable peak on your own than scrap for a great peak with others. In front of the bunker, chest-high sets were coming through, with the occasional shoulder-high wave that unfurled nicely before it hit the shallows. As I jogged to the water's edge, a flock of oyster-catchers took fright and fluttered away in a flash of black and white. They shimmered low over the waves, wheeled round and came in to land again, keeping a wary distance.

The waves were good, but it was tricky being in the right place at the right time. I was taking mostly right-handers, and although they were fine while they lasted, they kept closing down after only a few seconds. I decided to try the lefts, and paddled over to where I thought they would break.

I got bogged down in the first wave as it broke around me, but when I got back out, the next one was large and powerful, and I was in just the right position. I paddled hard and caught it well, angling my board left and taking the drop on a head-high peak.

But it was breaking fast. No time for acrobatics. No time for histrionics. It was a case of setting your line and going for it. In an instant, I was racing the wave headlong across the bay, one eye on the crest as it feathered and broke beside me, one on the bunker that had slipped quietly into the shallows as the tide rose. I was caught in that exquisite balance between enjoying the exhilaration while attending to the many physical factors that kept me riding. The wave was fast, but it was good and long, plenty of time to enjoy the thrill of the chase, the pure speed. No room for manoeuvres, this was a one-shot race, with both of us giving it our utmost. The wave ran its course, closing down a good distance from the start, and we collapsed into one another's celebratory arms.

After a good hour or so, I dragged myself up the long stairs to the van, exhausted. If everyone's predictions were right, tomorrow I would be in for a lot of pain. But at least I had had a good session. Carpe Undam, and all that. And as it turned out, the following day was small, which demonstrates the importance of seizing the moment. Surf now, for tomorrow may be flat.

The day after that the waves were back. Morgan turned up and we surfed the North Bay again. The waves were head-high and above, but fat and formless, and they petered out quickly. It made for a killer combination of difficult paddle for minimal reward, made worse by the current, which constantly swept us from the peak. Morgan resorted to hanging on to a large yellow buoy tethered in the line-out, while I flew past him in the grip of the current. It was a mediocre session, but at least it was amusing.

We got out and I persuaded Morgan to come and check Cayton in the rain. It didn't look great, and for once, we talked each other out of going in, when normally you do the opposite. Instead, I wandered over to the surf shop above the beach, and got talking to the young surfer working there. He knew Achilles and had surfed every break up and down the coast, and he filled me with renewed enthusiasm. When I left, I was determined to go in again, whatever the conditions.

The waves weren't great, and I didn't surf them well, missing lots or pulling back to avoid a pummelling. Perhaps I had used up too much energy in the morning, paddling fruitlessly against the current. I caught several, and took some decent drops from head-high waves, but invariably the wave vanished beneath me or I didn't hold my balance into the turn. Either way, it wasn't going well.

And then it went a lot worse.

Evening was approaching and I was starting to get tired. Without warning, I realised the wind had swung round and freshened up, blowing the waves out of shape and pushing me off the peak. I had been in for a while and perhaps I wasn't concentrating on my position, but I realised with a jolt that I was suddenly a long way from shore. I looked around to check again, and I was even further out. I was caught in a rip current.

Up to now, my experience of rips had been only positive. I knew the theory, and could spot them from the shore. I knew how to use them to my advantage to get out to the peak. This was the first time I had been caught in one unawares. Now I was being swept out to sea.

I told myself not to panic, but as the bunker on the beach grew smaller, it was a struggle to control my rising fear. Your immediate instinct is to paddle for shore as fast as you can. Dozens of people, mostly swimmers, drown every year trying to do just that, not realising that they'll never make it against the rip. They find themselves in turbulent water, and assume it's turbulent all the way along.

'Paddle parallel to the beach' is what you're supposed to do. Rips are usually narrow, like a river flowing out to sea. They form because all the water brought in by the waves needs to find a way back out, and gets funnelled into the easiest channel available. Once you've paddled across the channel, you'll find yourself in calmer, stiller water and can paddle to shore more easily.

What they don't tell you is that it's difficult to see the rip when you're in the water, so it's hard to tell you're in one, and even harder to see where it starts or ends. You just have to paddle to one side, even though it feels counter-intuitive. Eventually you will find yourself in slightly calmer water. Except calm is relative, and paddling to shore is not as simple and straight-forward as it sounds.

I managed to paddle out of the way of the rip, but I was still several hundred metres out, and the wind was trying to blow me further. I was exhausted after two sessions that day, and getting cold as the water tried to suck the heat out of me. The light was fading and even though I was clear of the rip, I was daunted by the task ahead. I had seen no one and no one had seen me. No one knew I was there. I have never felt so alone on a surf board. But it was my own fault. I knew the risks. If you surf alone, that's what's going to happen. I only had myself to blame.

I paddled and I paddled and gradually I started to get a little closer to shore. It felt like an eternity. My arms burned and my neck strained and my shoulders ached, and I berated myself for my stupidity. I tried to hitch a ride on passing ridges of swell, but they seemed to push me backwards, not drive me on. I made progress, but it

133

was painful, and painfully slow. There was no avoiding it, you just had to keep paddling.

Finally I got to within striking distance, and here the waves caught me. But instead of helping me in to shore, they washed me around for a while, insignificant flotsam tossed around in the white-water. Just because you're at the end of your energy doesn't mean you get a free ride. As dusk darkened the bay, I finally staggered on to the sand like a shipwrecked sailor. I had never felt so relieved.

Six

Norfolk

The next day I crossed the Humber, while Karen by the Indian Ganges' side did rubies find. My plan to be out of the North Sea by Christmas was looking increasingly fragile, but if I could tick off Norfolk, I could head to my parents' house for Christmas then continue south into Kent in the new year.

Reports of surfing in Lincolnshire were mixed, but I couldn't continue without at least having a look, so I decided to check out Skegness – much maligned Skegness. I found it fully deserving of all maligning, and anyway it was blown out. I continued on towards Norfolk.

As I drove, I was alarmed to see the fields were covered in an ominous sprinkling of fresh snow. The van had no heating, and it was starting to get properly cold at night. Cooking dinner warmed the van up, but the effect didn't last long. I mostly survived on a diet of thick vegetable stews that I cooked from scratch, along with rice or pasta. It kept me warm, but cooking created pools of condensation that streamed down the windows. When the condensation started to freeze, I knew things were getting serious.

To sleep, I wore thick pyjamas, thick socks and a thick woolly hat. When it was really cold, I even wore gloves. I had a warm duvet, a thick blanket and a charity shop anorak, several sizes too large, which I had bought in Thurso. In bed, I would wear it back to front so I could read without my arms freezing, then use it as an additional blanket to sleep.

Wrapped up like this, I felt remarkably snug in my steel sarcophagus, cocooned and safe, though it was difficult to keep your nose warm. Getting up to pee in the night was a bit of a trial, but by then I had usually built up enough residual heat to make a quick dash to the nearest greenery without succumbing to frostbite. Getting up in the morning was the hardest, when the still air in the van was cold to the touch and even sitting up to make tea was a shock. If I remembered, I usually slept with my clothes under the covers, to make getting dressed less grim.

Then came the laborious process of folding everything up and storing it away: pillow, blanket, duvet, sheet, under-sheet to block condensation, everything. And then folding the bed into a seat again. The key was to put everything away in reverse order, so it all came out again in the order you needed it. It became a real drag – though not as tedious as the inescapable and more precise ritual of making up the bed each night, which bored me rigid with its awkward routine and clockwork inevitability. If there's one task you can't put off until tomorrow, it's getting your bed out. But at least folding everything up helped get me warm in the morning.

WAVE 35: Cromer

I reached Cromer after dark, tired and bewildered by the labyrinthine one-way system, and went in search of fish and chips. I emerged to find that the wind had caught up with me, howling round the church tower, full of sleet and anger. It felt portentous, like Rome on the night Caesar was murdered, or Paris on Napoleon's posthumous return. By morning a fine layer of snow lay over the windows. This was no weather for surfing, much less for living in a van. Still, surfing was what I was there to do, and a van was what I was resigned to doing it in.

Sure enough, it was horrible. A heaving mess and very, very cold. The waves broke everywhere, and to get out meant a lot of diving through icy whitewash. By the time I reached the peak, my chest was clamped tight with cold, and my face raw. I had chosen the wrong board, my 6'5". It lacked the volume and stability for these dumping, fat waves and I was hurled around like a cork. A burst of driving sleet didn't help. After forty minutes, already very cold, I got out.

For the rest of the day, though, I felt a glow of pleasure, a warm tingle, part post-exercise euphoria, part sheer relief that I wasn't in the water. The wind dropped, the sky cleared and Cromer was charming.

That one dismal surf didn't feel like enough to tick Cromer off my list, so I decided to stick around. By morning, conditions were cleaner, though the air was still cold. No sooner had I got out past the breaking waves than the weak winter sun gave way to fat, fluffy snowflakes blowing horizontally across the top of the water. It was picturesque, certainly, but not ideal for surfing. Hail I had surfed in before; snow was a novelty.

Peering through the snowstorm, I caught a decent, shoulder-high right, and managed a few seconds on the face before it crashed down on me. As it did, my instinctive reaction was a delighted 'Great! Now I can go home!'

I stuck it out, though, and managed some actual, proper rides, including a nice left that broke head high, with a fast drop down the face, round a crumbling section, back on to the brown wall and up into a semi-floater as the wave closed down, leaving me in waist-high water, among the ankle-threatening flints that lurked on the sea bed.

Walking back to the van on numb feet was nasty, the thin rubber soles of my neoprene boots doing nothing to blunt the shooting pain of every stone and pebble. For all the protection they gave, I might as well have been barefoot.

I had planned to check out East Runton, but the next morning, everything was blanketed in snow, and I didn't want to risk driving. It was a decision I would later regret. The temperature was arctic but the sun shone low in the clear blue sky, and clean, head-high waves were breaking nicely beside the pier. Parents pulled toddlers along on plastic sleds, wrapped up like mini Michelin men. I struggled into my wetsuit, feeling a little out of place.

To my horror, when I pulled out my 6'10", I discovered a nasty gash on the rail. It must have clunked one of the treacherous flints that lurked in the shallows. Cursing, I grabbed my insubstantial 6'5" instead.

Earlier, the air had warmed slightly under the weak sun, but now it was back below zero and rivulets of melted snow had refrozen. I slithered down the icy ramp in a precarious parody of surfing, wary of dinging my one good board.

It wasn't a great session. The smaller board proved just as inappropriate as it had on the first day, and although the waves were better, I found myself continually pulling back from the yawning jaws of hollow monsters. Several sucked me over the falls, and one of them swallowed me whole, down into its cold, dark maw as I fell headlong,

138

not knowing where I was going or what I would hit when I got there.

Each time I was dragged under, any warmer water trapped by my wetsuit was sluiced out by cold, making it doubly miserable. I stuck with it, increasingly desperate, and finally caught a few. But by now I was properly cold, despite wetsuit, hood, boots and gloves. Eventually, genuinely afraid of hypothermia, I struggled out, disgruntled, and crunched back up the ice like a fire-walker. If the pebbles had been agony, the ice was worse.

I spent the rest of the day thawing out. That's when the pain really starts. While you're in the water, there's the initial sting before you go numb. Soon your feet and fingers hurt as the heat is sucked from them and the blood withdraws into your core to protect your vital organs. After all, you don't need warm fingers for survival. But it's later, when the blood cautiously creeps back, that the real pain begins, and no amount of coffee and porridge can make it any easier.

When it was really cold I could surf for about an hour, perhaps a little more. The pain would last for three. It was a dull ache that lingered on, especially in your feet, and made even walking agony for at least the first hour. I would find myself unable to force myself to move, sitting for hours in the ice-box of my van, entranced by the banal comfort of Test Match Special, the only programme, apart from Radio Norfolk, my ancient radio could find.

Somehow, though, the cold was manageable. You get used to it, and just wear more clothes without really noticing. When you're living in a snug, centrally-heated house, going outside is more of a shock. When you're outside all the time – and being in an unheated van is pretty much like being outside all the time, except there's no wind chill – you adapt. If I hadn't been immersing myself in sea water for an hour every day and later stripping naked for a wash, I would have been fine. All I could do was pile on more clothes and try and read or write with clumsy fingers. I lived in a short-sleeved T-shirt, a long-sleeved T-shirt, a sweatshirt, a thin wool jumper and a thick wool jumper. I had thick, lined trousers, two pairs of socks and, most of the time, a scarf and a woolly hat. If I got desperate, I put on my outsize charity-shop anorak, though it was cumbersome and turned me into a sumo wrestler.

No matter how cold it was, I always had a decent wash every day, standing in the plastic storage box I took my wetsuit off in, to stop too much water swilling around the floor. Heating the water would warm the air in the van by a degree or two and if you were quick, you didn't suffer too much for the privilege of keeping clean. If I surfed, then I washed straight afterwards, when I had peeled off my wetsuit and my skin was steaming in the still air of the van; if I hadn't surfed, I washed before I went to bed – a full body wash, not a quick splash. Like sleeping in a duvet rather than a sleeping bag, a decent daily wash made me feel more civilised, better able to cope with the other privations of the trip, social, physical and emotional.

It's true that it was hard going, facing the cold, night after night. It felt like genuine hardship, particularly during the long, dark evenings, as it got colder and steadily colder. But it was voluntary hardship. I could have ended it at any time. No one had asked me to be there. I reminded myself that I wasn't in Afghanistan or anything. I wasn't starving, and I certainly wasn't being shot at. I was just very cold, and it made everything more of an effort. It was tough but not impossible. And deep down, the masochistic part of me, the part that used to run marathons and climb mountains and ride a motorbike in mid-winter, secretly enjoyed the challenge. The same part of me that enjoyed surfing in Britain's icy waters. Or swimming in an unheated, outdoor pool when the temperature drops to single figures. Or, for five memorable days one January, swimming deep within the Arctic Circle, where the air was minus 13, and the salty fjord somewhere around zero. Living in a van in winter was a challenge, but the fact that I could end it at any time only made me more determined to stick it out. It's just a question of resilience.

Christmas was a different matter. I was definitely going home for Christmas. If the weather allowed it. I had surfed Cromer three times. That was enough. More winter weather was forecast, so when I woke to find sunlight glinting off the snow, I decided to make a dash for it while the roads were still clear. First, though, I had to check out East Runton, just in case. Not to surf, you understand, simply for reference. I was done with Norfolk. Or I thought I was.

When I got to East Runton, the swell was dropping and surfers were leaving. My mistake was to get talking to a local surfer, Mark, who had been surfing for twenty years and was still younger than I had been when I started. Over coffee in my van, he fired me with enthusiasm. Only surfing Cromer wasn't enough. I would have to give Norfolk another chance. Rats.

But not today. Today I had to get home to my parents' house before the snow returned, or face Christmas stranded in Sheringham. I knew blizzards were on the way, but the bright winter sunshine and Mark's convivial if lugubrious company made me linger. The sun was still shining as I set off, sometime around noon, but as I drove south, the sky soon covered over with the bone-white of

141

snow clouds. A dusting of snow started to fall. Soon it was a carpet, and getting worse. When I was still thirty miles from home, I came round a bend and felt the first flickering of a slide, as my back wheels tried to catch up with the front. It was a horrible sensation, new but unmistakable.

'Don't brake!' I seemed to remember. 'Keep steering in the direction you want to go!'

Like being caught in a rip, I knew the theory but had never put it into practice. I somehow managed to pull out of the slide and cut my speed without touching the brake pedal. But I was shaken by the lack of control and the fear of what might have happened.

It was dark by the time I reached my parents' house. The roads were covered in three inches of fresh snow and my nerves were shattered. My parents live at the top of a long hill and I was forced to abandon the van at the bottom. I trudged the last half-mile feeling like Good King Wenceslas, or maybe Good My Page. I suspect I looked more like Yonder Peasant.

WAVE 36: East Runton

As autumn had hardened into winter, I had grown used to the cold. A warm house made me soft again. For almost a month I found every excuse to keep off the road: Christmas, more snow, the surf forecast, a debilitating cold. As the days passed, I grew ever more reluctant to return to the fray. Eventually I could procrastinate no more. I had to complete what I had started. And annoyingly, that meant returning to Norfolk, four hours and 150 miles in the wrong direction, just because a little snow in Cromer had kept me from East Runton. I said goodbye to warmth and comfort, and headed back into the cold.

I slept above the beach and woke to the sound of surfers. Sweet music! After a month, I was desperate. I wolfed down a banana and jogged down to find one of the surfers already getting out. Too cold, he said, and looked it. Not a good sign.

To say it was cold was an understatement. It was grim. The air was perfectly still and the waves were more or less glassy, so you could get out without too much duck-diving. But where the water soaked through your gloves, it burned like acid.

Once the initial shock had faded, though, the waves made up for the cold. Chest high, opening nicely and peeling away for long rides. They were slow, it's true, but this was Norfolk. And after a month off the road, they were ideal – easy to catch, easy to surf, flattering my abilities and rewarding my unexpected return. I stayed in for an hour and caught a dozen or so long, lazy rides, with just a couple of others in the water. If it hadn't been for the cold, it would have been heaven.

Even after a leisurely breakfast, it was still ridiculously early on a miserable grey January day, a day for exploring, not sitting in a van moping. I decided to check out other spots in Norfolk to see what I might have missed. I left the beach and headed east, no real destination in mind. If I could get another surf in, great. If not, I could at least get to Lowestoft, the most easterly point in Britain, and the last place to surf before the inward curve of East Anglia makes surfing improbable, if not actually impossible.

I had taken months to cover the shoulder of Britain. I covered its curved buttock in a single day. It's a journey I highly recommend. Wide tracts of marshland bring in

143

migrating birds, interrupted by clumps of ramshackle housing unencumbered by taste or, apparently, planning law. It feels like the Wild West, all clapperboard and mud tracks, but unmistakeably English in its architectural inspiration, a combination of runaway beach hut, renegade summer house and grotesque garden shed.

WAVE 37: Lowestoft

Overnight, a gusting weather front blew in, bringing with it wind and rain. Lowestoft bills itself as the Sunrise Coast. The following morning there was no horizon, far less a sunrise. This was the Drizzle Coast, grey and blustery and no good for surfing. So I went surfing. It's the most easterly point in Britain. I had to.

It was always going to be rubbish, and sure enough it was. A howling on-shore wind was kicking up a mess of waves into unsurfable whitewash, chest high and seething. A couple of kite-surfers were out, which is never a good sign. The only suspicion of anything surfable was round the end of one of the groynes, where a sudden surge tidied up the mess for a brief instant. It was far from ideal.

I made sure I kept moving, catching whatever was going, no matter how unlikely or short-lived. I managed a few decent drops, and a couple of glimpses of green face. And because conditions were so unpleasant, and the idea of surfing so ludicrous, just trying to surf there became fun in a perverse way. Forty minutes was plenty, though. A dozen rubbish rides. Enough for honour to be satisfied.

144

Seven

South-East England

As I crossed the Thames at Dartford, the January sun shone and joy filled my heart. Forth, Humber, Thames - there was something exhilarating about these magical gateways. It felt each time that I was crossing my own private Rubicon, passing another milestone in my slow but steady progress around the map of Britain.

WAVE 38: Joss Bay

Kent isn't the most likely of surf destinations, but its eastern tip stretches just far enough to catch the occasional swell sweeping down the North Sea. If you could surf there, I had to go there.

The coast around this extremity of England is like a wheel of Stilton with large bites taken out at regular intervals. Each bite has a beach, edged by low chalk cliffs, their grey-white faces marbled with green. In theory, surf hits several of them. In practice, Joss Bay was my only option.

Even here, it was rubbish. Small, weak and pointless. It broke – low – all over the place and just dribbled towards the shore. At least Lowestoft had had the adrenaline thrill of battling the elements. This was just boring: small waves on a small beach beneath small cliffs. I got out, very unimpressed.

Later I watched a schoolkid ribbon his way down the road on a long skateboard to check the surf. The following morning, he reappeared with a surfboard and a friend. They clearly hadn't been surfing long, and even from the cliff-top I could see what they were doing wrong. With nothing better to do, I strolled down to watch, and perhaps offer a few tips.

At sea level, conditions looked a lot better. Not huge and not going far. But there were surfers out there (albeit beginners). And they were surfing (albeit badly). I ran back for my board.

Ryan and Kurosh were both about 15 and obviously bunking off school. Ryan had got a new board for Christmas and was desperate to try it. They were entirely self-taught, which explained their style, but being young and keen, they caught a few waves through sheer determination, although they should have been catching a lot more. Like many beginners, Ryan lay too far back, so his board was angled too steeply in the water, pushing against the water rather than gliding over it. Kurosh's position was better, but on every wave he stopped paddling too soon, before the wave had picked him up, so it always left without him.

These are the two most common mistakes every beginner makes. You see them repeated endlessly at every beach in the world. They lead to exhaustion, frustration and despair. People! Your board should be flat in the water, with only the tip of the nose peeking out. Think crocodile!

I politely pointed out to Ryan and Kurosh the error of their ways. Gratifyingly, Ryan immediately caught a great wave and surfed all the way to shore. It was the best wave he had ever caught, he said when he paddled back out, a big smile stretched across his face.

Above the beach, a gang of migrant farm workers were chopping kale in the bitter cold. Seeing them hard at work made me feel guilty that I wasn't doing something more useful or profitable with my time. At various times along my route I had felt an uncomfortable sense of privilege that I had the freedom to take to the road – although financially, living in a van was cheaper than any of the alternatives. The juxtaposition of the farm-workers' tough existence, digging vegetables in sub-zero conditions for miserable pay, and my own carefree way of life, however temporary, filled me with unease. Not for the first time, I felt that what I was doing wasn't real life.

For the moment I had more pressing things to worry about. I had had my engine looked at twice recently, hoping to make it run more smoothly and, if possible, more economically. Petrol was proving prohibitive, and the 300-mile round trip back to Norfolk hadn't helped. But once again the van was struggling. At first I thought it was just the cold. It wasn't. Reluctantly, I realised I had to get it fixed. As I retraced my steps round the M25, the problem grew steadily worse until I was crawling along at 40mph. Uphill, I had trouble reaching 30. I expected to be hauled over by the police at any moment.

'I noticed a certain lethargy in the engine,' Colin the mechanic agreed. Something to do with the distributor, apparently. He was able to fix it, and a week later, I was back on the road, all signs of lethargy gone from both me and the van. The surf forecast was excellent and I was finally about to turn the corner and leave the long, long east coast at last.

Except the van had other plans. Somewhere on a

147

country road outside Dover, there was a bang. The engine wouldn't engage and I was forced to freewheel into a lay-by. So much for the fantastic surf forecast. Exactly a week after my ignominious crawl along the M25 to my parents' house, I had to slink back once again – only this time I was racing along in a breakdown truck. Thank goodness for the RAC.

As if Neptune was laughing at my predicament, fantastic waves duly materialised on the south coast. Several websites commented on the great surf. In Kent and Sussex you get good conditions about twice a year. I had missed my window. It didn't improve my mood.

But that was the least of my worries. Colin couldn't fit me in for several days, and even then it wasn't clear he would be able to fix the problem. My van was finished, and me with it. It looked as if I was going to have to abandon the whole project half way. I certainly couldn't afford to buy another van. If I couldn't get it fixed, that was it.

For several days I slunk round in a cloud of gloom. I was stuck, and there was nothing I could do about it. What made it worse was that I was entirely unable to alleviate my wretchedness. Most of the time I'm cheerful and optimistic, and even when I'm not, I recognise that things could be so much worse. Life might not be perfect, but it's got plenty going for it. Depression I simply don't understand. Whenever I've felt down, it's nothing that a night's sleep – or better still, a surf – can't cure. I recognise there are clinical reasons for depression, and for genuine sufferers it's a life-wrecker, but I'm definitely of the "if you're miserable go for a run" school of self-medication.

This was relentless, though. I could see no glimmer of light, no silver lining, nothing but unremitting bleakness. It felt physical, a malign presence clinging to my back, shading everything in black. For those few days I finally glimpsed what real depression might feel like, a dark weight crushing you down, stifling any flicker of hope.

I was stranded, and had wasted six months and several thousand pounds on a pointless project that was going nowhere. At best, I had surfed the wrong coast. I was well into middle age, and I simply didn't know what I was doing with my life.

Just when things couldn't have looked more bleak, my father managed to put a large hole in one of my boards. I was incandescent with rage, and plunged even deeper into wretchedness. To his credit, he had the good grace to be mortified, though this was no consolation.

I repaired the board as best I could, and tried not to direct too much frustration at him. You can't really expect non-surfers to understand the unique fragility and precarious balance of a surfboard. And to be fair, we've all done it, early in our surfing lives, before manoeuvring a board out of the water became second nature. Surfboards look balanced, but the minute you turn your back they topple over like fainting guardsmen. It's why your first board should be third-hand, so you can learn the hard way how ungainly they are and how easily they get damaged.

My first board was a feisty, fabulous 7'6", second-hand but unmarked. Unfortunately I lived in a flat whose dimensions were no more than 7'5" in any direction. Whenever I moved it, I was in danger of denting the fibreglass, clearing a shelf or smashing a light-bulb. Sometimes all three. If you take care not to knock the nose, you damage the tail; if you focus on the tail, you knock the nose. You need eyes like a gecko until eventually you learn to move slowly and think spatially, to be aware of both ends of the board at once, as well as all possible obstacles and eventualities in your path; and when you've moved it, to make sure it's safely propped, preferably in a corner, never against a flat wall. By the time it all becomes second nature, your board will have more patches than an old bike tyre.

Repairing the board was relatively straightforward. It wasn't pretty, but it was watertight. Repairing the van was more tricky. The clutch had disintegrated in a dramatic puff of oily dust. I know nothing about clutches, but even I could see it was a shocker. I tried to be philosophical about the expense. Clutches have a finite life-span, and, like a fuse burning away, it was only a matter of time before it blew. I just happened to be there when it happened. It's the lottery of second-hand vans.

Eventually, Colin managed to fix it and I was back on the road again. Nothing could stop me now. Except, as I drove across the Thames for the third time in as many weeks, gentle snowflakes were starting to fall. Light flurries soon became a blizzard and before long I was driving through a snowscape. Surely I wasn't going to have to turn back yet again.

Where the snow was drifting on quiet Kentish roads, progress was difficult, and not just for campervans. At the point where several 4x4s were opting to leave a snow-blocked lane and drive across a snow-bound field, I had to turn round. Finally, by trial and error, I managed to find my way through, though I don't know how, and wouldn't be able to find that route again.

WAVE 39: Ramsgate

By the time I got to Ramsgate, it was covered in a pictur-esque blanket of snow that turned the marina into a Victorian Christmas card. To the north of the harbour, a low swell was running. A short way out from the snow-bound promenade, the fierce wind was whipping the sea into white manes, but closer in, low cliffs sheltered the foreshore just enough to let small, well-defined waves slip through. Everywhere was thick with snow, and the slope onto the promenade was a slippery trap. I decided to risk it, and crunched the van slowly down, full of trepidation. A few walkers tramped across the snow but otherwise the sea front was deserted, and I had the small, snow-filled car park to myself.

With snow on the ground, the air was somewhere around freezing point. The wind added extra chill. Chalk rocks slippery with seaweed lurked in the murky shal-lows, threatening to twist you over, so wading out was tricky. Then as you paddled, a fearsome rip washed you down the beach in a flash. Once again, you had to be quick or you were too far from any recognisable peak.

Even so, the first two waves were surprisingly good. A decent height and a decent amount of power behind them, and running for a reasonable distance, though they were perhaps a bit thick and chunky. I stayed high, sticking close to the pocket with a series of mini cut-backs and re-entries, more a wiggling zig-zag along the top of the wave than real turns.

Paddling back out, though, was almost impossible against the powerful rip. It was easier to whoosh back to the beach on your stomach and start again, though you still had to trudge several hundred metres along the sand.

And each time you were faced with that tricky chalk reef, which got trickier as the tide receded. It was a slow circuit, so the time between rides was overly long, and your time in the cold air felt even longer. And soon, as the tide dropped, the peak moved further out, until it was no longer sheltered by the cliffs and the wind started to mess it up. I caught half a dozen rides, none as good as those first two. But I was happy and invigorated, delighted to have got a session in against all expectations.

I left Ramsgate early the following morning. Everything still lay under a thick blanket of snow, and the road into Dover was strewn with abandoned cars. I was lucky to have made it to Ramsgate. Luckier still to have surfed there.

Finally I turned the corner of England and headed west. As I wound round towards Rye, the sky cleared. Sunlight glittered off the snow and the countryside was suddenly resplendent. My gloom of the previous week was gone, washed away by the waves, banished by the sunshine.

I stopped briefly in Hastings, where I had bought my beloved van, 3,000 miles and a lifetime earlier. I parked on the sea front, feeling the distance I had travelled; trying to gauge the journey still to come. The sea was motionless, a brazen mirror that mocked the idea of surf and surfing.

Further west, the snow diminished, the traffic increased and I joined the slow parade through Brighton. Even from the road I could see it was flat. Months later, I lived in Brighton for a while, and regularly surfed beneath the burnt-out (and often blown-out) pier, or at the ankle-twisting, board-chomping chalk reef in the lee of the marina. You can certainly surf there, and many people do, but it's usually tricky, conditions are rarely ideal and even on a good day it's unsatisfying and awkward. It's better than nothing, but only just.

I continued on to West Wittering, which I had last visited when I was still at school. The sexiest girl in my French class had invited me and my best friend to stay, and we spent three or four days jousting testosterone while she luxuriated in the attention without ever letting us near. One hot and lazy afternoon her mother propositioned me, I think, but I was too awkward and inexperienced to respond, or at least respond correctly. I think she propositioned my best friend too. He too failed. Youth is wasted on the young.

West Wittering this time was less exquisitely angst-ridden. But I did clarify the origin of the name: no sooner had I parked than a little old lady approached and spontaneously started wittering at me. It was fairly benign and I let her witter all the way to the beach. The sea was flat but I lingered for a while, in case she was lurking.

The forecast was flat for the next ten days, so I agreed to fly out to Barcelona for a week, to look after the parents of an American girl who had fallen out of a hotel window and was now in hospital. I thought I had signed up for a cushy job interpreting and facilitating, and catching up with old friends over tapas. Instead I spent two weeks at the bedside of a stranger who came within a heartbeat of death, while her family tore themselves apart with anguish and recrimination, and tried to work out whom to sue. It was the most gruelling experience of my life. It certainly put a damaged board and ruined clutch into perspective.

To say I was relieved when I finally got back on the road is an understatement. Two weeks had slipped by, and with them another window of decent waves. Whatever the trip was turning out to be, being stuck in a hospital corridor for fifteen hours a day on behalf of an unconscious stranger was its antithesis.

I resisted the urge to read too much into the experience. Sure, life is transient, precious and fragile. Sure, Carpe Diem and everything. I knew this. It's why I was living in a van surfing, while I still could. It's why I'm writing this. But the thought is so self-evident as to be banal. It certainly doesn't offer a blueprint for life. If you need a brush with death to remind you to live, you're probably doing it wrong. And anyway, it doesn't help you get through it any more easily. Did I drive towards my next beach glad to be alive? Of course. But most people do. Did I determine to get the most out of life? Of course. But what does that really mean?

What I *was* doing was living life in the present. Enjoying the now. But that was largely because the future looked difficult at best, and certainly didn't include the glorious freedom of living in a van surfing. So on I went. Where else was I going to go? I had to complete the trip. Half-finished it had no meaning. So even now I wasn't living fully in the present. I was caught up in the need to achieve, to pursue a goal, albeit a self-imposed one. Otherwise I would just have stayed in Thurso. Even now I was looking for a compromise between present and future; freedom and responsibility; being and doing. I continued, hoping to weave a purpose from a string of unrelated events. Isn't that what the examined life is?

To make it easier, I slowly realised that the worst was now behind me: the flat bits, the ugly bits, the cold bits. It wasn't warm but at least it wasn't arctic. It wasn't all beautiful but it generally had charm, and while it would occasionally go flat, surely it couldn't stay flat. Not for three weeks, as it had in Yorkshire. Not for two hundred miles, as it had from Broadstairs to Brighton. I was heading to proper surf country. Things could only get better.

WAVE 40: Boscombe Pier

At Boscombe, the artificial reef wasn't working, but beside the pier Mother Nature was throwing up perfectly decent waves instead. They weren't epic, but it was the first time since Yorkshire they been anything more than merely satisfactory. And there were surfers - six of them! It was more than I had seen – cumulatively, not collectively – since leaving Saltburn.

I surfed for an hour and a half, until darkness forced me out, cold but happy to be back in the water, even if the waves were unexceptional. The following morning, they were great. Cleaner, bigger, larger. The sun shone and once again I felt guilty to be surfing as gangs of cheerful workmen swaggered off to work.

The wind was blowing gently offshore, the sea almost glassy. I chatted to a local surfer as we caught waves in turn – or at least he did. I fluffed several, going over the falls, sending my board over the falls, getting up too late, the usual litany. Then a bigger set came through, and somehow I was perfectly placed. I went for it, caught it early and was up, staying high. Ahead of me, my new friend was also up, collapsing the wave in my path. Very correctly, though, he kicked out and left me riding. I got round the crumbling section and I was off, a long, long wave, staying in the pocket, weaving together small re-entries, keeping my speed up almost to the beach. It was the longest wave I had caught since Sandsend. Long enough to enjoy the sensation, to appreciate the situation, to relish the thrill. To marvel at the act of surfing, fully aware of what was happening around me. It was bliss.

Left to my own devices, I would have stayed out all day. But my arms had other ideas. Exhausted and out of condition, they eventually forced me to go in. I spent the rest of the day sitting in one of the beach cafés, basking in the exquisite exhaustion of two long surfs, and envying the young their tireless youth.

From the café, you could see where the artificial reef was from the occasional slap of white. Reefs work by creating a shallow platform below the water that abruptly forces the undulating energy of the wave to the surface, where it breaks in more or less the same place each time. They exist naturally, but are notoriously difficult to recreate artificially.

Even when it's working, the Boscombe reef isn't great for surfers, apparently. Too steep and abrupt. Better for body-boarders. And if that keeps body-boarders off the waves by the pier, so much the better. While I would rather have a body-boarder than a kayak in the line-up, given the choice, I'd rather have neither. They're like wasps at a picnic, irritating and everywhere. They want the buzz of surfing without any of the effort. Their reward is never to taste the true highs of surfing, although they probably avoid the real lows too. No, body-boarding is something I'm saving for my old age, once I'm too old even for long boards. Then it will be my turn to get in the way of all the real surfers. In the meantime, I'm happy to look down my nose at their clear lack of imagination or moral fibre.

The next day, I woke to a beautiful, rosy-fingered dawn. A fine frosting of ice filigreed the inside of the windows, and the sand crunched underfoot. It was going to be a beautiful day. Beautiful but flat.

I was meeting a friend in Lyme Regis, but as I limped

over the hills, I grew increasingly concerned about my engine. That certain lethargy was back. Once again my van was in danger of becoming a beach hut. At least a beach hut doesn't incur road tax.

I picked up my friend and we idly strolled among the fossils at Lyme. The entire beach tittered with the tapping of tiny mallets, as hordes of would-be palaeontologists hammered away, visibly hastening the erosion of southern England. On the Cobb, Lyme's famous stone wharf, a painted sign above one of the sheds reads:

'THE GODS DO NOT SUBTRACT FROM THE ALLOTTED SPAN OF MENS LIVES THE HOURS SPENT IN FISHING...'

I would like to think the same is true of surfing.

I had surfed Lyme Regis several years earlier. On the far side of the Cobb a decent wave had been breaking over large boulders, which unnerved me slightly. The distinct whiff of sewage did nothing to improve the experience. This time it was flat all weekend.

By the time I dropped my friend off, the van was really struggling. It was the same old story: cruising down hills, labouring up. In retrospect, the decision to trickle down the steep lane to sleep by the boatyard was questionable at best.

Sure enough, despite another beautiful sunrise, I soon regretted my decision. There's only one road out of the boatyard and it's up the longest hill in Dorset.

I took a brief run-up, gunning the engine to get some momentum, but within a few hundred metres I was in trouble. The van slowed and slowed. Soon it was barely crawling. It was certainly slower than walking pace. I know this because an elderly woman with two large bags of shopping was struggling up the hill on foot, and she was easily outpacing me. I was in real trouble.

Once again, I needed someone who could fix the van and not take three weeks over it. Eventually I tracked down a mechanic back near Boscombe who thought he might have the right part. It sounded a little vague, but my choices were limited. As the sun went down, I hit the rollercoaster over Dorset's pretty hills, hoping the downs would get me up the ups.

Ady's yard was a revelation, part elephants' graveyard, part operating theatre, part campervan showroom. The carcasses of several dozen VW vans in varying states of deconstruction or rehabilitation lined up along one side of the compound. A rank of gleaming vans stood on the other, tantalisingly out of reach – at least financially. A sharp metal whine screeched from a steel barn, where three or four mechanics were at work on, in or under various vans.

Whatever the problem, Ady knew he could fix it. Nothing was impossible. This was where I had been going wrong. My regular mechanic, Colin, was just that: a regular mechanic. To him, my van was a museum piece. He could apply temporary fixes, but only through the prism of new cars. To Ady, the van was a going concern that just needed a little attention. Within half an hour it was fixed.

The difference was phenomenal. Gone was the lumbering deadweight that drained my nerves and my wallet with every mile. In its place, an efficient speedster that filled me with joy. It was a pleasure to drive, making light of hills, and not just the down ones. I hit the road, destination Devon. Real surfing country at last.

Eight

Devon

I crossed the estuary at Teignmouth in the dark. The tide was out and the bridge felt ethereal, hovering above spectral sandbars, a ghost-crossing on a deserted night. I could feel my spirits lift with every metre. On the far side, I found a narrow lane that wound down through the trees to a small car park, with a glimpse of dark sea beyond. It would have to do. I was up at first light, and after strolling down to inspect the rocky, flotsam-filled inlet, I was on my way, eager to get through Torquay before the rush hour.

I had always imagined Torquay to be a rather depressing place. At sunrise that morning, it was fantastic. Pink light suffused the quiet air with a rosy glow, and everything was still. I had hoped to avoid the rush hour. I was so early, I had avoided all human life. It was a ghost town, a zombie city, a dawn for the dead. As I sped through the eerie silence, Torquay was unexpectedly thrilling.

Better still, I was surprised and delighted to see an unmistakable pulse pushing into the bay across a mirror-smooth sea. It didn't quite break until it hit the shore but it was enough to give me hope. I raced the zombies round the bay until I reached Paignton, where the promise of that unbroken pulse was gloriously realised. As the sun pulled clear of the horizon, it caught a single surfer in beautiful silhouette, surfing chest-high waves beside the pier. It was still only 7.15am. I parked, and watched, ready to join him.

Did I surf through the sunrise and seize the day? Did I forgo breakfast for something more fulfilling? Emerge from the water wet and smug, as most people were going to work? Alas, no. The lone surfer got out, and while I hesitated over a cup of tea, the tide dropped towards low, the waves fell off and breakfast called. I had been asked to look at a script. Better to work first, surf later, I thought. Except later, the wind freshened and started disrupting the waves. Had I learned nothing? If it looks good, go in! Better to surf now than risk no surf later.

WAVE 41: Paignton

Eventually, around midday, I made it in. It was unlikely to improve, and might get worse. The waves were shoulder-high and messy, and tricky to get into before they closed down. But the water was marginally less cold than I had feared, and I was marginally less unfit. A little out of practice taking decent drops, perhaps, but with the wave going nowhere, there was plenty of practice on offer. It wasn't the most skilful session, but it left me energised and elated. A surf's a surf, and I was still buzzing from the delicious dawn.

My elation increased as I drove into deepest Devon and the scenery grew ever more picturesque. The road swooped down through dappled glades and emerged, blinking in the sunlight, on the banks of the River Dart. Kingswear had been freshly painted to greet me, and in

160

the estuary, yachts and dinghies yawed in the fresh wind. If bridges made me happy, ferries thrilled me. Ever since that first, dark morning pushing off from Oban harbour, they had represented adventure and progress. As we pushed out across the estuary, I was euphoric.

Would my mood have been so intense if I hadn't surfed once already that day, and might possibly surf a second time? Probably not. Again I was reminded of the drug-like effect surfing has on one's mind and body.

The scenery had been pretty to the east of the Dart. To the west it was stunning: steep escarpments thick with lush grass, gnarled fences and brittle trees, enigmatic glimpses of unnamed coves and secret inlets. The narrow road clung to sharply-carved farmland which opened up around unexpected bends or plunged alarmingly down to sudden bays. I was in ecstasy, delighting in the journey, eager for the surfing to come.

WAVE 42: Bantham

From what I could tell, Bantham offered the best chance of a surf. I rolled down past the row of pretty stone houses to where a rustic gatekeeper stood sentry in a smart wooden hut, guarding the car park beyond. The sea beckoned, but the beach itself was hidden from view. I hate paying to park, especially if I haven't seen the conditions, so I inscribed an elegant circle and retreated to the top of the tiny hamlet, where a parking space had somehow materialised.

I walked down across the low dunes to find that the tide was in and the sea flat. Not so much as a ripple. Burgh Island sat in the middle of the bay, demure and inaccessible, oozing wealth and exclusivity. Walking back, I fell into conversation with Jason, head chef at the village pub. He seemed sure it would pick up as the tide dropped. I wasn't convinced, but when I returned a couple of hours later, sure enough, a small wave had appeared and the gatekeeper had gone home for the night. There really is no substitute for local knowledge.

A small but rowdy band of locals were sitting on the main peak hoovering up every wave, so I opted for a lesser peak which broke left and right, but closed down almost immediately. A short ride is better than no ride, I figured, at least until I could work on my assertiveness. It was breaking at around chest high but was neither fast nor powerful, a triumph of appearance over substance. But it was fun enough, even when I found myself clutching at white-water, and the bay was beautiful as the sun faded to a brazen medallion and dipped behind the island – or what had appeared to be an island. I now saw that as the tide drops, it reveals a narrow causeway, so that twice a day the marauding hordes can storm that prim and privileged enclave.

Gradually the locals left and I had the bay to myself. I paddled over to where the better waves were breaking and immediately caught one that made the session. It was a long, lovely right, still neither fast nor powerful, but with a nice open face that unfurled slowly for maybe fifty metres. For the first time in a while, I had that wonderful sensation of actively surfing a wave – albeit a small one – pumping rail to rail to keep up momentum and get the most out of it. Catching waves is great; actively surfing them, even better. I was tempted to go back for another. After two sessions, I was tired but not utterly exhausted. Sometimes, though, it's good to end on a high.

As the crimson faded to pale blue, I paddled back to the van. I had intended to look for somewhere more discreet to spend the night. Now, gripped by tiredness and capti-vated by the location, I was less inclined to move. For the next few days, I explored the area but returned to the same green lane each evening after the gatekeeper had gone home.

Then on Sunday morning, as I tucked into breakfast, a weathered face suddenly appeared at the door. The gatekeeper. He looked distinctly uncomfortable. 'I saw you here last night, so I know you've been camping here,' he said apologetically. 'The landowner wanted me to tell you that it's not allowed.'

When I left a little later, he was talking to a gaunt, patri-cian type in mirror shades and designer jeans, clutching a limp bunch of freshly-picked daffodils. The landowner, I presume. I offered them both a hearty 'Morning!' and a wide smile. The gatekeeper smiled back. The skinny aristocrat looked past me, pretending I wasn't there. To all intents and purposes, I wasn't.

I stayed in the area for another ten days, sitting out a brief lull then surfing various breaks up and down the coast, and even returning to surf Bantham a couple of times, either early, before the gatekeepers had arrived, or late, after they had left. But that was the last time I slept there, no matter how tempting. Mostly, I couldn't face being told off again.

Instead I alternated between Bigbury and Thurlstone, which both had empty car parks looking out over the sea. Perched on a cliff, Thurlstone has beautiful views across a wide bay, with an imperious stone arch and distant head-lands. There's not much there beyond a handful of dark houses, but twenty minutes away along the stumbling cliff-top was the village of Hope and its antique pub. So one evening, tired of listening to the wind, I chanced the walk and spent a couple of hours by their warm fire instead.

163

I was utterly unprepared for the depth of darkness when I emerged. The night sky was resplendent. No moon, no clouds, just a million brilliant reminders of our insignificance. Once again I felt my tiny concerns engulfed by the infinite. I found the sensation strangely empowering. In the grand scheme of things... there is no grand scheme of things. Whether you live to be a hundred or stumble over a cliff in the darkness, the universe will be equally unmoved. That I didn't stumble over a cliff in the darkness was largely down to luck – the path along the cliff-top was picturesque by day, but treacherous by starlit night.

Bigbury-on-Sea, in contrast, was more obviously inhabited, but with a generous car park above the beach where a shy van could sleep unobtrusively in mid-March. Plus it had a shower. Outdoors, shockingly cold and in full view, but still a shower. I couldn't believe my luck.

From there, Burgh Island was just a short hop across the causeway. But even close up, it felt exotic and mysterious. Built as an exclusive hotel in 1929, the gleaming art deco pavilion exudes opulence.

At high tide, the island is cut off from the mainland for several hours, so as a change from my solitary van, I decided to maroon myself there one evening. OK, it's hardly Robinson Crusoe, and if you had a dinner jacket and a hundred pounds to blow on dinner, I'm sure the time would pass in a flash. But once the water had covered my footprints, I was struck by the claustrophobic intensity of the island. Any island. You're stranded, with strangers, unable to escape. Whatever happens there, you're left facing the consequences.

Agatha Christie used to stay, and wrote a couple of novels there. It perhaps explains books like *Murder on the Orient Express* and *Death on the Nile*, about groups of strangers temporarily cut off from the outside world, and more obviously *And Then There Were None*, which is actually set on a small island.

It turns out Agatha Christie was a keen surfer too. Not in Devon, unfortunately. Surfing hadn't reached Europe yet. But there are photos of her in Hawaii, posing with a 12-foot balsawood board that looms over her like a tombstone. Perhaps that's why she liked Burgh Island, because she could sit at her desk and watch the waves, dreaming of surfing. I did much the same. Except instead of a luxurious cabin with hot and cold running servants, I had a beaten-up blue van. It was kingdom enough.

When dusk fell, I retreated to the Pilchard Inn, an atmospheric flint tavern beside the hotel, with stone floors, ancient settles and a roaring fire. Its wooden beams and rough walls have changed little over the centuries, and it's not difficult to conjure up smugglers and pirates plotting in dark corners.

As if its nooks and beams weren't atmospheric enough, overnight the weather rolled in, damp and drizzled and wreathed in fog. It carried with it whispers of piracy and skulduggery, of contraband smuggled into rocky inlets and hidden coves. The fog was too dense to see the sea, even from the water's edge, so I went for a walk to the river mouth. When I got there, the fog parted just enough to glimpse distant waves, and someone surfing them. The lull was over.

WAVE 43: Bigbury-on-Sea

The tide was on its way out, but I went in anyway. Later, the fog might thicken, the wind might freshen, the world might end. It was a long walk out over the damp sand, through shallow pools of seawater and silence. The sky was dark and low, and the fog lingered nearby. Waves were crashing in at around head high, fast but reasonably benign. A few surfers were in the line-up, but as I paddled towards the river-mouth, I found myself alone as a large set approached. I turned and paddled, knowing I couldn't afford to miss the first wave, and suddenly found myself up and surfing – though not without a bit of dancing around for balance, teetering on tip-toe like a character in a silent movie. The wave took me with it, though I was barely able to control my direction, and just clung on long enough to enjoy the sensation of riding it. 'I'm back!' I thought, as it shrugged me off a few seconds later.

I wasn't, of course. All morning I teetered and toppled, my feet too far back or too far forward. I was unfit and out of practice. But I stuck with it, trying to catch waves sooner, when they were more critical, reassured that the penalty for getting it wrong was minimal. If I needed practice, here it was.

The following morning, the swell had picked up. The sky was still heavy with the threat of rain, but the wind held off and the water felt fresh and clean, tingling with salt and cold. The waves were a little bigger, a lot stronger, much faster. Lots of exciting drops and vertiginous walls. Lots of clean, green face to grasp with a desperate hand, while the other clutched the outside rail for balance. It was more exhilarating than controlled, but it was progress. It felt like the real thing. I rarely managed to stand tall, but it didn't matter. It was all so fast and new! And timing was everything, as the wave dropped away, with or without you.

Eventually I caught a beautiful wave, early and well. I was up, high on a green face, as ahead of me the wave stretched out in a vertical sheet of fast-moving water. I dropped down the face and into a bottom turn, instinct taking over. Everything was happening too fast, but there was still time to appreciate the wave's smooth beauty and power, and to think actively about what I was doing.

It was a novel sensation, reminiscent of the single wave I had caught at Sango Bay, a feeling so new I didn't really know what I should be doing. Keep my line and race for the finish, probably. But instead, I pointed my board upwards and found myself cruising along the top of the wall for a moment. So far, so good. But now I really was in unknown territory. Instead of carrying on into a floater, or if I was really lucky, a re-entry, I must have gone a foot too far. Momentum threw me up and off the back of the wave, and it raced off without me. I fell back into calm water, shocked and dismayed – but delighted to have been on such a beautiful wave at all.

Later the weather closed in, wet and wind-swept, whipping up unruly waves that turned the bay into a seething riot of white. The outlook for surfing wasn't good. Only Wembury, just short of Plymouth, looked as if it might offer any protection against the gusting wind. I decided to investigate, itself not an easy option. Inland, the fog was thick and eerie, very *Hound of the Baskervilles*. The damp hedgerows were all I could make out, with the occasional gnarled tree that loomed out of nowhere like a tormented ghoul. I almost turned back.

When I finally made it, the tide was high and the air thick with fog, giving everything a mysterious, melancholy air. A sombre church on a low hill bristling with gorse kept watch over sinners and swimmers alike, while below lurked a dark, satanic mill, forbidding and apparently abandoned. The dense fog had coaxed dusk forward an hour, and in the deserted, drizzle-drenched gloom, it all felt very Gothic horror. I couldn't shake off the unpleasant sensation I was being observed, so I retreated to the sanctuary of my van. By ten o'clock, like all God-fearing folk, I was a-bed.

WAVE 44: Wembury

The following morning dawned still and grey. The drizzle held off, but the air was wet with its threats. The tide was still high and the lines of swell, though promising, were not yet breaking. I waited. Eventually a surfer headed in. Prematurely, in my view. But surfers are like amoeba. They multiply by binary division. When one goes in, another appears. Then two more. Then four. By the time I had struggled into my clammy wetsuit, there were eight. Soon after, I counted 17. Curses.

Wembury is basically a one-peak break. But what a peak! It breaks over a rocky finger that sticks out from the shore, with a short, sharp right over the reef, and a long, lovely left that powers on into the sandy bay. For a goofy-footer like me, it was perfect. But with so many people in the water, I was afraid I didn't stand a chance. Too many surfers, not enough wave. Fortunately, everyone in the water – the Plymouth Brethren, as I christened them – was exceptionally well-mannered. You just had to hold your place and hope that something came your way.

When it did, I couldn't quite believe what I was seeing. A perfect wave was gathering itself up as it rolled towards me, and no one seemed to have noticed. Like a cautious pedestrian, I checked left and right. No one was getting ready to paddle, so I turned and went for it, paddling hard, not knowing when another chance would come. The wave lifted me gently and I scrabbled to my feet. Two days at Bigbury had sharpened my timing and cleaned up my footwork. Here, the wave was slower and more forgiving. Plenty of time to find your balance and take a leisurely drop. Plenty of space to inscribe an elegant bottom turn. And then you were off, on a clean wave, well over head high, that reeled away towards the beach.

Unusually, I was on my forehand, able to watch where the wave was breaking, able to appreciate its beauty as it walled beside me. It wasn't as sharp or solid as the reef at Sandsend, no time for extravagant board work, no room for histrionics. But it was fast enough and solid enough to really feel its power beneath my feet as I sped towards the beach; and the last thing I had expected when I had peered out of my window that morning. I powered on, exhilarated and concentrating hard. I didn't want to mess it up.

Out of the corner of my right eye I watched the beach race towards me, all sharp rocks and physicality. Definitely terra firma. I needn't have worried. Five metres out there was a burst of energy as the wave exploded into chaos. It swallowed me up and spat me out as it hurled itself against the shore. I scrabbled to my feet, waist deep, and threw myself over the wave behind, before it could have another go at wrecking me on the beach.

After a long wait, when the next wave came my way, it was almost identical to the first – an easy catch, a leisurely bottom turn, then a long, walling ride to the beach, where a wary surfer could escape the close-down with a well-timed shimmy over the shoulder. That surfer was not me, so instead I went down with the whitewash. At least underwater, no one can see you grinning like a kid at a fairground.

The standard of surfing was good without being

ridiculous, and the atmosphere in the water was amicable. A bigger set came through, already crumbling as it reared above me. Buoyed by a run of decent catches, I reckoned I could make it. I paddled hard – the more so as another surfer was on my left, also paddling. I don't often fight for a wave, even if I have priority. Lack of confidence that I'll get it, perhaps. Or deference to the locals. This time, though, I felt I had put the time in, and wasn't going to relinquish my rights easily. I paddled and caught it, just as the white-water reached me. I half expected the other surfer to go anyway, seeing me about to be engulfed in foam and unlikely to make it out. He didn't, and I managed to get across the section and out onto a glorious clean wall. It was a fabulous wave, overhead and powerful, reeling well over a hundred metres to the beach, where the same explosive ending awaited.

After that my hit rate started to decline. More surfers, fewer waves, less energy. A couple of rights. A promising left, much like the others. Then the waves dropped off completely and eventually I was forced to paddle in, a disappointing contrast to the exhilarating rides earlier that had deposited me just metres from dry sand. A minor inconvenience, though. It had been the best session for months.

* * *

Overnight the wind stiffened. Back at Bigbury, I could hear the waves crashing from my bed. No chance of surfing where I was, so I decided to try Salcombe. It sits deep inside a narrow estuary, but I thought the strong swell might be enough to reach into its sheltered nooks.

On the way, I dropped in at the local surf shop, to look for a cheap board. Back in September, I had promised Karen I would visit her in Goa at the end of her journey around India, confident that by April my own odyssey would be long complete. Time had made a mockery of my predictions. I was still barely halfway round, but I couldn't reasonably cancel. Not if I valued the future of our relationship.

On the other hand, if there was the slightest chance of a wave, I didn't want to spend three weeks watching it from the shore. My 6'10" was too long for flying, and I certainly didn't want to risk my beloved 6'5" Phynix, hand-made for me by Leo in Peniche, with my name (misspelled) in pencil beneath the resin. Not for the sake of some Goan waves that might well turn out to be apocryphal.

What I wanted was a wide, flat board with plenty of volume that would float on a raindrop and catch ripples as if they were thundering reef breaks. Instead, all they had was a second-hand, machine-built epoxy 6'2". Not quite a BIC, but not far off.

On the plus side, it was durable enough for the journey, short enough for our national airline's stringent size restrictions and cheap enough that I could afford to ding it, ditch it or donate it without too much heartache. But was it long enough for a 13-stone intermediate to surf in gutless slop? I explained my predicament to the guy in the shop and he generously offered to rent it to me for three days for a mere £15, which he would deduct from the price if I decided to buy. If only all my doubts could be resolved as easily.

I was in no hurry, and decided to chance the tidal road that runs along the Avon from Milburn Orchard. It's not a road for anyone in a rush. It disappears completely at high tide, and only two lines of gnarled posts emerging from the water suggest it might return.

It was still under water, so I got out to have a look around.

Grey clouds hung low in the sky, and everywhere was thick with the suggestion of mist. Steep hillsides ringed with bare trees sheltered the river from any wind, and the air was unusually still. You could almost hear each water droplet drip from leaf to leaf. After the howl and bluster of Bigbury, it was delicious relief.

Beneath the overhanging branches at the far bank a cautious heron watched and waited. Among the reeds an egret stalked. A cormorant on one of the weathered posts stretched its wings and waited too. It was a scene of such exquisite tranquillity, I felt privileged to have stumbled across it, to adjust my plans to its imperceptible rhythm, its tidal pace.

A happy hour slipped by, as the heron watched and the egret stalked. I left the van at the water's edge and wandered up the narrow lane, shrugging off a gentle drizzle that thickened the air. The steep banks on either side of the lane were thick with ferns and grasses, laced through with ivy and the swollen buds of spring flowers waiting to blaze. They towered overhead like a walling wave, threatening to swallow up the unwary traveller.

Walking three metres below the level of the surrounding fields, you could sense unrecorded history all around, the trundling cartwheels and bellowing herds that had passed along these lanes century after century, etching them deep into the face of time.

An elderly couple arrived and shared my vigil. Finally a local driver pitched up, clearly familiar with the road, and drove on without a pause, sending a low furrow of wash from her gleaming wheels. I followed, brimming with exquisite melancholy from an hour of water-filled reflections on nature and time.

Time was still on my mind as I reached Salcombe, where the gloomy, fog-filled atmosphere invited introspection. I last visited Salcombe as a nine-year-old. We camped, as always, and spent endless days on a wide, sun-filled beach, while my father, far younger then than I am now, drifted around the bay in a red Mirror dinghy he had just finished building.

Relatively new to sailing, he made one important discovery that summer: if in danger, let go – the boat will slow to a standstill and point into the wind, reducing the risk of capsize. He did capsize once, I think, with one of my sisters, Claire, in the boat, aged seven. My mother was not impressed. I also remember he had a series of run-ins with a large rock that lurked in the shallows. It regularly scraped his centre-board at high tide, and occasionally, as the tide went out, threatened to bite a chunk out of the hull.

We probably went to the beach every day for a fortnight, taking the small ferry across the estuary each morning, bursting with excitement; then wearily back every afternoon, salt-kissed and sandy, lured by the promise of ice-cream on the far side. It was enough to imprint the beach on a young memory.

Now, as I drove into Salcombe more than thirty years later, I felt a sharp jolt. There was the beach on the far side of the bay, the perilous rock unmistakeable, the beach itself far smaller than my nine-year-old self had known it.

The memory had remained dormant for perhaps three decades. Just another idyllic summer holiday of childhood, when the sun always shone, the days were as endless as the beaches, and the sun-drenched corners of Britain seemed as warm and exotic as the Mediterranean. When childhood still lasted forever.

The abrupt reminder was bitter-sweet. The memory made me warm with happiness, but I felt genuine sadness at the irretrievable disappearance of time. It was a delicious glimpse back to a golden childhood, charged and carefree. Yet it brought its mirror image, the unwelcome reminder of mortality, of the implacable ravages wreaked on each of us, year on year. Here was one of a thousand memories that resurface just rarely, poignant reminders of what we have lost. A memory that might have belonged to someone else, so distant was it, and so unfamiliar to the man who now remembered it.

The rock still lurked in the shallows, threatening eternal youth. I was no longer that youth; was not even the youthful parents who had taken me there thirty years earlier. I was an ageing repository of memories rattling around in a VW van, desperately trying to create newer, fresher memories, to replace the ones that repeatedly faded with time until they lay forgotten or obscured, without a rock of ages to haul them from the depths.

And what is surfing, if not this same experience in microcosm? The fleeting flash of brilliant now, then the gradual forgetting. It leaves us nothing for the future except memory, and sadness that we are no longer young. Each wave is like youth itself, absorbing and everlasting, until suddenly it's gone. And nothing will bring it back.

So we repeat what we can no longer remember, and this time cling to the memory harder, so it can't race away without us, or disappear in a million drops of water we can't quite clutch or comprehend. We remember the wave as we ride it; but yesterday's wave? Last year's? Only dimly. Only sometimes. Only with sadness. I surfed to be pure now. I write about it to stop the now fading away entirely.

I wandered like a ghost, with the ghost of my childhood

174

walking with me, hand in hand. We didn't linger. Beyond that one bay, Salcombe was unrecognisable. Gone the relaxed and sandy idyll I remembered; in its place a claustrophobic ghetto for Chelsea weekenders and yachting Yahs. Like much of Devon and Cornwall, it had been sold to the highest bidder. No one, I suspect, had built their own boat.

As I left the village, I took one last look at the beach with its rock across the bay. The estuary was still beautiful in the mist, timeless and unspoilt. A school of dinghies raced across the bay. Perhaps the ghost of my childhood father, a young man of 34 or 35, raced with them. If so, I hope he avoided the rock.

WAVE 45: Salcombe

Just outside the village, the road plunged down a leafy hillside to a small beach, where the dejected ruin of a modest fort clings to the rock like a demoralised cormorant. The fog was thickening, and the far side of the bay kept drifting from view. Low waves were breaking in crystal-clear water, just enough for a gentle surf wreathed in mist and nostalgia.

Conditions called for as big a board as possible. My 6'10" would have been perfect – plenty of volume for the catch yet agile enough to get the most out of each wave. But I needed to try out the 6'2" I had just rented, even though it would probably mean a less exciting session. The waves weren't great, and didn't merit such a small board, but if there were any waves in Goa, they would probably be like this, small and weak. Inadvertently I had stumbled across perfect test conditions.

175

As I paddled out, the small board felt skittish and jittery beneath me, not helped by the choppy wash of the incoming tide. The waves were about waist high, but as they formed, they cleaned up nicely, offering a decent face. No point – or penalty – waiting for the perfect wave; as soon as something reasonable came along I turned and paddled, unconvinced I would actually catch it on such a small board.

Amazingly I felt the lift as the wave took me. I pushed up, conscious I had to watch my feet. My first foot found its place as normal. My back foot, to my surprise, did the same. I was up and riding! Once moving, the board was fast and responsive. Perfect! It was even more skittish now, but at least I knew I could surf it. Though I still wasn't convinced it was worth schlepping a board – any board – all the way to India.

Everything about the place conspired to create a dramatic atmosphere: the ruins, the mist, the low hills on either side of the estuary, the clean, clear water and gently-shelving beach. Everything about it was the opposite of wild, but that was fine. Physically and mentally, you don't want to be fighting the elements every time you surf. Sometimes it's nice just to relax and splash around.

The board had proved to be a success, but when the three-day trial was over, I decided to take it back. Dragging it all the way to India was a ridiculous idea. Impractical, expensive and pointless. At the last minute, though, the thought of missing out on any waves, however small, was worse. Instead of handing it back, I bought it. As things turned out, it was a fantastic decision.

In passing, I mentioned to the guy in the shop that I was intending to surf at Hope Cove. He politely suggested Thurlestone instead, a suggestion I immediately discounted. I had slept there for several days and hadn't seen a ripple. But as I drove off, I passed a signpost: Thurlestone 2½ miles. I might as well go and have a look.

WAVE 46: Thurlestone

Whether it was surfer serendipity or just the law of averages, I got there as two surfers were about to leave. Five minutes later I would have missed them. There was surf, they confirmed. Try the first small bay by the golf course.

I picked my way down the track and sure enough, a small but shapely wave was peeling across a beautiful little beach, hidden and intimate, scattered with tiny shells as small and translucent as fish scales. It reminded me of the beaches of my childhood, a private paradise lit by an ever-setting sun.

To the left as you looked out to sea, a low finger of rock slipped discreetly beneath the water, stretching out into a gentle reef. Clear lines of swell were breaking over this submarine pavement and unfurling across the bay before finally shuffling onto the sand like an exhausted walrus. My arms were still recovering from the battles of the preceding days, so this was the perfect break, gentle and forgiving, but with powerful, well-formed faces for weaving lazy lines and gentle turns. As the sun sank and my shoulders ached, I made the most of a light session on a new and pretty beach.

WAVE 42 bis: Bantham Revisited

Now, finally, time had overtaken me. I had to leave for India and the unknown. In truth, I didn't want to go. Karen was out there, waiting, and with her, difficult questions about the future. I wasn't ready to face them. I wanted to stay in the van, on the road, in the privileged postponement of real life as I continued to surf around the country. But I had no choice. I had to go.

Before I went, there was just time for one last surf. Sunset at Thurlestone had been divine and I went to bed looking forward to a similar session in the morning, before the long drive home. I woke to a beautiful dawn, but the waves were too small, and for once I couldn't wait. Instead I headed back to Bantham. Surely there would be something there, even if it was only thigh-high slop.

It was still early, but if I was to catch it before the tide got too high, I couldn't afford to hang around. Certainly no time for breakfast, just a quick banana for energy.

As I came over the top of the dunes, I caught my first glimpse of the bay, dark blue beneath a pale sky, with the island forming an elegant backdrop. And waves I couldn't quite believe.

Overnight the swell had picked up, but the insistent breeze of the previous week had swung round and was blowing lightly offshore, stroking the waves into clean lines that peeled elegantly across the bay. After a week of relentless grey skies and nagging wind, of frequent rain and on-shore slop, it felt like a mirage. They were big and powerful: well overhead on the sets and thundering eloquently as they curled over into explosive oblivion. It was stunning.

Only three surfers were out, and clearly making the

178

most of the conditions. With relish, I prepared to join them. I warmed up and headed for the rip alongside the rocks, which whisked me effortlessly out to sea and into the line-up. I had spent a week tightening up my timing and honing my fitness, and if my arms were a little weary, enthusiasm and mental energy would make up the difference. It was going to be a great session!

Except it's never that simple.

I watched as the three surfers each caught a wave with apparent ease and disappeared towards the shore behind a monstrous wall of water. Now it was my turn. I was alone on a blue expanse, with a thundering leviathan rumbling towards me. I paddled closer, to where I thought the next wave would break. But the next wave broke early, before it reached me. Afraid of getting pummelled and pushed out of position, I decided to go for it anyway, before I got swept into the impact zone.

I turned and started to paddle. The water rose in a smooth curve beneath me as the shoulder of the wave approached. Before I knew what was happening, the smooth blue shoulder I was trying to accelerate down shattered into a hammering cloudburst of chaos. White-water devoured me, swallowing me deep into its dark throat. I struggled to push myself up and onto my feet, but the forces pressing down on me, and the jittery dance of the board beneath me as it balanced on a thousand jets of water, jostled me impossibly and I came off.

The wave took me anyway, dragging me for a metre or two before my deadweight anchored me and it let me go. I spluttered to the surface and looked around. The wave hadn't taken me far, and if I was quick I could recover my position with relative ease. I hauled in my board and started to paddle. Almost immediately the next wave in the set broke over me. I ducked beneath it, and felt the torrent at my back. When I emerged, the third wave was almost upon me. I paddled and dived again. Again it pummelled me.

Each wave was pushing me gradually into shore, but worse, the cross-current was taking me further from the take-off, and into the dreaded impact zone, where every wave breaks over you and traps you in an unwinnable contest for clear water. I paddled urgently towards the calm expanse of blue no more than thirty metres away, but whenever I thought I was about to reach it, another wave broke and pushed me back. My arms, tired when I had got in, were not equal to the task, and grew less equal with every stroke, as I felt my energy drain away.

Eventually I realised there was only one alternative: paddle for shore and catch the rip back out. It felt counter-intuitive, three hundred metres against thirty. But the three hundred were fixed and finite; the thirty endlessly renewed, a constant distance that was unlikely to diminish without a superhuman effort or a sudden lull.

I headed towards the beach. It wasn't so bad. It was even – let's admit it – a little fun: the quick whoosh towards the shore on the powerful white-water then a hasty wade through the shallows and an easy paddle out along the rip. In under five minutes I was back at the peak. Five minutes I would otherwise have spent fighting the current in the impact zone and getting swept further along the beach.

Was it my imagination, or had the waves grown while I struggled? They were fabulous! They rose from nowhere, small ridges that pushed in past Burgh Island and suddenly grew into towering walls. Each wave announced itself with a gentle shoulder – itself a sculptural arc of beauty that pushed through the water like the prow of a ship, growing steeper and taller until the wave was upon you.

They were majestic and imposing, and I was desperate to catch one. This wasn't going to collapse into a 'nearly' session.

I sat and waited and when the prow started ploughing the water towards me, I turned and started to paddle. But again I was out of position. I was never going to make it. Too steep, too fast, too scary. At the last minute I made the panicked decision to pull out. I was still out on the shoulder, so rather than spin round and sprint for safety, I took the laborious route, paddling round in a slow arc, like a turning barge.

Too slow. The wave caught me and grabbed me by the ankles. It was going to pull me over the falls for my audacity. For a giddy instant I felt like a 19th-century daredevil going over Niagara in a barrel. I just had time to push my board away. The wave took me in its swirling grasp and swept me over. Thundering water cascaded around me, hammered over me, pummelled on top of me. It gave a final tug of my ankle as it tried to drag my board from me, and then it was gone, steaming on towards the shore, leaving me to scrabble back to safety before the next one arrived.

Except it was already too late. I was already out of position. I made a half-hearted attempt to paddle out through the next two waves, but I could feel myself being pushed further and further from the peak. With a sigh, I swung my board round to face the beach, and set off on the long circuit back to the rip. Back to square one.

As I paddled out again, I watched the other surfers and thought about what I was doing wrong. The problem was simple. I had never come across waves like this in real life, just in magazines or on surfing websites. I had certainly never surfed any. I wasn't prepared for the delicate balance of the rising shoulder, or the sudden speed with which it seized the unsuspecting or inexperienced surfer. These waves seemed to rise and form so delicately, so beautifully, and then were gone so fast in their abrupt explosion of energy and violence.

In the videos, surfers seemed to catch them effortlessly, matching the perfect, smooth wave with perfect, smooth surfing. I was beginning to realise it wasn't that simple. Just because the wave was perfect didn't make it any easier to catch. Quite the opposite. Not only did you have to be in the right position, you had to be angled exactly right, neither too directly towards the beach (it picked you up and hurled you down), nor too closely along the wave (it shrugged you off like a leaf). And you had to be moving fast enough, whether by paddling or gravity, for the wave to take you. I paddled into position, determined to be more courageous, to risk more by putting myself in the critical position to catch the wave – or be hurled under again.

A wave started to rise ahead of me and I went for it, concentrating on what I was doing, not on what might happen if I got it wrong. One moment I was paddling strongly before the grinding plough of water, the next I was lying high on its shoulder, speeding on a steep trajectory downwards, head first. Before the idea of struggling to my feet on a board fast approaching vertical could flash through my panicked mind, the wave had tipped me over. This time I went plunging properly over the falls, upended like a twig and hurled down the face with only my board and fear for company. The wave cascaded over me and I was cartwheeled into darkness.

With every failure I was growing increasingly dispirited. I was fast approaching the critical point when despondency and exhaustion take over and you no longer hope for a great surf, you just want to salvage the session in any way you can. Yet again I was in danger of being swept up the beach, but just when it looked as if I would have to do the circuit of shame again, a small wave came through. It was nothing like the glorious set waves, but I was in no position to turn it down. I needed anything I could get. I caught it. If nothing else, it reminded me I could still ride a wave standing up. Better still, it took me back to the rip.

Whether it was this gentle boost to my flagging confidence, or an incremental step in my understanding of the wave, or whether it was just blind luck, my fortunes suddenly changed. I paddled back into position, a little more wary now, but determined not to let fear get the better of me. This time I was in exactly the right place, out on the shoulder, ready to catch the wave good and early.

To my left, a wave was already starting to break. It wasn't one of the largest set waves, but it was a decent size, growing steadily as it came to meet me. I paddled hard, certain I was just going to get bucked off again, but hoping that somehow I could hold on. Gravity took me, rushing me down the face and I started to get to my feet. It took an age – so long, I was convinced I would reach the bottom and the wave would go without me. I hauled myself up into a crouch, holding onto the rail with my outside hand, fighting for balance. My front foot was out of position, too far back. Somehow I managed to jerk it forward without falling off.

And suddenly I was riding! At long last, after an hour of floundering and failing among the most beautiful waves I had seen in England, I had finally caught one. I was on a clean, fast wave, head high, not as powerful as some, but walling up beautifully as I sped down the line. I had no thought except to hang on and not mess it up, enjoying every second.

In the end, though, I must have out-sprinted it, ending with a whimper not a bang and finding myself trying to surf along what was now only a low, gentle hump. I slowed and sank. Behind me the peak was still steep and surfable, and speeding towards the shore without me. Curses! But I had surfed a good fifty metres or so. I couldn't help smiling. I had finally got one.

While every error in the line-up was punished by the current, success was rewarded. Each wave deposited you conveniently close to the rip, ready to go back and do it again. I had caught one. My luck had changed. I'd understood what to do. My next wave would be far more straightforward, wouldn't it? I returned to the peak full of renewed energy, ready to put my new-found knowledge to good use. And almost immediately went over the falls again.

As I paddled back out, I watched the incoming waves carefully. I was just in time to see one of the surfers catch a beautiful, clean, arching wave that curved up and over like a rolling scallop of smooth perfect water, twice his height. It curled up in a towering scroll of smooth marine blue, while behind him scrunched a spiral of immaculate, thundering white. He stayed high up on the wave, close to the curl, describing elegant lines full of grace and poetry on the beautiful blue face. I was open-mouthed with admiration. That was the wave I wanted.

I reached the line-out and waited. A wave started to peel towards me, but I was afraid I was too late for it, too far down the line. I went for it anyway, paddled as hard as I could – and suddenly, almost before I had thought about jumping to my feet, and certainly before I knew what my feet were doing, I was up and riding again. For a second or two I stayed in a crouch, left hand gripping the rail until I was sure of my balance. I straightened

184

up, and found myself perfectly poised, speeding along the face of a huge, clean wall of water, vertical and very nearly hollow. It was well over my head, with the top just starting to curl over, sprinkling me with drops of water. And it was enormous - a real leviathan. Not just tall, but wide, like a great wedge of dark blue sea, a massive mountain of moving water propelling me along its splendid, arching flank.

Everything was happening too fast to do anything except speed ahead, soaking up every instant of the experience, as time slowed and my world, my existence, my entire being were absorbed by what was happening around me. And what was happening around me was the most glorious wave of my life!

I surfed on, entirely focused on the wave, and on surfing it as best as I could, concentrating too hard on the experience to analyse it or even feel it except as an intense rush of pleasure that I didn't dare look at too closely because I was too intent on the unfolding movement of time and space opening up before me. I was on the wave of my life, and I didn't want to mess it up.

Ahead, the wave threatened to crumble before I got there. But the combined knowledge of all those rubbish waves in waist-high slop paid off. I dropped down a little, and made it round the crumbling section, then back out onto the clean, dark blue face again, determined to make the most of every metre, really enjoying the sensation of being on such a fine wave.

It was a good long ride, perhaps a hundred metres. And it was fast, without the flow and ebb of waves I had surfed at Sandsend or Lagide. Just a long race to the finish. But it was so satisfying! The shape, the size, the sensation of latent power...everything about it. I stayed with it to the very end, and as it finally closed down, surfed out the white-water as far as I could, not stopping until it finally petered out in the shallows.

For a moment, I looked back, tempted to have another go. But my arms had been failing me for a while already. I didn't think they had the power even for one last attempt. And today of all days I didn't want to end on an anti-climax. I floated up the beach back to the van as the enormity of the wave I had just surfed sank in. A real wave of real consequence. It felt sublime.

Nine

Goa

Back in August, I had had no idea how long my circuit of Britain would take. Easter had seemed like a reasonable deadline, and I had happily agreed to meet up with Karen at the end of her own journey of discovery. I had failed to consider the various delays, distractions and breakdowns that might beset me, and now, much as I was looking forward to seeing her, I was dismayed to have to interrupt my odyssey when I still had so much to do. Short of jilting her at the platform, though, I had no alternative.

Karen met me with garlands of flowers and we checked into a rickety hut beside a quiet beach. The next three weeks were an idyll of delicious food in ramshackle beach cafés, afternoons spent writing in the shade, sunset walks along the water's edge, and, to my relief, surfing.

For the first few days, conditions were distinctly unpromising – small, wind-blown slop that shuffled onto the sand like a drunken tourist. But at sunrise, I soon discovered, the winds were still, the water glass-smooth, and on the next beach along, five minutes away, a nice wave broke and called me from my sleep each day. I would stumble out of bed, pad across the sand, paddle a few metres round the rocks and surf for an hour or so while Karen slept. Then back for fresh fruit, masala omelette and chai. The word idyllic is overused, but this was pretty close.

By ten, a stiff breeze would start to blow on-shore, and surfing became impossible. I found it strangely liberating. You didn't have to spend the day wondering if it would get better. It wouldn't. You had to get your surf in early, then you were free to get on with your day. It was especially liberating if what you wanted to do was write. It's difficult to write when you've got one eye on the waves.

I was happy to surf alone, and after several days concluded there were no other surfers around. So I was startled one morning to find another surfer already in the water. Lee was tattooed, overweight and garrulous, a bon viveur who spent half the year playing guitar in Dubai, half lounging in Goa. He had identified what he wanted in life, and this was it. He surfed an immense BIC longboard and would sit way out, waiting for the bigger sets to roll in rather than bother with scraps, as I tended to do.

'Here we go, chaps!' he would declare to a seemingly flat ocean. He would paddle for an unpromising bump, laboriously and inelegantly haul himself to his feet and surf an unexpectedly large wave with improbable skill and even style. It was a masterclass in patience, and I often think of him when the sea goes flat, and try to emulate his optimism.

The beach was usually deserted, especially at dawn, but one morning, I arrived to find it had been transformed overnight into a tacky resort, garish and paper thin, complete with beach café, jet-ski hire and banners. Bollywood had arrived! They didn't seem to mind me surfing, and whenever I thought the distant camera was pointing in my direction, I tried to catch as many waves as possible. One particularly long wave even earned a round of applause from the German hippies drafted in as extras, which embarrassed me – though I was quite pleased with the wave, a nice left-hander, waist high and fun, ending in a floater close to the beach. It was the first time my surfing had ever been applauded, and almost certainly the last. After a few days, the circus left town again, and I was left to surf in peace.

Surfing the same wave every day was a revelation. I had grown used to surfing somewhere once or twice, then moving on. Three weeks was unprecedented. I got to know the wave well and could tell when to go and when to wait, where to sit, where to avoid. It must be how locals feel.

I got a bit cocky, and surfed it almost onto the sand a few times. And a few times my cockiness was suitably rewarded: I had my scalp scraped almost bare when one wave imploded before I had a chance to kick out. Another time, a few metres from the beach, the bottom fell out of the wave without warning. One minute I was riding a nice right, the next there was nothing below me except sand. My board took a dive, and in the ensuing melee the tail must have caught, because somehow the nose jabbed me hard in the ribs, just below the heart. The resulting bruise deepened like a Turner sunset. After that I avoided going too close to the shore.

While I usually surfed the next beach along, I did surf my own beach twice, once on the first day, once on the last. On our first afternoon, at the far end of the bay, a small, fun wave gave a brief shriek before closing out, and it was possible for a desperate surfer to catch a few short rides. I came off one wave and saw that people were staring. Some were even pointing. It took me a moment to realise they weren't pointing at me. Behind me, a dolphin was swimming idly past. It didn't come particularly close, so I can't really claim to have surfed with dolphins, but its presence was electric. After that, we often spotted it at

189

sunset, when it lazily patrolled the bay and we lazily kept pace with it along the sand.

On our final morning, I returned from surfing the far beach as usual to find a rideable wave breaking beside the rocks, fast and walling and irresistible.

"Just a couple," I told myself. But I was soon hooked by the short-lived shot of adrenaline it fired into my veins. You could hang on to a low rock, let go at the last minute and paddle straight into the wave's gaping jaws. If you timed it well, it would hurtle you thirty metres along the shore and hurl you on the sand laughing. It was fabulous, and I would have stayed all day, until Karen wandered down to suggest it might be nice to spend our last few hours in paradise together. And so it was. Though I couldn't help glancing back at the wave from time to time and surfing it in my mind.

Ten

Cornwall

Back in England, I was running late. I had planned to be in Cornwall by February, March at the latest. It was now mid-May, and summer was already warming my back. Cornwall was resplendent: the hedgerows ablaze with flowers, the beaches ablaze with sunshine, the traffic wardens ablaze with zeal. Summer isn't a good time for surfers anywhere. In Cornwall, even less so. Too many people in the water. Too few places to camp. There were actual campsites, of course. But by now it had become a point of honour as much as finances not to use them.

To resume my route, I returned to Wembury, and the memory of those great left-handers that cold, wet morning back in March. On a calm, sunlit evening in May, with the water gently lapping the shore, it was difficult to believe this was the same beach.

WAVE 47: Church Cove, Gunwalloe

I made seafall again at Gunwalloe, a few miles short of the Lizard Peninsula. Around the beach, low hills create a natural arena of muted greens, broken only by the stone

191

tower of a medieval church sheltering from the worst of the Atlantic weather. My blue van seemed as incongruous as a spaceship.

Dusk thickened, and I wandered the eerie green moonscape like an alien, homesick and in need of human contact. There was none. Not a soul. Just a cowshed that gave a muffled bellow from time to time. I felt like a ghost, haunting an abandoned universe; an avatar trapped in a computer-generated landscape devoid of real life. It was an unnerving feeling, unworldly and disembodied, though there were worse places to be stranded alone for eternity. Especially if the waves picked up a bit.

They didn't. In the morning, low ripples rolled lazily onto the narrow sandy beach, ruffled by a light breeze. But I ran into a South African with wet hair and a long board who had found something that was just about surfable and was going back in. I asked if I could join him.

The hill that sheltered the church concealed a narrow strand of twisted rock and polished stones. The map doesn't even mark it as a beach. But beyond the seaweed-slippery foreshore, a low, weak wave was washing over sand as the tide came in. Shallow rocks lurked below the surface, but there was just enough time to catch a few waves before the tide came too far in and the rocks grew too perilous.

By any objective criteria, the waves were mediocre. Clean but crumbly, and curtailed by the fear of what lay below. On the other hand, the sun was shining, the water crystal clear and I could finally surf barefoot in Britain for the first time since October. After six weeks off the road, it was fabulous. Context is everything.

Like a rally driver ticking off check-points, I couldn't go on without making a detour to the tip of the Lizard

Peninsula. It's the most southerly point on mainland Britain and far prettier than nearby Land's End. I spent a rather melancholy day there, writing and watching my fellow reptilians. Almost without exception, they represented the two poles of British energy and body mass: sprightly walkers in bulky boots trudging the coastal path, or pasty sedants waddling the shortest distance from car to gift shop and back. I scoffed, though essentially I did little more. I did cast envious glances at the walkers, however. Not that I could ever consider emulating them. The urge to surf would be too great. The coastal path will have to wait until I'm too old to surf – unless I'm too old to walk by then too, which is quite possible.

WAVE 48: Godrevy

From the Lizard Peninsula, the sea seemed flat. Praa Sands, utterly unruffled, confirmed the verdict, so I cut across to Gwithian and then up to Godrevy, within the sweep of Virginia Woolf's famous lighthouse.

The idea of surfing beside such a famous edifice was very appealing. *To The Lighthouse* is one of my favourite books, partly because it's all about one of my favourite pastimes, procrastination – they spend the first half of the book talking about doing something and never getting round to it, and the second half wishing they had – and partly because I once spent an overcast Sunday in Barcelona reading the book aloud to a Catalan woman I was trying to impress. (The following week she was teaching *Moby Dick*, which might have been more of a challenge.)

The tide was on its way out, and the waves didn't look

great, and I was going to wait for the tide to turn. But by midday I couldn't prolong the agony. I had to go in. Most surfers clung to the peaks by the café and only a few stretched towards the lighthouse, deterred, perhaps, by the rocks and the walk. But if the peaks were a little less sharp, they were a lot less crowded. As always, it was a reasonable trade-off.

The waves weren't perfect, but the location was fabulous. Yet again, I silently thanked the National Trust for their vigilance and enterprise. As a surfer, you might have little interest in stately homes and ornamental gardens. But they protect dozens of coves and virgin beaches, and this alone makes membership worthwhile.

The following day, in a burst of optimism, I took out my shorter board. It was a disaster. The waves were overhead and too fast. Nerves and close-outs conspired against me. I made a couple of hair-raising drops but didn't feel in control, and the wave agreed. Finally my leash snapped and I had to swim for shore, bringing the session to an abrupt end.

The third day dawned foggy and calm. My joints ached and my throat was sore. I didn't want to go in. Through the fog, I could hear the waves as they crashed, but everything was muffled and distant. I walked down through the maze of rocks, which deadened the sound still more. Even at the water's edge, everything was strangely quiet, each wave breaking in quiet isolation. But the waves looked great: head high, clean and powerful, and coming in at a nice long interval. I really liked the location, but after two mediocre sessions, I didn't feel I had done it – or myself – justice. Sick or not, I had to go in.

I warmed up and paddled out, feeling eerily disembodied, not really part of my surroundings. Further down the beach, I could just distinguish a few lonely figures in the fog. Out at sea, dark clouds threatened storms and violence. After falling off more waves than I could remember the previous day, I was nervous. Mentally and physically, I wasn't ready for another hammering.

But the water was stunning in the subdued light. It was remarkably clear and a deep, dark green, almost black. As it rose up to form the steep wall of each pristine wave, it was like black glass, sheer and flawless until it shattered into a million bright shards. And from the very first wave, I knew things were going to be alright. Some days it just clicks. A good left, head high, with a steep take-off into a sheer black wall. It was a short ride, but crucially, I was controlled enough to kick out over the lip before the wave could engulf me. I was back! I paddled out again and caught a right. Longer this time, and more powerful, with another fast drop. Then along, weaving up and down the face, threading together turns, top and bottom, controlled and aware of my surroundings. This was bliss.

If I was captivated above the water, it was nothing to what lay below. As I dived under the looming curl of a wave, I opened my eyes to see a whole new world, blurred but beautiful: deep caverns carved from dark green water, black pits and emerald columns, swirling vortices of chaos as the white-water plumed past. Everything silent and serene. I was mesmerised. This was where the mermaids lived. I heard them singing, each to each. They sang to me and I sang back.

WAVE 49: Porthleven

I don't know what possessed me to check out Porthleven. Hubris, probably. It's Britain's second most famous reef, after Thurso, and from what I had heard, far trickier. But the fog and drizzle showed no sign of clearing and I had nothing better to do. I should at least go and see it. It wasn't as if I was actually planning to surf there.

The fog was even thicker on the south coast than it had been on the north, and the village had a Gothic, gloomy feel. It felt like a Scottish November afternoon, not Cornwall in May. I parked on the quayside and peered through the mist. The stone pier seemed to disappear into the fog. A few fishermen were casting their lines into the gloom, and a couple of people walked their dogs. On the smallish wave close to the harbour wall, two body-boarders were taking death-defying drops that threatened to dash them on the rocks. Was that it? The famous Porthleven? It wasn't what I had expected. And it certainly wasn't surfable. Except as I watched, a surfer jumped in. So perhaps it was.

From Arrifana to Biarritz, I've watched intrepid teen-agers catch gaping shore breaks and felt a tinge of envy at their speed and athleticism, to say nothing of their lack of fear. I would be washed onto the sand before I could even consider my feet, let alone stand. But those so-called one-manoeuvre waves looked positively leisurely compared to the curt brevity of this wave. This was a zero-manoeuvre wave. And one which crashed onto rock, not sand. So much for surfing Porthleven, I thought.

Then through the fog on the far side of the harbour, I caught a glimpse of something. A smear of white against the grey, a black smudge. Nothing, more a fold in the mist than anything definite. I stared. A moment later, there it was again. Surfers! I had been looking at the wrong wave. Out there, wreathed in fog, that was the famous Porthleven reef. And irresistibly, it was calling my name.

Full of trepidation, I struggled into my wetsuit, still wet

from the morning surf. At least my three days at Godrevy – and the three weeks in Goa – had given me confidence. And confidence is half the battle. Maybe more.

I didn't fancy a leap into the unknown, straight off the pier, so I opted for the cowardly route, out past the death-wish teens on their flying body-boards and round the end of the pier. Then a long, lonely paddle through the thick sea mist, with thoughts of wild rips and ruthless fishermen to distract me from what was waiting when I got there.

The air was still and the sea like shifting steel, dull and slow. Ahead, the wave slowly materialised out of the gloom, each set sharper than the last, rising gently from nowhere before hurling itself on the dark rocks. Above, the tops of the cliffs faded from view, hidden in the fog, and when I looked back towards the village, the small church above the harbour had almost disappeared, while the pier was just a dark blur hovering over the water. The only signs of life were the wave itself, and four surfers taking it in turns to slice down its sheer face and race along its speeding walls.

I watched and waited. Partly good manners, partly fear. Everything about the day was slow and sluggish, muted by the mist. Everything except the wave, its cascading lip the only brightness against the grey. It peaked at about head high or a little higher, then hollowed over into a short, steep right and even shorter, steeper left that seemed to crash dangerously close to the rocks.

The take-off area was small, but soon I found I was in the right place. A low line was pushing towards me. Each of the four surfers had caught a wave, and were either paddling back or sitting too wide. This was my wave. It grew with every metre, doubling, tripling, quadrupling in size. I was still in the right place. This was still my wave.

I turned and took a couple of leisurely strokes, ready to spring nonchalantly to my feet, as I had seen the other surfers do.

What happened next was far from nonchalant. In a flash, I found myself staring down a sheer wall of water, five feet high and close to vertical. Another flash and it had tipped my board up, and tipped me off it. I was tumbling headlong down the sheer face of moving water, heading for the reef below. I wasn't prepared for the force and violence of the water. It pushed me down and exploded around me, and made it very clear this was no place for leisure and nonchalance. 'Paddle hard. Paddle early.' Had I learned nothing? I spluttered to the surface, suitably chastened.

More surfers were starting to arrive, paddling in from the quay as I had done, or picking their way down the vertiginous cliff face. This was bad news. The waves were regular, but too widely spaced. Not quite enough for half a dozen of us – especially when you're the least competent in the group. I determined to catch one while I could, and made my way back to the peak to wait.

Soon a wave came. I paddled hard and early. Much better. But shaken by the speed of the wave, I committed the classic coward's mistake, and tried to get to my feet too soon, before the wave had properly picked me up. I found myself fumbling around on all fours, wobbling on its shoulder as it shrugged me off and rolled on without me. This was worse. This was ignominy. This was the sure sign of a novice. At least when you go over the front, you've shown commitment, courage and desire.

I remembered Tup's words in Thurso: 'You've got to really want the wave, or you won't catch it.'

By now, the new arrivals were in the line-up. Suddenly I was one of eight. Then ten, then twelve. The atmosphere, though, was friendly. Almost everyone knew each other. It was just after six and they were dropping by for a surf after a day's work.

I had been over the falls, and been shrugged off the shoulder. I couldn't afford to screw it up a third time. Except I did. A rerun of the second wave, scrabbling to my feet to find that I was stationary and the wave was rolling off without me.

This was bad, not just for my confidence but because it alerted the line-up to my incompetence. When you arrive at a break, you get the benefit of the doubt and – if you're polite and the locals aren't morons – you get a share of the waves. But if you screw it up once, and definitely three times, it sends out a message. Not that you're not a good surfer – although that as well – but that it's not worth giving you the wave because you're not going to do anything with it. Leaving you a wave means leaving the wave unridden, and when there are several surfers in the water and the sets are slow to arrive – and even when they aren't – no one wants to do that. I burned with embarrassment and bitter self-recrimination: 'How could you get it wrong again? Why are you such a coward? Great waves, great place, you're in the form of your life and you can't get a wave?' It wasn't pretty.

I paddled back and took my place, a respectful distance from the peak, hanging off the end, hoping to pick off a smaller wave if any came through unridden. None did. Or when they did, I was too far from the curl, and couldn't get into it. The more I tried, the harder it got, and the more my shoulders burned with the effort – just as my eyes and throat burned with shame and frustration. Eventually, damp and very dispirited, I accepted the inevitable. I turned and paddled for the quay, hoping the mist – or even the sea – would swallow me up.

I retreated to the van, and spent the night on the quayside, sleeping fitfully. Out on the reef the waves exploded with a boom that echoed around my brain. I was full of regret and self-reproach, tormented by my failings. By dawn, there was just one thing I wanted to do. I had to go back and face my demons.

The mist had lifted slightly, but the morning was still dull, and I was exhausted. Exhausted but determined to do better. There were a few people out already, and the atmosphere was a little less friendly. But I had spent all night rehearsing what I would do. No more fear. No more cowardice. Just go for it.

'It's only water,' I told myself. 'Water crashing onto rock,' whispered my cowardice.

I went for it. The wave picked me up, and I glided forward, my board slicing through the mirrored water like the prow of a ship. Stupidly, I looked down. Big mistake. The wall was close to vertical. I didn't want to fall down it. I pulled back, and let the wave go without me. Not a good start. Not what I had planned.

I went for it again. Again I sliced through the wall. Again the wave was suddenly vertical, but this time, I was committed. I started to jump to my feet. Too late. Gravity took over. I just had time to push the board away before I fell headlong down the face, towards the reef below. The wave piled down on top of me, and I was spun head over heels. I came up, disorientated.

'It's very tight in there,' a lone body-boarder commiserated as I rejoined the line-up. He wasn't wrong.

I was determined to catch a wave. I paddled, hard and early. Caught the wave. Struggled to my feet...and felt the lip whack me on the back of the head and send me flying. This was getting ridiculous.

Then suddenly my wave came. Not quite out of

nowhere – they all came from the same quadrant. But unexpectedly. As it rose towards me, I simply turned and paddled. And without warning I was on my feet. It was as simple as that.

It was sublime. All that falling and frustration, and now I was being propelled along a glass-smooth, vastly powerful wall of water that glistened and shone and rose up to meet my board as I surfed. It all seemed so effort-less, almost dreamlike. A different world. I just held my balance and let it take me – it was all I could do; all I needed to do.

For a terrible instant I was worried the wave had propelled me too fast, and I had outrun it. But just as I was resigned to sinking too soon, it peaked up again, and again I was off, surfing to the very end, where it faded gently into deep water. I kept my momentum, and steered the nose of the board gently over the small hump and back towards the line-up before finally sinking. No drama. Just a burst of adrenaline and an over-arching sense of relief. Two days and nearly four hours of desperate trying and I had finally caught a wave. And a fabulous wave to boot.

By now the tide was falling. I was almost out of energy, my shoulders were burning but I wasn't ready to go in just yet. I stuck around for a second wave, smaller this time, but welcome reassurance that the first hadn't been a complete fluke. Several rocks loomed large and close below my feet as I flew, magnified by the glass-clear water sucked up into a smooth arc that propelled me towards the shore. When the rocks loomed too close, I took my leave, frustrated, delighted, exhausted, with barely enough energy to paddle back across the harbour-mouth to the quay.

WAVE 50: Gwynver

Of all the places I visited on my trip, Land's End was the most disappointing. It's an enclave of tacky profiteering and witlessness, and really not worth a visit. Nearby Sennen, on the other hand, is one of the prettiest beaches in Cornwall.

Technically, I didn't actually surf Sennen during the trip, though I have since. Instead, I surfed Gwynver. At high tide, it's a different beach, separated by a scattering of rocks; at low, it's the far end of the same beach. The water is exquisite: from the cliff-top, a beautiful Mediterranean turquoise; from a surf board, as green and clear as the Caribbean. The waves were exquisite too. I surfed there three days in a row, and each time they were fabulous: clean, sharp and a reasonable size. There was a decent interval focusing their power, and a gentle breeze that whispered them into sharp definition. And on the first afternoon, something special happened.

At first the waves had been difficult to get into. Just when you thought you had a wave, it backed off. You had to be in exactly the right place and paddle hard. Once you were up, they were slow and lethargic, until they reformed on the inside.

Then without warning, everything changed. The tide was dropping, and the swell started to hit a different bank. Suddenly the waves were big, fast and hollow. Fortunately, after Goa, I was pretty fit, and after Porthleven, I was familiar with fast and hollow. A set came towards me and I started to paddle. I felt the lift as it picked me up, and suddenly I was on my feet, high up on a steep wave that seemed to have jacked up out of nowhere.

There was only one way to go, and that was down. I was convinced I was going to somersault over the nose, but it was too late to back out now. I didn't fall though. Instead, I took a vertiginous drop, speeding to the right, my trailing hand instinctively grabbing the rail as I stayed in a low crouch and flew down the face of the wave as everything accelerated around me.

And suddenly, nothing made sense. My brain couldn't compute what was happening. The angles and planes of water and sky were all wrong. Gravity, plus the fact that I was standing on a fast-moving board, were telling me one thing. My eyes were telling me another. Around me, the water started to stretch and dance in ways I had never seen before. Nothing was in the right place. Everything shone and glittered and curved and curled around my field of vision. It was only a millisecond, but I was disorientated. No wave had acted like this before. Nothing in the physical world had.

Before I could work out what was happening, the wave closed down around me. I found myself in a situation that was much more familiar: being tossed around by churning white-water. I struggled to the surface, bemused by what I had seen, and pulled my board back in.

As I paddled out, another set pushed in towards me. I was curious to see what the waves were doing as they broke, and instead of stretching to get clear, I waited just where it was about to break. The water peaked up, clean and sharp, and started to break above my head. I saw the glass canopy stretch up and over, taut and glistening. The wave rolled past and pulled me up its clean face, towards the peak. I watched as it curled over my head, and in a flash I was staring down an open cylinder of glistening silver that stretched along the entire length of the wave to infinity.

203

At the last minute, I felt the water wrap around me as the cylinder started to wind itself up, and with a burst of white, it was gone. The wave rolled on towards the beach and I bobbed out into the sunshine, no longer watching from inside the wave, but shrugged off its back. I felt I understood what was happening now. I just needed to make sure.

Usually when you try to repeat the magic of a wave, it doesn't work. Every wave is different. Often you're in a different place. Or the angle is wrong. Or you paddle too fast or too slowly. Or a whale shook its tail a hundred miles away and disturbed the rhythm of the swell. Who knows?

But for once, I managed it. The next wave wasn't identical, but it was close enough. Again I caught it good and early. Again I found myself high on the wave, a vertiginous drop gaping below as if a crevasse had just opened to swallow me whole. Again I took a drop that must surely catapult me headfirst into the water. And again, suddenly, the universe around me shifted, and I was surfing in a different world. A world of steep vertical lines carved from dripping steel and molten silver.

It was breath-taking in its beauty, in its steepness, in its suddenness. Instinctively again I stayed in a low crouch, hunched into the curve of the wave, one hand clutching the rail, the other stretched out ahead of me like a blind man feeling his way into this bright new world. The wave started to curve above me, shading me from the sun with an emerald umbrella of water that stretched out like silk, translucent against the sunlight. It curled me in its mermaid embrace and held me there forever. It was an image I knew from a thousand photos and videos, the elusive arch as the wave starts to wrap into a barrel. The surfer's grail. But it was the first time I had experienced it for myself. While swimming, sure. While paddling too. But while surfing? While moving through this magical tunnel of light and movement? Never. It was sublime.

I can't claim it was a barrel, though. A cover-up, at most. And a brief one at that. In another instant, the wave snapped shut, dashing the liquid arch into a million drops of water. But for an instant, I had gazed into eternity.

By the following day, the waves had lost their magic glimpse of brilliance. In return, they opened up for longer rides. It was a reasonable exchange: an instant of the sublime for a few seconds of speed. Both were exhilarating and adrenaline-filled, both exquisite. Different in their subtle challenges and intangible pleasures, but it was still paradise.

By now, I was surfed out. Exhausted. I was going nowhere, happy to sit in my van on a quiet cliff-top and admire the view. But then I got a call from Tup, a fellow surfer I had met in Thurso, diametrically the furthest point from where I was now. We had shared a frustrating surf and gone for a couple of beers, and now he was off to Gwynver and did I want to join him?

Surfing round Britain is a lonely business. People are less or more friendly, depending on the day, the place, the intensity of the wave. But it's a transitory relationship. A few words, a shared smile, a brief exchange of condensed biography. Like castles in the sand, it's a fragile structure, wiped clean with the incoming tide. You find a new beach, you make new friends, you move on. Meeting up with a surf buddy was an unaccustomed pleasure.

Surfing with friends – even vague acquaintances – adds an extra dimension, especially when you're both surfing well. They spur you on to surf better. They cheer your triumphs, shrug off your failures, act as witness to the ephemeral poetry of the wave, guardians of a memory that is difficult to hold on to, and to which you yourself were only a partial witness. Most of all they make a solitary activity sociable – though when it comes to the actual surfing, it's still just you and the wave.

It also made me realise how far I had come, both geographically and athletically. Back in Thurso I had been inexperienced and unsure. I had been an intermediate surfer at the lower end of the scale. Now, by repeated exposure to different waves in different situations, by battling with difficult conditions and my indifferent technique on a daily basis for nine months, I had improved. I was still intermediate, let's be clear. But on a good day I like to think I was upper intermediate. Or at least a good solid middle.

One wave in particular changed how I felt. Nothing special, a shoulder-high left-hander that I casually caught without really thinking. A wave came, I was in the right place, I automatically turned, took a few instinctive strokes and suddenly I was off and riding, heading down the beach on a glorious wave. Tup, no slouch himself, was evidently impressed, and mentioned it a few times. Up to then I had had no benchmark. I had good days (Gwynver) and bad days (Porthleven) but no mark against which to measure my progress. Now I realised how much I had improved.

After Tup left, I stuck around, sitting in the van reading, eating, listening to the radio. The usual post-surf stuff. I got talking to Juan, a Spanish architect in his fifties who lived in London but had a second home in Bodmin as a surf base. As we chatted, he calmly munched his way through an apple, a banana and two peaches. Perhaps that's the secret of surfing longevity, a healthier diet.

My own post-surf diet revolved around toast and Wagon Wheels. If it was still early, porridge, followed by toast and Wagon Wheels. If I was feeling healthy, muesli, usually followed by toast and Wagon Wheels. Any time I was near a shop, a pastie, followed by toast and...you get the picture. Over the year I probably consumed twice my bodyweight in Wagon Wheels, and still lost a stone. Before starting the trip, I hadn't had one since I was a kid. Perhaps living in a van, there's a subconscious association with travel and adventure and trundling through Indian country in a covered wagon.

A couple of mornings later I got another call from Tup. There were no waves, but did I want to go shark-hunting? I had visions of an elemental struggle with a mighty fish, a robust counterpoint to my struggles with the waves. Of being Hemingway. Did I want to go shark-hunting? Hell, yeah!

Tup, a professional photographer, had spent the previous day photographing sharks from a small plane. Now he wanted to paddle out and get some shots from the water, and he needed someone to get up close to give them some perspective. And not in a philosophical way. Basically I was bait.

Fortunately these were basking sharks, the gentle giant of the shark world. They might be seven metres long, but they just laze around with their mouths open, living on plankton. Unfortunately they are very unreliable. Like the waves at a fickle reef, they can be there one day and gone the next, depending on slight changes in wind and tide.

Undeterred we scanned every bay from Sennen to Penzance, scrambling up rocky headlands, speeding down deserted lanes, striding across empty beaches. It was like chasing waves, but without the anxiety. On a wave hunt, your desperation increases with every flat cove and unruf-fled vista. Today, with no prospect of surfing, I could sit back and enjoy the ride, visiting bays and beaches I would otherwise struggle to find. The scenery was excellent and Tup the perfect guide. Which was fortunate, as rumours of sharks turned out to be unfounded. So it was Tup's aerial shots from the previous day that appeared in one of the tabloids, illustrating that standard summer filler: 'Huge shark appears off Cornwall (but fails to eat anyone)'.

WAVE 51: Porthtowan

I left glorious Gwynver and headed north up the shoulder of Cornwall, trying to make up time. Porthmeor was flat; Portreath was small; I ended up at Porthtowan. Any porth in a storm.

A sluggish, grey afternoon hung heavily over a scrappy pebble beach between two crags, and the waves too were scrappy, jacking up all over the place, then just as abruptly crashing to a close-out. Hidden somewhere in the rocks, an unseen blowhole announced the arrival of the larger sets with a whale-like snort. A dozen surfers scrapped for these scrappy waves, no one much more than competent, while in the shallows a handful of learners turned each ride into a tricky slalom.

WAVE 52: Chapel Porth

The following morning, Chapel Porth, a few miles further on, couldn't have been more different. Here the valley is uninhabited, with just the ghostly hulks of abandoned mines to guard the cliff-tops, and a small café and car

208

park beside the beach. The water, too, was deserted, and with good reason. The tide was way out, beyond a wide expanse of sand that linked various small coves together, and a brisk cross-shore wind was kneading the waves into a heavy, heaving mass, shapeless and shifting and well above head high.

Trying to surf was like wading through dough. By chance you might find yourself below a crest just as it rose up ready to roll, but you needed a snap decision and a rushed take-off to have any chance of catching it. I tried, mostly to no effect. When I did catch a wave, the white-wash hammered down on my back like an avalanche, and by the time I was on my feet, I was surrounded by seething chaos. The face, what little remained of it, stayed just out of reach. I persevered for a while, enjoying the rolling challenge, but when I realised I was unlikely to get a proper wave, I gave up and headed for shore, catching a small reform as consolation.

I surfed there again a week later. I had left my 6'10" in St Agnes to be repaired and had to return to pick it up. This time the tide was in and the sea calm, with a gentle off-shore breeze grooming it clean. Small sets arranged themselves into pristine lines that peeled elegantly across the bay with pin-sharp precision, abrupt and powerful but easy to catch if you were quick. A lone jellyfish appeared from time to time, caught in the clear wall of the wave as it rose, iridescent in the early morning sunlight. The waves were only waist high, but still fun, and a long interval meant that paddling back out was simple. Even on my shorter board I caught dozens, left and right, revelling in the beauty of the narrow cove.

As I got dressed, I was approached by someone who had happened to take a few shots of me from the cliff-top. It's almost impossible to get photos of yourself

209

surfing, especially when you're travelling alone, so I was delighted. To my dismay, though, they seem to show an ungainly amateur struggling precariously to his feet, rather than the lithe athlete walking on water I have always seen in my mind's eye.

WAVE 53: Fistral Beach, Newquay

I had been hoping to avoid Newquay. Sure, it has a reputation as Britain's surf mecca; sure, it has at least one outstanding beach break; sure, it would leave a gaping hole in my narrative if I missed it out. But pretty much everything I had heard about the place suggested it was appalling. I suppose that alone made it obligatory.

More pressingly, I had to find a launderette. Karen was coming down for the weekend and the least I could offer her were clean sheets. I duly spent a couple of hours watching my sheets spin around in a whirling vortex of white-water. It made a pleasant change from finding myself in a similar situation.

Sheets duly cleaned, I strolled down to Fistral Beach to take a look. There were a lot of people in the water, a good hundred or so, maybe more. But it's a long beach, and they were evenly spread: several dozen were fighting it out at the northern end, where the waves looked a little better and a little longer; several dozen were bobbing around the southern end. In between, decent waves were breaking and there were plenty to go round. I decided to give it a go.

When I returned with my board, it was after seven. The low sun burnished the water and stretched the shadows of departing beach-goers. Most learners had dragged themselves home, so the shallows were surprisingly clear, at least until eight o'clock, when a horde of munchkins tumbled into the water like ducklings, all wearing bright swimming caps to stop them floating away.

Thick walls of swell were pounding in at around head height. A light cross-shore wind, with maybe a hint of on-shore, thickened them up a little, making them easy to catch but a little choppy, and giving some of them a false peak and a double drop, like a heartbeat: when you caught the wave, there was a short initial drop followed by a deeper, steeper one to watch out for. But the faces were clean and strong, and though they closed out after twenty or thirty metres, they were fun and sufficiently dramatic.

At the far end of the beach, where the local pros were slugging it out, the atmosphere looked ugly and competitive. Among the surfers in the middle of the beach however, the mood was friendly and relaxed. It felt as if everyone was on holiday, so no one could lay claim to the break as their own, and everyone was patient and generous rather than edgy and aggressive. In short, I was pleasantly surprised. Even the location was prettier than I had expected, with an imposing hotel on one headland and elegant townhouses on the other, and a raised golf course acting as a *cordon sanitaire* between beach and town. Over the next hour, I had a blast. Great waves, plenty of them, and the sense that I had underestimated Newquay as a place to surf.

It was only as I drove away that the other Newquay reasserted itself, a tacky resort full of bargain-basement souvenir shops and Benidorm bars. Mobs of marauding teenagers emerged at sunset like drink-seeking zombies, roaming the streets clutching cider and alcopops. As the last rays of the dying sun dazzled my rear-view mirror,

I headed out of town, feeling like the lucky survivor in the final reel, relieved I didn't have to stay and face the hungry hordes.

I wasn't entirely out of the woods. I needed somewhere to sleep, and everywhere north of Newquay was comprehensively guarded against vagrants in vans. I continued on with an increasing sense of urgency. The road coasted over pretty farmland, thick with golden corn, but the sea felt distant and the car parks blind. Where the road dropped steeply to sea level, closely-packed villages offered no welcome to strangers. Eventually, as the light faded completely, I reached Trevose Head, and spent a troubled night dreaming I was about to roll off the bare headland and into the sea below, watched only by the silent lighthouse.

WAVE 54: Booby's Bay

Fistral had been a pleasant surprise, but it was a relief to return to a quiet beach, far from cars, shops and teenage drinkers. Booby's Bay is not the most inaccessible beach in Britain, but it's still a decent trek down country lanes, over fallow fields and across a stretch of golf course to a grassy path that runs along the low cliffs. From there you clamber down stepped slate slabs slippery with iridescent weed and wet with rock pools, to find clear water and a pretty shore line.

After Chapel Porth and Fistral the day before, I was tired, but for a while I made the most of the deserted bay. Clean, head-high waves were peaking nicely, with a fast, steep drop that opened into shining green walls: a moment of exhilaration before the wall collapsed. In the bright sunlight, the sea bed shone, and I couldn't resist opening my eyes as I duck-dived, to watch the emerald blues and mustard greens shimmer through blurred eyes.

At Fistral, with so many other surfers in the water, I had had to challenge for every wave, and take drops I might otherwise have left. It had sharpened my timing and boosted my confidence, and now I went for waves that earlier would have filled me with doubt. Catching them only boosted my confidence further, and for a while, I had a great time, catching short, dramatic rides in a beautiful place on a beautiful day.

WAVE 55: Sandymouth Bay

Karen had met me off the train in Goa with garlands. I met her in Barnstaple with a damp van and a wet wetsuit. Luckily, she is very understanding.

Foolishly, I had failed to buy a map. For an itinerant surfer, maps come just below surfboards and wax on a list of essential kit, showing not just where to surf but where you might sleep. Buying the local Ordnance Survey had become part of my routine. I would arrive somewhere new, search out the bookshop and stock up for the coming weeks. This time, though, I had got ahead of my library, and we spent a frustrating couple of hours following hopeless lanes to unsuitable dead-ends, trying to second-guess the road atlas.

Increasingly desperate, we finally stumbled across a general store with one remaining map among the tinned peas and birthday cards. I fell on it like the Holy Grail. And like the Grail, it led to our salvation, guiding us to Rockymouth Bay, a beautiful cove where we spent three days clambering on rocks, cooking mussels and, of course, surfing. At least, I did. Karen doesn't surf, though she is perfectly happy sitting on a beach with a book, which is something. It's not actually called Rockymouth Bay, of course, but to name it here would be a betrayal.

This wasn't Goa, though. The clouds came rolling in, the wind swung round and suddenly fleeces were more appropriate than flip flops. Widemouth Bay was howling, and even the eager swarm of learners – usually so resolute – were cowering on the beach, afraid to brave the mess. Just one solitary surfer was out, making heavy weather among the heaving waves. If I was tempted to join him, the desire quickly vanished.

Sandymouth Bay the following morning was still rough and troubled. Foolishly I decided to give it a try anyway. I hadn't missed two days in a row for a while. A strong rip insisted on pushing you towards the unwelcoming rocks to the north, and thick algae, whipped up into egg-whites, dripped off your chin like bubble-bath. I caught a couple and called it a day.

WAVE 56: Rockymouth Bay

On day three, Rockymouth Bay was calm and almost glass-like, with head-high sets that pushed in like billowing silk. It looked glorious. A local surfer, Pete, was just getting out, glowing. He gave me a brief guide to the bay's highlights – a great left breaking off the rocks on the left, a handy rip alongside the rocks to the right – and after a quick warm-up, I headed in.

Like many coves in Cornwall and Devon, the bay is a slender cranny in the steep cliffs that run along the coast. At high tide, the beach almost disappears, but as the water drops, it reveals sharp rocks running out to sea like dragon's teeth. Only a brief patch in the centre of the bay is safe from their bite, at least until low tide, when several separate bays link up in an unbroken strand that extends for miles.

With so many rocks and so much water washing around, it was a bit hairy, particularly the handy rip along the northern edge. But once you got out, it was fabulous: big and clean and very flattering. As I caught each wave I was looking where I was hoping to go (along the face of the wave), rather than where I feared I would end up (falling into the depths below). It was a sign I was surfing confidently, and I was tempted down to the southern end, to try the left Pete had promised.

It was hard to get over there and took real effort and determination to leave a decent peak and fight the cross-current. When I eventually made it, the south side felt even more hairy than the north. The rocks were sharper and seemed closer to the line-up. I had seen them at low tide, but hadn't really memorised their topography. Now, with a full tide, only the tips emerged. The rest lurked beneath the surface like a bad memory, with no indication when they might leap out and maul you.

But Pete was right. The left was fantastic. It drew itself up to just over head height, smooth and silvered in the grey morning light. I turned and paddled, and as the first wave caught me, I looked down its clean line to my left, where it rose in a gentle shoulder that stretched away beautifully towards the far side of the bay. In an instant, I was off, swooping down into a controlled bottom turn, grazing its smooth, long face with my fingers. Then up again, slicing the wall of glass in two, careful not to make any abrupt movements that would throw me off.

On I went, swooping and rising, carving controlled turns from top to bottom of this beautiful moving mass as it continued to draw itself up, smooth and elegant, until it filled my entire world.

I knew what I was on, I recognised a great wave, and knew that for once, I was perfectly in control. It was a fabulous feeling. It filled me with the moment, focused all my attention on the present, on the now, as I glided along, supremely aware and intent on just one thing: surfing this wave with my entire being. Time itself slows and stretches, and for a brief eternity, the wave rolls out and you surf it forever, unaware of past or future except that it involves this wave, this moment. It felt like paradise, like poetry, like surfing the very fabric of time. This is why you surf, for this glimpse of eternity, this moment that makes you immortal, that wraps you in the universe and wreathes you in the infinite. This is the essence of surfing, and for this instant, you are infinity. You are pure essence. It felt sublime. It *was* sublime. It was everything.

And then the wave ends. The infinite is over. Eternity ends. A hundred metres and a lifetime from where I had begun, I glided gently over the brief hump of swell, all that remained of the towering wall of energy that had connected me with the whole of time and space. Ahead of me was calm water. But I was in ecstasy.

WAVE 57: Puttsborough

It was half-term and my friends from Newcastle were on holiday nearby, along with two other old friends and a combined sextet of kids. I waved Karen off at the station

216

and went to find them, playing cricket on Puttsborough Sands.

On the way, I had a look at Croyde. It was the first beach I had ever surfed in Britain, one blustery New Year's Day several years earlier, when I was still living in Spain and surfing the warm waters of the Mediterranean. While my friends slept off their hangovers, I slipped away and rented a board, eager to test myself against the chilly waters of Britain.

A filthy on-shore gale was howling, turning the sea into a seething mess. But I had driven two hours to get there, and went in anyway. Only one other person was out, a learner trying to catch waves with his board sticking up like the hull of a speedboat. I suggested he move forward a few inches and he immediately caught a ride all the way to shore. It was only a mini-wave of white foam, but for a learner, that's enough. As he stepped off, almost on the beach, he turned to check I was watching. Of course I was! I gave him the fist-salute of congratulation. Welcome to the brotherhood. It was the most warming aspect of an otherwise chilly day.

Now, in late May, the weather was warm, the half-term hordes were swarming and the waves were small. I continued to Putts, where my friends were staying right on the beach, in a beautiful house belonging to a wealthy aunt. After months railing against the privatisation of Britain's coastline and the iniquity of second homes suffocating our coastal communities, for the next three days I found myself staying in one. Or near one – they offered me a sofa, but I preferred my van, parked in the drive. Less as a protest, more for the peace. Six kids in holiday mode? The shock would have been too great.

After so much solitude, I revelled in the energy and excitement of a family holiday by the sea, even someone else's family. The house was a modernist gem, and having spent several days beside Virginia Woolf's lighthouse, now I felt I was caught up in the novel itself, surrounded by plans and picnics and the paraphernalia of days at the beach. It was bliss. Apart from the surfing, which was a dismal failure.

In sharp contrast to the warmth and laughter around the breakfast table, the beach was cold and lonely, wreathed in thick mist. Galloping horses emerged like ghost riders, silent on the wet sand. I had the marrow-deep shiverings of an incipient cold, but I dragged myself into the water anyway, lured by smooth waves and compelled by the expectation of my hosts. It was a pitiful display. One of those days when nothing goes right, despite apparently good conditions, large and clean, though overly steep. Being on the wrong board didn't help – my longer board was still being repaired, and I missed the extra second or two it offered, and the resulting confidence that you will catch the wave and not be hurled aside like flotsam.

So I was hurled aside like flotsam. I fell down mirrored faces, or failed to get into the wave, or if I did, I got my feet confused. Whenever I did manage to stand, the waves closed out and I was left with a draining paddle back. I persevered, though my only reward was a few brief rides at the expense of plenty of effort.

I tried again in the afternoon. The high point was an early catch on a fat wave, to find myself standing tall above a six-foot drop. I wasn't convinced my board would hold it – it looked too steep, but I was committed. I pushed on, pressing ahead on my front foot to take me forward. It was as if I had pressed the button in a lift, going down. I took a breath-taking descent that felt like free-falling into the abyss. As I reached the bottom, ahead of me the wave threw down a high curtain of water. The abyss was where I ended up.

Eventually I accepted I wasn't going to improve without some decent rest, and went to eat ice-cream on the beach with my friends. They remained distinctly unimpressed by my display – and by extension, I felt, with how I had spent the preceding nine months, though they were polite enough not to say so. I didn't want to outstay my welcome at Great Aunt Maud's modernist gem, and after three days of hijacking someone else's family holiday and three disappointing sessions in the water, I left, slightly rueful at the missed opportunities.

There were more frustrations just around the corner. It turned out that my brake lights weren't working, so instead of speeding back down the coast, I had to head inland, to a VW mechanic near South Molton, where I camped on a quiet country lane, so I could take it in the next morning. That was the only night of the trip I would sleep away from the coast, surrounded by the smells and sounds of farmland. It was pleasant and peaceful, but it didn't feel right. I was supposed to be by the sea.

I spent the morning pacing the forecourt at South West VWs, another fabulous campervan boneyard run by enthusiasts. No amount of pacing could accelerate the repairs, and it was midday before I was off again.

WAVE 58: Droskyn Point

The surf forecast was excellent and I raced back south to resume where I had left off. Along the way, I checked various spots, hoping to catch some of the places I had missed on the way up. Croyde was heaving; Crackington Haven was dumping; Crantock was flat. Finally, at around six, frustrated by a day lost to repairs and the road, in beautiful sunshine I reached California.

Or so it seemed as I parked on the cliffs above Droskyn Point and found myself surrounded by golden youth, wide smiles and colourful, clapped-out surf mobiles. Even the beach looked Californian, corduroy to sunset. Clean lines of swell pushed in to the beach as if the sea were a pond and the sun a giant pebble tossed into the middle. From the cliff-top, the late afternoon sun sharpened each line, accentuating its sinuous beauty with light and shade. They were small and fairly weak, but peeling perfectly, and after three sessions of turbulence at Puttsborough, this was fine.

My body ached, and I was tense from several hours' driving. A quick surf was exactly what I needed. I teetered down the perilous stone steps carved into the cliff, picked my way across the low rocks at the bottom, sharp with mussels and slippery with seaweed, and stepped onto the sand, where the water was already knee deep under the incoming tide.

Dozens of surfers stretched out along the beach, so I picked a less crowded spot just below the cliff, and for once managed to assert myself in the line-out, catching my due, no more, no less. The waves were clean and perfectly formed, and even on my smaller board, easy to catch. You had to paddle hard, of course, but it was easy to hit the right spot, which made it bliss after the marathon struggles of the previous days. I took mostly lefts, with a few reasonably long rides, and waded back out each time, revelling in the easy-going charm of the place and as always, relieved to have gone in.

I continued south to resume my route at Chapel Porth,

then back to St Agnes the following day to pick up the board I had dropped off a week earlier. It wasn't ready, of course, so they gave me directions to the workshop, where a dust-covered young surfer in a mask was sanding it down with a degree of care and precision that the modest repair fee barely merited.

While I waited, I dropped in at the headquarters of Surfers Against Sewage next door. If I had managed to surf around Britain without contracting gastroenteritis, conjunctivitis or rabies, and without stepping on so much as a soggy tampon, let alone a radioactive syringe, it was thanks to their hard work campaigning for cleaner beaches. It felt only right that I should go in and thank them personally.

WAVE 59: Watergate Bay

My whole body ached, but I was feeling the pressure to keep surfing new spots. As I drove up past Watergate Bay, it looked vaguely surfable. It's one of Cornwall's most iconic beaches. I had to go in.

The beach is long and wild and surprisingly unspoilt, with dramatic cliffs and a scattering of rocks to break the gorgeous monotony. Only the ugly café and surf complex that squats by the entrance to the beach mars the experience.

To avoid the crowds, I walked up the beach a short way in search of a solitary peak, looking forward to an easy, late afternoon surf to wash away the grime. Now that I had my larger board back, it should have been easier – easier to catch waves, easier to balance, just easier to surf.

Instead, the bigger board made me lazy and complacent

221

and I didn't make the most of some reasonable waves. Too often I got bogged down in white-water, or fell off for no reason. You can't really expect to surf well if you don't make the effort. I gave myself a stern talking to, the waves got bigger and things started to improve – at least until two teenage boys invaded my peak and carried on a teenage boy conversation. Even when they were thirty metres apart and I was between them, they kept up their tedious dialogue. To make matters worse, not only were they catching my waves, they were surfing them better than I was. Bloody half-term. My mood darkened and after a frustrating run, I caught a mediocre wave back in, defeated.

By now an apocalyptic haze hung over the beach, tinged pink by the evening sun. The cliff-top road through featureless cornfields, familiar from a week earlier, was now like driving through pink candyfloss, with the sun a muffled marshmallow low on the horizon. Tired and rather dispirited, I headed for Trevose Head, where I knew I could sleep undisturbed.

The following morning, mist hung heavy in the still morning air, with no sunshine to lighten it. A mile away, I could just make out Constantine Bay, where white manes broke against a gunmetal sea. I had surfed Booby's Bay, but was eager to try its neighbour. I packed up and rattled down the hill to take a look.

WAVE 60: Constantine Bay

Close up, Constantine was a dramatic sight. The fore-shore was a seething mess, with cross currents rushing from all directions. But once you got out, it was oddly

222

still. Still, apart from the silent monsters that emerged from the slate surface of the sea to tower over a dozen waiting surfers. I paddled out easily enough and took my place among them.

The water was dark grey, almost black, and merged with the canopy of mist that encased us in our own muffled world. Only the slash of white as each wave broke softened the darkness. They were big and fairly terrifying. Several were twice the height of the surfer riding them. Some even bigger. On the other hand, they were quite fat, with long, long faces, so they weren't desperately steep or fast. Even so, you had to grit your teeth and really go for it.

It was thrilling and nerve-racking in equal measure. The waves promised exhilaration and doom. The mood in the water was quiet, almost reverential. We all recognised these were spectacular conditions – not just the waves, but also the intense, muffled atmosphere and gloomy, muted monotones. It was like surfing at the end of the world, alone and isolated and awaiting the cataclysm.

And when you caught a wave, you were even more alone, as the wall of water separated you from the small band of survivors on their tiny rafts behind you; while ahead was seething chaos, with only the vague suggestion of land somewhere beyond. But you were rewarded with a glass-smooth face and the eerie sensation of silence and stillness that washes over you as you fly down the face of a roaring mass of water, etching your line against the infinite.

I caught a left, clean but short-lived. It took me by surprise, as I half expected to be pitched down the face. It petered out too soon, but it gave me confidence, and a little later, when a huge right reared up just where I was sitting, I turned and paddled. I was sure I was too late and would be swallowed up. Instead, I was on my feet and taking the drop down its snow-smooth surface, slicing over its pristine face as the crest towered high above me, menacing and omnipotent. It held my fate as if I were a mouse in the palm of a giant hand. But I surfed it out, revelling in its smooth beauty, before it could clench its fist on me. The wave softened, but then reformed, still shoulder high, still clean and just as exhilarating, until finally the giant snapped its fingers and was done. Then a third wave, just as big, though this time the reform was heading left, so I switched direction and went with it, surfing up and over the shoulder at the last minute, as it exploded in a violent crunch that tried to take my legs away.

And that was it. My mojo left me. I was repeatedly out of position, or caught under the impact zone, or unable to achieve escape velocity on tiring arms. But I was happy enough, as I clambered up the rocky ledges slick with seaweed, with the roar of those fabulous waves echoing around me in the mist-filled bay.

I spent the day revelling in the exquisite discomfort of exhausted limbs, my whole body tingling with the memory of those few fabulous waves. Nothing to do but eat and read and watch waves, as I slouched and slithered in my seat, unable to find a position that was comfortable for more than a few minutes.

I was getting more and more weary – a deep weariness that had nothing to do with fitness and everything to do with age and the intensity of the past few weeks. Mentally, too, the insistent schedule was taking its toll. I only had a few days left before I had to break off again – just enough to complete this section of coastline, and with it the English part of my trip. I would be sorry to leave the West Country, but I was looking forward to an enforced break. I couldn't let up yet, though. I needed to keep going, to get more beaches under my belt.

WAVE 61: Harlyn Bay

By late afternoon, Constantine was a desperate mess, so I drove over to Harlyn, on the opposite side of Trevose Head. It faces north rather than west, and offers shelter when westerly gales make the rest of the coast unsurfable. At high tide, the beach almost disappears, a pretty curve edged by rocks, with lush green fields sloping gently down to create a ridiculously picturesque scene of rural tranquillity. Even the distant caravan site slipping down the curve of the hillside doesn't disrupt the idyll. The only drawback is that it needs a decent swell to reach round into the secluded bay. And big though Constantine had been, the direction wasn't quite right. Even so, sheltered from the westerly wind, Harlyn offered two things that Constantine didn't: a mellow evening surf and a new beach to add to my tally.

A little too mellow, perhaps. I've surfed it since, when it's been clean, powerful and challenging. That evening, it was only one of those things. I messed around in the clear water, never more than waist deep, catching baby waves that dribbled me into knee-deep shallows, then wading back for more. It was barely surfing, except in the most generous definition, and the contrast with the morning's surf couldn't have been greater. But I was happy enough. Sometimes you have to recognise your limits.

By morning, the wind had picked up. Booby's and

Constantine were even less appealing. Time was of the essence. I only had a few days left. I pushed on north-wards.

WAVE 62: Polzeath

I wanted to surf Polzeath for several reasons, most of them nostalgic. I had distant memories of a family holiday when I was seven or eight, and can still remember surfing my first waves there, on a length of plywood that curved gently at the nose but was painfully sharp everywhere else.

Then a few years ago, I spent a long weekend with a now ex-girlfriend, Emma, staying in a caravan belonging to her aunt. Beautiful November sunshine, low and ethereal, glanced off the water as if off bronze, and fabulous waves pulsed into Polzeath's wide bay – at least fabulous by my Barcelona standards. There was only one problem: I couldn't rent a decent board. They gave me a foam beginner's board, and I spent a frustrating morning catching great waves then trying to find a rail with which to surf them. Being a foam board, it had none.

By lunchtime, frustration got the better of me. One of my long-standing surf buddies, Jo, once told me she had bought a BIC board one weekend in Ireland in similar circumstances. At the time, I had been horror-struck by the indulgence and expense. Now it seemed like the only reasonable response.

Fortunately, I didn't have to buy a BIC. For the same price, the surf dude offered me a 6'11" epoxy board. I was hesitant, but desperate. Two waves later, I was thrilled! I spent the afternoon catching fabulous lefts that far outshone anything I had surfed in Barcelona. Maybe that was when my real passion for surfing started.

The bay at Polzeath is impossibly long and flat, so the tide comes in half a mile, and on spring tides covers the car park. When it's out, the sea feels remote – a thin strip of silver buzzing with flies who turn out to be surfers. Amusingly, a handful of wrinkled oldies in sagging swimmers still persist in surfing on what are essentially tea trays, waiting waist deep to catch white-water and the occasional reform with a short length of weathered plywood. When I was a kid, these wooden boards were pretty much all there was. Now they're just for obstinate eccentrics.

A brisk on-shore wind was blowing, whipping up the waves, but they still had enough power and shape, and anyway it was a beach I had to surf. The water was busy, but the standard was average at best, with only a handful of surfers catching anything decent. At first, I wasn't one of them. Fat, shoulder-high waves were tricky to catch, or devoured you in abrupt, unpredictable collapses.

I moved to the southern end of the beach, and as the wind dropped, I suddenly found my rhythm. They were still tricky to catch, with the false start of fat waves that don't want to let you get over the bump. But once you did, they walled up well. And as with my last visit, they peeled left for what felt like miles.

To underline yet again the difference that confidence makes, suddenly I couldn't put a foot out of place. For once, I found myself catching outrageous waves and surfing them surprisingly well, in full control, until they faded out, way up the beach. The penalty for getting it wrong was zero, and as a result, you could relax, so you didn't get it wrong anyway. My surfing shone, and I had a great time, catching long, long lefts, fast and zingy, around shoulder high at the catch, a bit of a delay as they stood up, then pumping along, surfing rail to rail to keep up my speed and race past a couple of sections as they crumbled; then up into a floater as the wave finally closed down, a hundred metres from where it had started. It was heaven. And once again, Polzeath had etched itself on my memory.

I got out, beaming, grabbed a pasty and headed out of town. Much as I had enjoyed surfing there, it's full of braying posh kids trying to buy into the surfer vibe. Newquay is awful, but at least it's democratic. Polzeath rhymes with death, and it's no place to linger unless you've got a trust fund. A few weeks later, David Cameron was on the front page of several newspapers, carrying a body-board there. This tells you all you need to know about Polzeath. And about David Cameron. And indeed about body-boarding.

WAVE 63: The Last Reef in England

I had one day left, maybe two, depending on circumstances beyond my control. Before I went, I had my eye on somewhere more challenging: a rugged semi-secret cove somewhere between Devil's Hole and Tense Rocks. Both would prove to be extremely apposite.

With limited information, I scoured the Ordnance Survey map and found somewhere that looked like the right place. Even so, I got comprehensively lost and almost stuck down a narrow farm track trying to find it from the south.

The following morning, I approached from the north, walking a mile along the cliff-top under a glowering sky.

Rain had made the long grass slippery and I slithered under the awkward load of wetsuit and board. A barbed wire fence added further iniquity, ripping my trousers beyond despair. It all felt rather ominous.

The bay itself was no less ominous: a jagged grin backed by tormented cliffs and pierced by sharp shoals. In the middle, a large wave broke just beyond knuckles of rock that slipped beneath the water with malicious intent. Apart from the steady, well-spaced lines of swell, nothing moved. If this was an arena, it was a deserted one. Not a soul in sight, and none likely to appear.

A small patch of sand caught between ribs of sharp rock was the only thing resembling a beach. To get to it involved a steep scramble down the rocky path, a clamber down vertiginous wooden steps, a teeter across a slippery slate slab and then a precarious wobble across loose rocks.

The idea of surfing alone at an unknown, isolated reef with no one around made me tremulous with foreboding. But it was a measure of how far I had come, emotionally as well as geographically, that I would even contemplate going in. It felt like a culmination of my experiences so far, from solitary beaches and ragged reefs in Scotland to sizeable waves in Yorkshire and Devon. I was confident in my ability to beware of danger, but not overconfident. I knew that one submerged rock, one unwary rip, and I could be in a lot of trouble.

I approached with caution, trying to ignore the malevolent grumbling of rocks that rumbled around in the undertow. As I paddled out, nerves gripped my stomach and tightened my shoulders. Voices whispered in my ears that this was all folly. I was exquisitely aware of how alone I was.

Out in the water, it felt even more solitary, as if I had

stepped off the edge of the world. Under a low, dark sky, everything was reduced to shades of black and grey in the dark morning light. The vivid green fringe that lined the cliff-top was the only sign of life. There was not so much as a seabird for company. I could have been surfing on the moon.

Summoning the courage to paddle out alone was one thing. To catch a wave, quite another. I didn't know where to sit, and I was very concerned about the fossilised spine that stretched out from the cliff in a direct line with where the wave was breaking, and which emerged from the water in a couple of places in the form of sharp, misshapen vertebrae. The only consolation was that by riding a wave, I would be putting clear water between me and the sunken monster. Too much, though, and I would be tripping over its neighbour.

I paddled hesitantly for a couple of waves, less in the hope of catching one, more to see what was happening: how it was breaking, where I would be heading if I fell. Then mustering as much commitment and courage as I could, I paddled for one in earnest.

To my surprise, I caught it. It was just over head high, but fairly slow, crumbling softly at the peak, and with a long, reasonably innocuous face. I stayed high, and managed to steer down the face, heading right, one eye on the shore and its voracious rocks, one on the unfurling wave that stood grey and expressionless at my side.

It was great, but I kicked out early, well before it ended, not sure what lay below its grey surface. I was still chest deep, and surprised to find I was standing on sand. The sharp edge of my fear softened slightly. I paddled back and waited for another wave. The sea was calm, almost glassy, and a long, long interval made paddling easy, and wave choice straightforward. It only broke in one place. You just had to be there when it did.

The next wave was a little bigger, a little fiercer. Again a straightforward catch, just below the peak as it started to furl over, to find myself high on a benign slope of water that bore me no apparent animosity. I swooped down the smooth face and into a wide bottom turn, heading right again. It was glorious.

My pleasure was heightened by my surroundings, and the feeling of pushing my limits, my experience. Here I was on this wildest of waves, somewhere at the outer reaches of the universe. I was surfing at the Tannhäuser Gate; off the shoulder of Orion. I was the last man alive, and the luckiest.

I surfed the wave for longer this time, lured towards the shore by Sirens, and the knowledge that it was only sand beneath. Except it wasn't. When I eventually kicked out, I found I was on rock, sharp and uneven. I was still waist deep, though. A wave was bearing down on me and as I dived beneath it, the top of my foot scraped something jagged. A cluster of mussels maybe, or a rash of barnacles. Whatever it was, it shouldn't have been that shallow. It sliced a sharp stave into my skin, which flapped and smoked wisps of blood for the rest of the session as a constant reminder of what might be down there.

I caught several more, but now I was concerned about hidden rocks again, and saw them in every unexpected boil and gurgle as the wave rose and sucked up the water in its path, ready to hurl itself down again. It was an unnerving experience, and it didn't get any more comfortable.

Eventually, a couple of locals turned up, one friendly, one not. Their arrival filled me with opposing emotions: relief that someone would notice if I drowned;

231

disappointment that my solitary surf was over. I surfed with them for a while, until tiredness made my paddling slower and my judgement worse. Fear of unknown obstacles below and my automatic deference to other surfers conspired against me, and my wave count dropped. I was fully aware of the irony that in the safe sands of Polzeath I could catch outrageous waves at appalling angles, while here I failed to catch waves that were arguably easier. Surfing is all in the mind.

As more surfers arrived, I caught a final wave to the shore and its ominous rumbling boulders, dragged myself up over the steep shelf at the water's edge, and off on the long walk back to the van, my trousers flapping.

I was delighted to have surfed at such a portentous, out-of-the-way reef. It was utterly unlike anywhere I had surfed before, wilder, more challenging, more demanding of all my experience. To have surfed it felt like a milestone, a real achievement. This was The Last Reef in England. It was an appropriate end to this section of the trip, and a suitable farewell to England.

Eleven

Orkney and the North Coast of Scotland Revisited

Wales was next, but if Cornwall in May was tricky for an itinerant surfer, the idea of the Gower in August made me shudder. Conveniently – if you can describe anything in Aberdeen as convenient – Karen had a family anniversary to attend. Thurso was just a few hours away, and in the months since leaving, I had increasingly felt the need to return. I just needed to persuade Karen.

The solution was Orkney, a short ferry ride from Thurso, with its Stone Age villages and Viking tombs – and plenty of deserted beaches to surf as well.

After the Hebrides, I was expecting Orkney to be wild and rugged, whispering with the memory of its earlier invaders. I was disappointed to find it well-groomed and well-to-do. If the Hebrides are jagged boulders hurled by a vengeful god, the islands of Orkney are smooth stones perfect for skimming. Even the Neolithic village at Skara Brae, older than the Pyramids, older even than Stonehenge, somehow seems divorced from its past. Its well-tended hobbit-warren of dwellings has become a tourist tick-off, like a model village or interesting cave. It's difficult to imagine them as the real homes of real people who lived 5,000 years ago.

It's worth a visit, of course. But I was interested in another ancient site, one that predates even Skara Brae: just in front of the village, at the edge of Skaill Bay, is a reef. Just across the bay, another. Both have a reputation for world-class waves when conditions are right.

WAVE 64: Skara Brae

Conditions, of course, weren't right. It was August, so I wasn't expecting much. I certainly wasn't expecting a fun session, surrounded by seals, surfing liquid glass.

Outside the bay, the outer reef was a seething mess, but inside, a clean, shoulder-high peak was breaking, with nice lefts and rights rolling smoothly for twenty or thirty metres, groomed clean by an acquiescent off-shore breeze. Rather than walk half a mile round the curve of the bay, I foolishly chose to paddle. It was a slow haul, and attracted the close attention of several territorial seals. They stared at me with an air of menace that left me spooked. One in particular, a gnarled grey beast, cruised past malevolently several times with an expression like an aggrieved pensioner, getting closer each time.

Fortunately, the reef must have been no-man's-land, and while I was surfing, they just eyed me from a distance, still cruising like seadogs but never coming too close. And by then I had other things to think about - not least the jagged rocks speeding below my feet.

The water was crystal-clear, and magnified every barnacle, every filament of eager kelp. I was unfamiliar with the sublime beauty of pristine water speeding over an unknown reef, and as I raced along, the dappled effect of the lighter rocks was slightly unnerving. I shouldn't have worried. Surfing over them, they seemed danger-ously shallow, but when I came off, I was still only waist deep, standing on kelp-covered boulders.

I was reminded once again how important it was to acquire the cumulative experiences of different reefs. Had I not surfed Thurso, the kelp would have unnerved me; had I not surfed Porthleven, I would have been troubled by the sensation of surfing over shallow rock you can see so clearly. More clearly, in fact, than when you're sitting on a board. On your board, the moving surface distorts your vision. When you're surfing, the power of the wave sucks the water up into a sheer pane, smooth and unblemished. It becomes a liquid magnifying glass for everything below, making it even more beautiful, but at the same time more threatening.

The few waves I surfed well were fabulous – as strange and unusual as anything I had surfed up to then, and given an added frisson by the solitude, by the isolated location, and by the ghostly whispers of Neolithic locals who long ago looked out as these same waves reeled across their reef. Here, more than in the carefully exca-vated hypotheses of the archaeological site, I sensed the past, and my link with it.

WAVE 65: Whitemill Bay, Sanday

I surfed at Skara Brae a second time, on smaller waves. Then we caught the ferry to Sanday, at the north-eastern edge of the archipelago, past fertile islands and barren rocks, and tiny islets inhabited by stoic, sea-faring sheep who would be left to graze everything in sight before being shipped off to their next floating pasture. Busy sea birds intent on silent destinations criss-crossed the straits. Gannets dived and plunged around us.

At Whitemill Bay, a seal colony barked and basked on sand as white as sun-bleached bone. A mile down the beach, I found a small wave to surf. A few seals popped up to have a look, but they were friendlier than their Neolithic cousins, and left me to it. Or maybe they were less impressed with a display which, with the exception of one glorious left-hander, was distinctly underwhelming.

The waves might have been mediocre, but the location was fabulous, on the northern shore of one of the northernmost islands of Orkney. A rarely-surfed beach, stuck out at the far reaches of the empire, where surfers, and even people, were few and far between. It was worth going in just for that.

WAVE 66: Brims Ness

Karen had to return to London, but I still had two bits of unfinished business in Scotland, which had captivated me with its great waves, deserted beaches and dramatic landscapes. One was Thurso, of course. The other, by some distance, was the most isolated beach in Britain.

Back in September, I had shot past Sandwood Bay in a hurry, desperate to get to guaranteed waves. Later I had crossed it off my list. It had seemed too far, too isolated, too unlikely. Also I didn't know what shape the trip would take, what this journey was. Back then, surfing Sandwood had seemed unnecessary. Now it felt essential.

I didn't go straight there, though. I wanted to get my fitness back up, and to surf a few old friends: Melvich, Strathy, Brims...

Brims! As if! I hadn't surfed Brims Ness before, and I can't really say I've surfed it now. Instead I spent a suicidal hour or so wondering at the wave's sheer and savage beauty as it crashed around me, and fearing a grisly end on the shallow rocks a few feet away.

After a sobering series of near-misses and timorous pull-backs, I straggled back onto dry land with a couple of ugly scrapes to my board and a useful lesson: if no one else is in, sometimes it's for good reason.

I retired to Melvich for a couple of days to restore my confidence. Then, on a stormy Saturday, when surfing was out of the question, I made the beautiful, wind-battered drive along the roof of Britain once more, heading west. It was time for Sandwood Bay.

WAVE 67: Sandwood Bay

Sandwood Bay is the last beach in Scotland before you get to Cape Wrath. The nearest road is four miles away, across rugged moorland. If you get into difficulty, you're on your own. It really is the most isolated beach in Britain.

I reached Oldshoremore, the closest village, late in the afternoon. The wind had dropped and the weary sky, streaked with fading storm clouds, glowed pink and gold with relief. Highland cattle grazed impassively above the beach and seagulls wheeled in delight. I found a rocky cove as far from the scattering of tranquil cottages as possible and tried to sleep, with only nerves and the gentle murmur of waves for company. I didn't know what to expect the following day, I just knew it wasn't going to be easy.

I woke early to a still, bright morning, and cooked bacon and eggs to steel me for what lay ahead: the long walk in, whatever surf I found there, the long walk out again. 'The condemned man ate a hearty jailor,' I remembered with amusement.

I wasn't condemned, but I was certainly nervous. I had surfed alone on deserted Scottish beaches several times, with little expectation that anyone would pass by. But somehow the distance to Sandwood Bay made it feel more dangerous, as if there were degrees of isolation. In reality, the risk of drowning or getting into difficulty was the same whether help was one mile away or five. I suppose if I broke a leg or slashed my head, it was further to crawl or stagger for help, but I tried not to think about it. I did pack my first aid kit, though, just in case.

I loaded up my bag with food, water, wetsuit and towel, laced up my walking boots, slung my board over my shoulder and set off, pausing only to take a heroic photo of myself at the small sign pointing the way: Sandwood! I felt I was embarking on a major expedition.

Soon I was out onto open moorland, with ominous hills to the north and a couple of picturesque lochs to lift the spirits. A soft quilt of golds and greens, lightened with a haze of purple, settled over the land as far as the eye could see. The air was still and there was no one in sight. For a pleasant Sunday stroll, it would have been difficult to beat. As the prelude to a surf, it was alarming. Not only was I in the middle of nowhere, there was no indication I was anywhere near the sea.

After almost an hour of rolling moorland, on one of the steeper sections of path, I met a couple of Spanish backpackers coming the other way. They had spent two nights pinned down by the fierce wind and were bolting for safety with the determination of escaped convicts.

238

Twenty minutes later, the path rounded the hillside and I caught my first glimpse of Sandwood Bay, majestic, wild and entirely deserted. To my relief, the royal blue cloak of the sea darkened with pleats of swell as it reached the beach, then frayed into an ermine fringe of white. Even at half a mile I could see there were waves, and large ones. My anticipation grew, but so too did my trepidation.

After its gentle meander over the moors, the path dropped abruptly towards the sea, then disappeared entirely among a rash of crater-like dunes with sharp rims and sandy bottoms that pocked the edge of the beach. Lost in this lunar wilderness, I was disappointed to see that someone had tossed a plastic bag of rubbish into a hollow, too lazy to carry it back with them. May their bones rot in hell.

The beach itself was immense, a few hundred metres wide and almost two miles long. It felt good and desolate and far from civilisation, untouched by the damaging hand of man. From the water's edge, you can see the cliffs that stretch up to Cape Wrath, a mere six miles to the north, and can just make out the lighthouse. To the south, a rock stack, Am Buachaille, towers above the waves. Half-way along the beach lurk two low islands of rock, and to the left of them, two clear peaks were peeling nicely, with a clear channel between them, perfect to ride out on.

I warmed up and waded out, delighted but still nervous. Even in the channel, trying to get out was a challenge. A seething wall of white-water raced towards me and I was taken aback by the sheer power of the waves, unlike anything I had felt. The beach took the full violent force of the North Atlantic head on, with nothing to mitigate its savage power. If you tried to dive over the wall of white-water, it seized your feet and left you floundering. If you tried to dive under it, it pushed you back and tried to snatch your board. Careful timing was the only option. Even so, by the time I reached the safety of clean water, I had been swept a hundred metres along the beach.

But it was fabulous out there: a heavy, nicely roiling sea, with big, lazy waves in no hurry to get anywhere, well above head high and often more. I rolled and pitched on the ocean main, watching to see what the waves were doing, drinking in the wild majesty of the panoramic shore. Just being in the water at this wild, distant beach at the far corner of Britain, far from anywhere, felt fantastic. Well worth the walk, the drive, the time, the effort.

The peak was moving all over the place, and the insistent current was impossible to conquer, so there was no time to hang around. If you saw your wave, you had to go for it. I took the first wave good and early, overhead, with a bit of a peel, heading left. It was a straightforward catch and suddenly I was up and riding, not very fast, not really going anywhere. But it was nice and clean and controlled, and I had a real sense of riding the ocean, not just its extreme edge.

I drank in the view from my privileged vantage point high on the crest of the wave, and surfed carefully, no heroics, just enjoying its power. But I was wary, too, of getting sent through the spin cycle and sucked into the undertow. As soon as it started to crumble, I rode over the top and paddled back out.

The next wave was fatter, less defined, and took a while to get into, as I paddled and paddled and waited for it to pick me up. Eventually it did, but by then it was ready to burst. As I got to my feet it exploded under me, and I found myself on an unintentional floater above a seething morass of white-water. I held on for a moment, struggling for balance as I plunged down and through the explosive chaos. Then fell back for a dark pummelling.

To get back out, it was easier to coast to shore and walk to the channel than to fight against the full Atlantic. It gave me a chance to admire the view, to drink in my location from dry land. I paddled out again relatively easily. More pitching, more rolling, more waiting. Savouring the sensation of floating just off the island of Britain, almost all of which stretched before me, south and east.

The next wave was late too, breaking round my shoulders as I struggled to catch it. I managed to get clear of the foam and out onto the face as it reformed for a short, exhilarating ride along a sheer wall, with the churning jaws snapping at my heels, hungry and desperately ferocious. It was a brief ride but fabulous, different to the others but just as satisfying.

Soon, though, the wind picked up and the waves started to lose their shape. I caught a couple more, struggling against the current to stay in the right place as the peak started to move around, unpredictable and capricious. I decided to try surfing the reform, where the breaking wave gathers up its strength for a second assault. Here, the shape of the waves was better, less touched by the fingers of the wind. It was tough but rewarding, messing around in chest-high water, fighting in the shallows for occasional snatches of surf as the undertow pulled at my legs. Not the same as the glorious sensation of powerful green faces, but energising to wrestle with the waves against that wild backdrop of dunes and cliffs, so exposed and far from the rest of the world.

Eventually I dragged myself from the water, tired but with enough in reserve for the long walk back, and utterly entranced. Sandwood Bay was sublime.

So sublime, I could barely drag myself away. Instead I messed around, taking photos and exhilarating in my surroundings for an hour or two. But happy though I was, there was no avoiding the four-mile trek back. Eventually and regretfully, I had to set off, turning back to look over my shoulder every few minutes to capture once more a view I might never see again.

If the walk in had been a nervous expedition full of joy and anticipation, the return was a slog. Happy and contented but still a slog, as I dragged my weary body back to the van, with a damp wetsuit and leaden board. A couple of times I had to stop, simply too tired to carry on. Getting there had taken a jaunty hour and a half. Getting back, with the exquisite, all-over exhaustion of surfing, two and a quarter.

Almost four hours of hiking for a couple of hours of surf. Anywhere else, you might think twice. For Sand-wood, the sense of achievement was immense. It was absolutely unmissable, almost indescribable, possibly unrepeatable. Utterly worthwhile.

Back at Oldshoremore the south-facing beach was flat but so beautiful and serene I was tempted to stay. Durness, though, was a four-hour drive away, and if I wanted to surf Sango and Can of Beans before heading to Thurso, I couldn't really hang around. I made a cup of tea and hit the road.

The last time I had driven the deserted road towards Durness, back in September, I had been in a tearing hurry, desperate to surf. Now I was calm and relaxed, glowing in post-surf ecstasy, able to appreciate the harsh beauty of the landscape, carpeted in gold. Memory triggered memory, and from somewhere came a recollection of the small beach I had glimpsed just to the east of Cape Wrath, overlooked by giant cliffs and guarded by a double rock-stack. Kervaig Bay. The second most isolated beach in Britain. I realised I probably ought to surf there too.

WAVE 68: Kervaig Bay, Cape Wrath

The next morning I was up early, ready for another expedition into the unknown. Low cloud covered the tops of the higher hills, but it was dry, with barely a breath of wind. The same grumbling ferryman packed us into the damp crate of his tiny boat and on the far side we trooped into the same rusty minibus for the rattling ride up to the lighthouse. They dropped me off in the middle of nowhere and once again I found myself alone in the wilderness, standing at a crossroads holding a surfboard, wondering if I was mad.

Kervaig Bay was about a mile away, down a rocky track through the heather, alongside a stream that chuckled with delight. I too was delighted, if a little anxious. I didn't want to miss the last bus home, and I didn't want to be swept off to Iceland. Both seemed possible.

The tide was about half-way out, with attractive waves breaking nicely, perhaps chest high. But to my astonishment, I wasn't alone. Three men were struggling to haul a large wooden boat over the sand. So much for a solitary surf.

The boat was a heavy, clinker-built skiff and they were trying to heave it above the water-line, safe from winter storms. But despite an elaborate block and tackle, they were making little headway over the soft sand. To see a fourth pair of hands appear so unexpectedly filled them all with visible delight.

The waves looked good but the tide was dropping. They wouldn't stay good for long. If I wanted to surf, I had to get in quickly. But of course, I had no real choice. I had to help them with the boat – although I did so in the painful knowledge that the longer I delayed, the worse the waves would get.

"If you can't help someone in need, who can you help?' Robert Young had told me cheerfully back on Harris, almost a year earlier, as he helped me retrieve my van from a ditch. I put down my board and rucksack and took my place alongside them.

As we heaved, they told me their story. They had rowed round the cape three days earlier and had been heading for Durness when the storm caught them. They had been lucky to find this narrow cove. It's the only break in the cliffs for ten miles. Had they missed it, they would have been in real trouble. Even so, the boat had capsized in the surf, throwing them out close to the rocks. They were lucky not to have drowned.

'Set your hand to the plough and don't look back,' my father, a farmer's son, sometimes says. I set my hand to the rope, though from time to time, I would look back at the sea. A pang of regret ran through me with every breaking wave.

For over an hour we heaved and strained and sweated and cursed as the boat crept forward inch by hard-won inch until finally, barring hell or freakishly high water, the boat was judged to be safe, and the three men set about gathering their stuff. By now, the tide was far out. The gentle banks of sand that had been coaxing the waves to break so elegantly were well above the water line. With low tide approaching, the waves were crashing close to shore in a sudden burst of frustrated energy. Not good for surfing. Not good at all.

Ideally I would have waited for the tide to turn. But for once, I was not master of my own destiny. Miss the minibus and I would be stranded on Cape Wrath for the night, four miles from a draughty lighthouse, twelve miles and a cold swim from the van. If I wanted to catch a lift, I had to surf now, or not at all.

On the other hand, the beach was beyond beautiful. Edged with wild meadows and moorland grass, and at the foot of the tallest sea cliffs in Britain, it looked straight towards the North Pole.

Just beyond the waves at its eastern edge, two immense rock stacks emerged from the water side by side, linked by a single, fallen mass, so they looked like a cathedral rising solemnly from the waves. Overshadowed by the immense cliffs, it was only up close that you realised the true scale of this natural temple. To call the view awe-inspiring barely does justice to its monumental beauty, its sombre majesty.

The water was clear, tinged with brown from the peat washed from the hills, giving it a dark emerald tint. Loose kelp floated around the shallows but otherwise the seabed was sandy and smooth. Just off-shore, so close I could see their eyes, dozens of gannets wheeled and dived like darts.

As I feared, the waves were past their best. The few times I managed to get to my feet, the moment had long gone. More often, I was hurled violently over the falls and dumped into shallow, kelp-filled water. To add injury to insult, as I let one wave go, I felt a sharp flick around the cheek. A jellyfish had rewarded my indolence with a passing swipe across the face that left it numb and tingling for the rest of the day. Time after time, I fell or was sent flying by the power of the wave.

Then, somehow, amidst all the frustrating abruptness and violence, amidst this scene of majestic beauty, my perseverance paid off. Somehow I managed to ride the perfect wave.

It was a fast catch, of course, early and high up, then a frantic drop and suddenly I was whistling along a hollow wall of shoulder-high water that curved over me as I crouched. It was fast and frenzied, a carved-out scoop of hurtling water sculpted perfectly for me to surf. Behind me, I sensed it snapping at my heels. But all my focus was ahead, watching my path, aware of its subtle beauty, its magnetic power, the elegant translucence of the emerald water as it walled up around me. I was just able to admire it over my right shoulder as I raced it to the shallows, relishing every millisecond of exquisite precision, even as I knew it was about to expire. I was seeing every detail in the miraculous slowing of surf time, and I was able to take it all in, the green curving wall, the fraying curl, the expectant slope that rose ahead; and above, the towering cliffs. Once again, the universe slowed and I surfed a wave that lasted forever.

It lasted forever and was over in seconds, dashing me back to earth, back into shallow water some fifty metres and several light-years from where I had started.

I paddled back, hoping to repeat the wave. For my trouble I was hurled and churned and spun around the shallows. What little I did catch was over in a flash, poorly caught and poorly surfed in ever worsening conditions. But no matter. The location, and that one wave, made everything else – the time, the effort, the expense – absolutely worthwhile.

I dragged myself out and admired the gannets wheeling around their rough-hewn cathedral: Notre Dame des Vagues, with its voracious, diving congregation. The three men had left, and at last I had the beach to myself. I savoured the isolation, wolfed down some food and watched the gannets wheel and dive before setting off on the steep trudge up the track to the desolate intersection, hoping the minibus hadn't gone without me.

* * *

If I had been surprised to see three men and a boat at Kervaig, at Sango Bay the following morning, I was amazed to see a long-distance cyclist towing a surfboard. Vitas was from Germany, and was cycling to Ireland, surfing along the way. For salty discomfort and relentless exposure to the elements, he might as well have been rowing the Atlantic. After a battering by the waves, I can't imagine having to get on a bike, especially on that windswept coastline. It's stunning, but there are long, long hills between its distant villages. We shared a mediocre session and I fed him tea and cake to help him on his way. Then I couldn't resist Ceannabeinne. It was just too pretty. I surfed it twice, afternoon and morning, but it was rough and heavy, and neither session improved my record there. Then finally, it was time to face my demons at Thurso.

As I turned into the familiar farm track at Thurso East, I was amazed to see an unmistakeable van parked outside one of the cottages. Achilles again! I jumped out and we greeted one another like old friends. I had last seen him in Scarborough back in December, but it seemed almost inevitable I should meet him again here.

'It will probably pick up later,' he told me. 'If you want to go in, you should,' he added in his bluff Yorkshire way.

From the farmyard, it didn't look promising, so I was surprised, a short while later, to see a large figure casually striding over the rocks and paddling into the line-out. Achilles, of course. I should have known. He had the power to summon the waves at will. What had looked small and unpromising now revealed itself to be a solid, surfable wave, breaking a little higher than Achilles himself, and Achilles was at least six foot. It was a bit messy, a bit crumbly, a bit fat. But it was a wave.

Nervous and excited, I changed and picked my way to the water's edge.

Things didn't start well. My first wave I fell off. The wind had dropped a little, but it was still blowing across the wave, making things a little unruly. Panicked that I would be caught inside, I pulled in my board and scrabbled for open water.

I had seen Achilles take several waves left, which seemed counter-intuitive on Thurso's majestic right. But when a left came along, I took it, happy for anything to boost my confidence. It was fine – not very big, not very long, but at least I caught it. I made sure not to get too close to shore, and deliberately fell off backwards, taking care not to plunge too deep. Even so, I was a little alarmed to find that the water only just covered my knees. At least I had proved to myself that I could catch a wave. I paddled back, relieved. But determined to stick to the rights.

A right came. I paddled. It was a struggle to get into, and alone or elsewhere, I might have let it go. But I didn't want to embarrass myself in front of the mighty Achilles, or get psyched out by this most mighty of reefs. I paddled hard, until eventually it took me in its powerful grasp and I was up, nice and early, riding a decent, head-high peaty sea monster, rough and scaly. It wasn't a massively long ride – the reef wasn't really firing – but it was enough to boost my fragile confidence.

Another followed. And another. They were bigger waves than I thought I would have been capable of, and I was up on my feet fast – out of fear, mostly. But the glorious sense of relief that I was surfing again at Thurso – even modest-sized Thurso – was electric.

In surfing, as in so many things, success breeds success. For once, everything went right. And surfing with Achilles was a real pleasure, as we attempted outrageous

248

waves and cheered one another on. Even when I found myself caught inside a couple of times, standing on limpet-encrusted rock in knee-deep water, with the whole of Thurso bearing down on me, it was merely alarming rather than out-and-out terrifying. The seething, peaty froth was powerful, but it wasn't the baying monster I had seen on bigger days.

The session was fabulous, surfing huge ramparts of peat-brown water, sliding down wall-like faces, feeling a glow of pleasure whenever Achilles called me into a wave with an unexpected – and touching – 'Go on, our kid!'

The sky had been overcast for several days, but as night approached, for a moment the dying sun emerged and bathed the cliffs of Hoy across the water in a beautiful blood red, shadowing every crag in jet black. It sank below the hills, turning the sky to the west a glorious, glowing orange.

Achilles got out and once again I found myself alone at Thurso in the thickening dusk. But where before I had felt disappointment, despair and self-loathing, now I was filled with happiness and delight. I had calmed my Thurso demons. If I wanted evidence of how far I had come since I had set off nearly a year earlier, here it was. A proper session at Thurso, surfing to my full potential. I was thrilled.

Twelve

Wales

My Scottish adventure was complete. England too. Next was Wales, and regretfully, the imminent end of my odyssey. But crossing the Severn Bridge made my heart soar. It always does. The elegant lines of the bridge, the glimpse of muddy shore foreshadowing the surf to come, the sense of a clear border into an exotic new country – it all combines to create an uplifting flight into the unknown. Although 'exotic' might be overstating the case.

As a child, I spent a summer holiday or two camping in the Welsh rain. All I remember is damp canvas and being dragged through incomprehensible slate mines on miniature trains as my parents struggled to keep us dry and entertained.

When I returned, thirty years later, it was to live, not visit, thanks largely to Emma, the now ex-girlfriend who had had already re-introduced me to Polzeath. After fifteen years, I had finally tired of Barcelona, and Cardiff seemed like a reasonable alternative. At the very least, it wasn't London.

In Barcelona, I used to cycle to the beach with a board under my arm. In Cardiff, it was a 25-minute drive. The waves, though, were incomparable. If I hadn't moved to Wales, I wouldn't have known the pleasure of regular, reliable waves; I wouldn't have progressed from mediocre surfer to proudly average; and I wouldn't have embarked on this whole trip. Wales will always remind me of waves.

WAVE 69: Rest Bay

Three or four times a week, I used to head to Porthcawl to surf at Rest Bay. It's not the best break in the world, or even in South Glamorgan. The peak shifts, the current pulls, the crowds swarm on sunny Sundays, and at high tide the beach shrinks to a rock-filled handkerchief. But it was close, convenient and reliable, and it has the best chip shop in Wales. Nothing gets you through a cold session like the thought of fish and chips.

I surfed ankle-dampeners and ugly monsters; glassy shoulders and on-shore mush; crowded peaks and deserted seascapes. In rain and shine, in fog and wind, I surfed Rest Bay. And I loved it!

In fact, I was so familiar with Rest Bay, I would have been happy to miss it out. It felt too familiar for this journey of discovery. But when I got to south Wales, as so often, it was the only wave around.

After surfing nearly seventy new places in all imaginable conditions, it was strange to return to a beach I knew so well. I was a different surfer, more experienced, more aware. Surfing the same beach, you might not notice your progress. Returning for the first time in two years, the difference was significant. My timing was sharper, my wave selection better, my control more consistent. I still wasn't a fantastic surfer, but at least I wasn't the worst surfer in the line-up, which made a nice change.

251

Conditions were average: chest-high waves peeling well, though lacking power, a slight cross-shore wind, bright September sun. Not the most rewarding waves of the trip, but it was uncrowded and easy, and a fitting way to mark my return to Wales and to launch the final section of the trip.

There were other places I wanted to surf nearby. Two of them, Ogmore and Llantwit Major, I had tried to surf, but never had the knowledge or the patience to catch when conditions were right. A third, Southerndown, was one of my favourite beaches, small and intimate, and overlooked by intriguing cliffs and the razed remains of a small castle. It was usually smaller than Rest Bay, and prone to tricky currents and hungry locals. But when you got it right, it was a delight.

I still remember the first decent wave I caught there, soon after moving to Cardiff, one glorious afternoon. It was chest high and clean, and I was up good and early, wondering if I had missed my moment. But then I pushed down on my front foot and felt the exhilarating thrill as I suddenly dropped down the face and shot along the wave. It was a revelation! Up to then, I had been clinging to waves, hanging along for the ride. This was the first time I had actively pressed down on the accelerator pedal. Things were never the same again.

WAVE 70: Ogmore-by-Sea

I got to Ogmore as the tide was starting to drop. A dozen surfers were catching waves similar in height to Rest Bay, but it was seven o'clock and getting dark. As usual, I had missed it. Instead of continuing on to Suds, I decided to stick around and see what would happen in the morning. I parked by the river mouth and watched the surfers, as a beautiful sunset spread its rosy fingers over the bay.

At six o'clock the following morning, it was dark and misty. I stuck my head out of the van, but could neither see nor hear any waves. Half an hour later, though, the sound of car doors slamming roused me. Two surfers were getting ready to go in. And if they were going in, I was going in.

I picked my painful way across the riverbank and cast myself into the cold, fast river, paddling briskly to get across before it swept me too far out. It was still grey and misty, but as I got closer, I could just make out five or six surfers in the water, spread out at decent intervals, with a Stand Up Paddleboard cruising for ripples a little further out – never a welcome sight, though to be fair he mostly stayed out of everyone's way.

I took my place in a convenient space and was happily watching what the locals were doing when I looked up and realised I was well-placed for a left. I paddled, with no great expectation of catching it, but suddenly found myself surfing a head-high wall that seemed to be roaring in my wake. The combination of a larger board and a slow wave made for a leisurely ride, and I just stayed in the pocket, amazed at the sizeable wave that seemed to be chasing me in.

It was a left, but the rights were where it was happening. Head high, with clean faces groomed by a light breeze, they rumbled in like rugby players, big and boisterous, but quite friendly once you got to know them. I fluffed a couple, fell off a couple, but eventually it happened. It was the same height as the first, somewhere just above my head, but much more powerful, and reeling off into the river-mouth, fifty or sixty metres away – plenty of time to enjoy the sensation of rolling along on an easy-going wave, to listen to its growl and admire its off-white mane.

Eventually the tide dropped and the waves faded, but by then I had caught several decent rides. It was still ridiculously early so I decided to search out another nearly-wave from my days in Cardiff: Llantwit Major. Several times I had made the picturesque trek out to Llantwit and its boulder-strewn reef. Each time, I had found it flat. And while it was closer than Porthcawl as the curlew flies, the slow country roads meant it took far longer to get there, and just as long to get from there to anywhere else. Every time you went, you gambled two hours of your life. And every time, it seemed, you lost. In the end, after several fruitless visits, I gave up. It just didn't seem worthwhile.

WAVE 71: Llantwit Major

Now, things were different. If you're going to be sitting in your van all day reading, writing or arithmetic, time takes on a new meaning. When you sleep wherever you want, place becomes relative. If necessary, I could stay all week. Of course, now that time wasn't an issue, I didn't have to sleep there at all. There were waves, and plenty of them. To the right, a heaving mess of ugly brutes; to the left, a speeding toast-rack of clean lines that rocketed across the reef.

Full of trepidation I hobbled over the ankle-turning, skin-grating, barnacle-covered cobbles to the water's edge. The reef seemed fast and the waves full of force, but they were neither very big nor very hollow: mostly chest high, with a few shoulder-high sets.

When my wave came, I paddled hard, felt the lift, and

was on my feet in a fleeting instant. In the next instant, I overbalanced and fell. Not a great start, but by now messing up the first wave was my standard routine for new reefs. At least I hadn't pitched over as I paddled, which was my main concern; I didn't get mugged by the wave behind, which was my next concern; and I was in chest-high water, standing on barnacle-covered boulders, which was my third concern. The reef was fast, but I had survived the first fall unscathed. I could relax.

Sure enough, the next wave was better. At least I stayed on it, riding until it closed out, twenty or thirty metres away. The next one, the same – up and riding until it closed out. But I was reasonably happy. They weren't huge, but they were nice enough and dramatic enough and a wave is a wave. If only they would hold up a little longer, rather than closing down so soon.

It was then that I realised why they were closing down. It wasn't the reef. It wasn't the wave. It was the locals. They kept dropping in! On every single wave! Every time I took off, there was someone taking off in front of me, twenty or thirty metres further on. And as every surfer knows, this is the worst thing you can do. The person already surfing or who is closer to where the wave is breaking has priority. It's their wave. If you catch it ahead of them, or sometimes if you just paddle, the wave closes down and their ride is over. You've just stolen the ride from them. It's very poor etiquette.

To be fair, I wasn't getting special treatment. They dropped in on one another too. But that didn't make it any more acceptable. I tried various tactics. I moved up the reef. I moved down the reef. It made no difference. I took big waves and small waves. No difference. What I didn't do was drop in on anyone. I don't see the point.

Finally, as my frustration mounted and the swell

dropped and my arms started to ache, I decided to call it a day. From nowhere, a wave appeared, and for once, there was no one ahead of me. It was fabulous! A long, long wave, reeling for eighty or ninety metres down the reef. I weaved together careful turns, top and bottom, making it round a couple of sections that were starting to crumble, and following it all the way to the end. It was ace - a really satisfying ride. But it made me realise how much better the session might have been, if it hadn't been for the uneducated lunks of Llantwit Major, the most tiresome oafs I had the misfortune to meet on my entire journey round Britain.

WAVE 72: Rhossili

A few days later, I picked Karen up in Swansea and we continued on west, to the Gower. Caswell Bay, flat; Langdale, flat; Fall Bay: flat. Mewslade: flat, or almost – a sporadic shore dump sporadically dumped two reckless optimists on the shore.

At Rhossili, from up on the headland the waves looked reasonable. They turned out to be fat and lazy and lacking any energy in a gusting on-shore wind. I caught a couple, more by chance than design, but they didn't stand up to scrutiny. After half an hour I trudged back up the hill, wondering, for once, if it really had been worth the effort.

WAVE 73: Sumpters

During my time in Cardiff, I had signally failed to surf

– or even find – the famous string of reefs that lurk off the Gower coast. From time to time I would study the map like a 17th century explorer, but decided they were probably not for me. Even if I managed to find them, I probably wouldn't be able to surf them. Now, though, things were different. I was determined to surf one - if I could find it.

I studied my guides and pored over the map, and decided to try Sumpters, the easiest and most accessible of the named reefs. A line of vans suggested we were in the right place, then along a well-worn path to a rocky beach beside an equally rocky bay. There was no one around, which worried me a little, but it was a beautiful, cloudless day and the late September sun glanced low off the Bristol Channel, turning that murky strait into the Mediterranean.

I left Karen to bask on the rocks like an exotic Scottish lizard and made my way to the water's edge and along the sandy-bottomed stream that trickled out between the rocks. Two surfers were out at Port Eynon, to the east. It looked appealing, but I was determined to stick to the plan.

Shapely waves were curving in and peeling across the reef. At first they were only waist high, but soon increased to chest high as the tide dropped. I was nervous, alone on an unknown reef, but conditions were sublime, clean and glassy. And if anything happened, Karen was on hand to summon help.

As per usual, I fluffed the first wave. Then for almost an hour, I could do no wrong. I caught plenty, mostly rights, amazed and delighted to find myself up and on the face. They weren't fast, but they were clean and generous, and pushed in smoothly, with a gentle but forceful insistence that flattered my surfing and made me happy just to be there.

From out on the reef, an imposing view of the Gower's picturesque cliffs stretched west to the Worm's Head. In the middle distance, I could see other reefs firing. Somewhat to my chagrin, they all looked bigger and more explosive than Sumpters. But more crowded, too, and for a first attempt, I was happy to have the place to myself.

Eventually a local turned up, who was friendly in conversation but kept taking off on waves when I had priority, which irked me somewhat, not least because I had let him have a couple early on. I hadn't noticed it during my time in Cardiff, but poor etiquette was clearly the defining characteristic of south Wales surfers. Then a long-boarder in a helmet arrived, which dented my spirits further.

But for once, the new arrivals spurred me to paddle harder, to take early catches, to make the most of average waves, ending with an above-average one, a long, rolling right that unfurled off into the channel, sixty metres away. I waded back to dry land, delighted to have finally surfed one of these famous reefs.

WAVE 74: Pete's Reef

Emboldened, and with conditions holding up the next day, I decided to search out a second reef. Again I studied the map, and headed for the same hamlet. There isn't really anywhere to park, and local residents have clearly endured decades of thoughtless intrusion by unwelcome surfers whenever the reefs are firing. Every house bristles with no parking signs and traffic cones, and when I tried to turn in front of one particularly well-guarded gate, a white-haired ogre shook his fist at me.

From here, it's just over a mile across featureless heath, with fat blackberries to delay the greedy surfer, and a soft dirt track to make the going good. As I reached the top of the cliff, high above the reef, a lone surfer caught a wave and gave a whoop of delight that echoed up the hill like a gunshot. At least I knew I was in the right place. As I watched, a dark shape detached itself from the cliff side. Another surfer watching and waiting. He headed down towards the reef and I was able to follow his route: along a steep, grassy sheep track, down a precarious rock path, through jagged mouthfuls of petrified sediment and onto rounded cushions of smooth stone worn into gentle curves.

From my recent experiences, I was expecting a frosty welcome from the two surfers on the reef, but both were friendly. Back at the village, I had been *persona non grata*. Once on the reef, I was part of the team. I sat out a few waves, watching how they broke and letting the two surfers get on with it. Sets were well spaced, and often with just two waves. They reared up to chest high then broke at shoulder high, sometimes head high. And they seemed horribly close to the rocks. I was still nervous, and the nearby rocks didn't help.

Soon, though, a three-wave set came through. One each. The third wave was clean and walling up nicely, with my name written across it. I had no choice. I had to go for it. I paddled and took off – but somehow the nose of my board got caught in the water. My weight was a fraction too far forward, perhaps. Too late to readjust. As I went to stand, it dragged me down and into the water. I had a moment of panic – I was heading down, straight towards the reef. Sure enough, as I flailed around, my arm grazed hard rock.

The wave rolled me over, dragging me further into

shallow water. I tried to stand, but the next wave was upon me. My feet made brief contact with the rough rock below. No comforting kelp here. From a brief touch, I could tell I didn't want to try and hold on – my feet would have been sliced like sushi. Instead, I let myself be rolled around, trying to stay face up, bouncing along on my bum. Not very decorous. By now I was no more than knee deep. Not somewhere I wanted to hang around. A lull allowed me to scrabble inelegantly towards deeper water, push over a couple of small waves and haul myself back onto my board so I could paddle for safety. Panic over.

After a short wait, another set appeared, clean and shapely and about head high. The other two took their waves. The third wave arrived again. I had to take it. I paddled hard. I had learned something at least. I fully expected it to tip me up and dump me down, but I paddled hard anyway, taking care to keep the nose of my board above water. I was committed, locked into the moment of doubt, the instant when you surrender control completely, when you wait with anticipation to see whether you've made it onto the wave, or whether you've been pitched off into the depths.

Amazingly, the wave didn't pitch me off. Amazingly, I was on my feet and riding. Amazingly, my feet were in the right place. I was off, on a fast, exhilarating ride, the wave vertical beside me, the reef beckoning below. Fast? It was like a rocket, shooting me along, precarious on my tiny platform. An instant of adrenaline-filled ecstasy, almost too fast to take in. Just the mirror-like wall propelling me, framing my world, pushing me into the future, absorbing my present, erasing my past. It was all now.

And in a flash, it was over. An eye-blink. Almost before I knew what was happening, I was gliding over the low shoulder and into the deep water of the channel, suffused with a euphoric blend of relief, delight and wonder.

I paddled back to join the other two, trying not to grin too openly, and took my place in the line-up again. There was a long wait for the next set. Rather too long. Instead of gaining confidence, I grew more nervous. I had seen what was involved, what you had to do. I had seen the steepness of the wall and the proximity of the reef, and it all seemed so improbable. OK, I had caught one, but that had surely been a fluke. It was never going to happen again. Part of me wanted to get out now. Quit while I was ahead. But I knew I wouldn't be happy if I did.

The lull dragged on, and the first surfer got out. Another took his place. One out, one in – if only it always worked like that. On cue, a set arrived. This time I was second in line, not third. Even more pressure. Even more reason to go. The wave was bigger than the previous one. I paddled. Hard. Again, I was up and riding. Another rocket ride, taller, steeper than before. And with what looked like a flat slab below me. I tried not to look. Tried to focus on keeping my line. Tried to hang on, until the wave had catapulted me out and over the shoulder, with the gentle come-down of flat water after the precipice that went before. Glorious.

By the time I had paddled back, another set was coming through. And this time there was no one there. No one to force me to take it. No one to make me improve my game. But I knew what to do now. I knew I could do it. I went.

Again, the split-second instant between paddling and riding. The exhilarating acceleration along a burnished mirror of sculpted water. The gravity-defying, universe-stopping, time-freezing rush. It was just fantastic! Again,

261

it was over in a few seconds, and I was out to the slow pastures of the channel.

By now, I was utterly delighted. One wave might be a fluke. Three was sublime. Whenever I paddle out, all I want is three waves. Just three, I tell myself. Three is the difference between a great session and no session. Sometimes, on tricky days at tricky breaks, I've had to content myself with two. Sometimes, with one.

In retrospect, I should have got out then. As more people arrived, I lost my confidence, or my mojo, or maybe just my opportunity in the line-up. For the next two hours, all I got were scraps and smaller waves. Our numbers grew, first six, then nine, then twelve. All good surfers, all very competitive – with the exception of one timorous soul who hung off the shoulder and was never in danger of catching anything. I felt bad for him, mostly because on another day, that might have been me.

Eventually, the tide started to come in and the waves got worse. I was exhausted from paddling for waves and failing to catch them, from trying to get into waves when I was out of position, from paddling then pulling back. I began to despair, and even contemplated paddling back to dry land. I was saved by a smaller wave, which, while mediocre, at least allowed me to ride back to the channel with my head held high. Or highish. It was consolation of sorts.

* * *

As I was on the Gower, I decided to call on a friend of mine, Ian, a film-maker in his sixties who lives in a chilly farmhouse overlooking Broughton Bay. Or not quite overlooking. It sits behind the dunes, a few metres above sea level. So while it's only about 400 metres from the beach, you have to stumble across 390 of those metres if you want to check the waves. Not a major expedition, it's true, but not something you want to do in your pyjamas on a Welsh winter's morning.

Several times when I was living in Cardiff I cat-and-goose-sat for Ian, rattling around in the old stone farm-house trying not to be driven mad by cold, boredom and the exquisite isolation of spending a hundred hours with only cats, geese and a banshee wind for company. At least the geese made me feel welcome, and would hang around the kitchen door honking hopefully. The cats would just slink past, eyeing me with suspicion.

A couple of times, I chanced the impressive rips of Broughton Point, which offered decent, opportunistic lefts when everywhere else was howling. But you had to be quick. If not, you would soon find yourself dragged two hundred metres into the bay, where a moraine of pounding close-outs waited. Even paddling for shore wasn't easy. The tumbling whitewash was little help, and once you had paddled free of it, you found yourself caught in a lagoon seething with unseen currents that seemed to sweep you in circles as you struggled for dry land.

Broughton one December was my first experience of the tremulous pleasures of surfing alone in harsh conditions, with no-one in sight and only flighty flocks of migratory birds to witness your solitary battle with the elements. The damp grey of a dismal afternoon faded to an early dusk, and I found myself chilled to the bone, with ice-cold spray lashing my cheeks as I struggled to hold my position and my sanity.

There is nowhere that feels more alone than out among stormy waves. I shudder when I contemplate the miserable fate of sailors washed overboard. If I had been

263

swept away, no-one would have noticed until my friends returned to find their cats hungry, their geese anxious, their guest gone. But I stayed out there until I could barely paddle, with the occasional reward of a lucky wave that made it all worthwhile.

It was always dusk on the Gower that winter, and almost always grey. Except once, one morning in February, when the sun shone brightly and the memory of the previous day's storm etched itself on the face of the sea in deep furrows. It was still fickle and tricky, but I caught some reasonable waves and at least the light was with me, not against me. Eventually, after a decent session, I paddled for shore.

As I waded through the shallows I was filled with a sublime sense of calm. The moment felt serene and spiritual, almost overpoweringly so. It emanated from the natural beauty of the bay and resonated through my happy, tired body, connecting me with everything around me – and something beyond. The entire universe, perhaps.

The feeling didn't seem coincidental or casual. It felt like a revelation, a glimpse of something ineffable. If I was looking for religious guidance or a sign in which to believe, if I was looking for divine visitation and a moment which would justify my beliefs or prove the existence of God, this was it. For the few instants it lasted, I was aware of something else, something greater than the material world around us, something unseen and all-powerful. An energy, a presence, a higher power.

It brought back a previous glimpse of the sublime, in the Alps late one afternoon, skiing with my father and one of my sisters, Lucy. We had caught the last lift up to the top of the mountain and were skiing easily through silent pines, alone apart from the occasional skier who whooshed past. We took our time, savouring every delicious moment. Again I was suddenly filled with immense calm and contentment. The physical experience of skiing through a deserted landscape became a spiritual one, the more so for being with two of my loved ones. It was a moment of magical beauty, almost ethereal. Like being on a wave, it seemed to last forever. And, like being on a wave, it seemed to connect us to the universe, with the immeasurable energy of the infinite, an energy that will continue flowing long after we have reduced ourselves to space dust. Once again, the thought brought comfort and reassurance. We are nothing. We return to nothing.

WAVE 75: Llangennith

Round the corner from Broughton is the Gower's most well-known beach, Llangennith. Or Gennith to its friends. It's a beautiful beach, wide and dramatic, stretched along the tip of the peninsula from the Worm's Head at Rhossili up to Broughton Bay, backed by dunes and bracken-covered hillside. It faces west, and catches any passing swell – and all the passing wind.

Unfortunately, I've never really got on with Gennith. If you're riding a foam beginner's board and don't mind a little wind chill, it's as good a place as any to learn the basics. But with so many other excellent breaks nearby, for an intermediate surfer with aspirations its appeal soon fades. You can't even check conditions properly without paying for parking at the campsite gate, half a mile from the beach. You can catch a glimpse from the village, another half-mile inland, but that only confirms the colour of the sea, not anything useful like wave size, state of the tide or wind conditions. There isn't so much as a flag – the fluttering ensign of campsites everywhere – to check which way the wind is blowing.

Of course, you can always ask at the surf shop in the village, but without fail they will tell you that Gennith is your best bet. Often – and I know this from personal experience – this is an outright lie. On one notable occasion, when I was still new to Wales and fairly new to surfing, Llangennith was a howling mess, savaged by wild winds and pounded by insurmountable whitewash. But when I asked about alternatives, I kept getting the same answer, repeated like a mantra: Gennith is your best bet.

Knowing what I know now, I could name half a dozen breaks nearby that would have been better that day, with more shelter or better orientation. Not that I blame anyone for keeping quiet about their chosen surf spots – particularly a surf shop. No-one would thank you for sending hordes of muppets to a little-known cove or tricky reef. As a former muppet, I recognise that you learn by finding surf breaks yourself, discovering which places work best under what conditions, and, more importantly, what you are capable of surfing and when you should stay dry. Even so, I left the shop fuming. One thing is to be vague, another is to lie.

This time, I was pretty sure Gennith would be fine, so I bit the bullet and paid the fee. They eyed my van with suspicion and I had to assure them I wouldn't be camping there. It was the first time I had set foot in a campsite all trip. It felt like enemy territory.

From the dunes, the waves looked fine. Fairly clean, chest high, apparently peeling nicely. From the water, it was a different proposition: flat, formless and closing out. Better than Rhossili three days earlier, and fine for the surf school bouncing in the shallows, but far from ideal. It was choppy and lumpy and if you weren't right in the pocket, either it passed you by or engulfed you in whitewash. After four waves, none of them noteworthy, all of them brief, I decided to change boards. But as I walked up the beach, I thought, "You know what, even with a bigger board, it's not going to be great. I'm tired, I've done enough, I really don't need to go back in."

So I didn't. I sat in the van and watched as squalls of rain and surfers blew in and blew out again. And although I checked conditions several times over the next few hours, for once mind and body were in agreement. It just wasn't quite worth it.

WAVE 76: Caswell Bay

Before I left the Gower, I really wanted to surf Langland or Caswell. Maybe both. Caswell is the prettier beach, small and welcoming. But the car park is blind and claustrophobic, and full of nocturnal activity of one sort or another. Sleeping at Langland is more exposed, but at least you have a view of the bay. Not that there was much of a view at seven o'clock the next morning. A downpour was hammering on the van, the road was a raging torrent and the bay was flat.

Back at Caswell, a few waves were coming through, small and formless. I could have justified giving it a miss, but by now I was a full-blown addict. I had to get my daily fix. I sat in the lovely warm café for a while, hoping conditions would pick up. When they didn't, I went in anyway. Half a dozen rides, none very exhilarating, but all I could expect under the circumstances.

WAVE 77: Freshwater West

I left the claustrophobic lanes of the Gower and headed for Pembrokeshire, where glorious sunshine dipped the landscape in autumnal gold. At Freshwater West, head-high waves were rolling in, ruffled by a light on-shore wind. I was tired, but the forecast for the next few days wasn't great. Better to get in. Get one in the bag, as Karen always said, quoting her sister Morag, a photographer, for whom getting a shot in the bag is essential. You can always improve on it later.

The beach is stunning: long, wide and unspoilt, backed by farmland, with low cliffs looking out over the green-tinged sea and golden sand. Only the tips of chimneys at the oil refinery beyond the hills to the north spoil the view, and from beach level, they too disappear. I changed on the grassy cliff-top and clambered down a steep, short gully to the sand.

Low fingers of rock, uncovered by the dropping tide, reached out jealously towards the water's edge, and an MoD Keep Out sign warned of unspecified dangers just where the best waves were breaking. Far down the beach, a surf school was straggling back to the car park with awkward boards, while another surfer sat well outside the supposed danger line. I headed for a point close to the line, though it wasn't long before the current had swept me just inside it. Fortunately I survived to tell the tale.

The waves were big and fat, with a lot of water moving around, and you really had to be under the curl to catch them. I made the mistake of paddling for one mountain that was already breaking some twenty metres away. It engulfed me like an avalanche, and though I managed to emerge from the front, I was on my knees. My knees! The shame! I rolled off before anyone noticed.

The next one was more promising, but in my haste, I managed to fumble my hand position, and slipped off at the crucial moment. So far, so incompetent. I paddled for several more, but either they were too fat and didn't pick me up, or too steep and I pulled back, afraid I would tumble over the falls.

Eventually, a large, likely-looking wave arrived, peaking up well, just to my left. I had seen – surprise, surprise – that you really had to paddle hard and get up fast. I paddled hard and started to get to my feet, but even as I did, I wasn't sure I could make it. The wave seemed to open up beneath me like a chasm. But by then, it was too late. I was committed. I just managed to point the tip of the board a couple of degrees to the left, and I was off.

I took the drop, a wild, unknown descent, sure I was about to plunge the nose into the water and send myself cartwheeling over the top. Somehow, though, as I dropped down the choppy face, using all my strength and all the intangible experience I had acquired over the preceding months, I just managed to force the nose round and fit the board into the tight curve of the wave, driving it round into a desperate bottom turn, certain I was about to be thrown into the water.

As I did, I looked up into the face of the wave. The sight was astounding. From nowhere, a gaping maw had opened up and now towered above me, slavering to snap me up and swallow me whole, board and surfer together, in one tasty mouthful. It was magnificent - a snarling, salivating muzzle. A dragon's jaw hungry for human flesh.

The peak of the wave hung above me, a good few feet above my head, engulfing me in a roaring cavern. It had swallowed the sun, which turned the translucent water into an emerald cave, glittering with treasure and delight. Not quite a barrel, but very nearly, just lacking a dripping curtain to complete the circle, but still hollow and gaping, and the closest I had come to that watery grail. It was fabulous.

But alas, I only had an instant or two to appreciate the majesty of the moment, the magnificent sensation of being caught in the dragon's maw. Even so, it seemed like an eternity. Time enough to take in every shimmering detail, every splash and ripple, to enjoy the glorious feeling of the wave's power roaring all around me. In another instant, it would be gone.

As I powered along the face of the wave, hurtling to escape from the cave, the jaws snapped shut, swallowing me whole as promised. I was engulfed, sent hurtling down into the dark maelstrom, delighted. Welcome to Pembroke! Here be dragons!

WAVE 78: Marloes

Freshwater West was fabulous, but my time on the road was coming to an end. I had to keep moving. The next morning, Tenby was flat. So was Manorbier. I continued on north, stopping briefly in Pembroke to admire the dramatic castle, then across the hectic estuary of Milford Haven and west to Marloes. It's a million miles off the beaten track, but I had heard it was worth a detour.

I parked at the National Trust car park a mile or two beyond the village, and squelched barefoot over the fields. Then winced and hopped along a newly-laid path, sharp with grit and agonising gravel, down to the beach.

It was worth the walk, though, if not the hot coals. At high tide, it's a series of small sandy coves, rocky and dramatic, with huge slabs tumbling vertically down to the sand to cut each cove off from the next, and jagged teeth reaching out to sea. The water was clear, which was fortunate, as more rocks strew the shallows.

To my alarm, as I got there, a fisherman was eyeing up the peak with interest. I had no time to lose.

In Barcelona, when the swell came from the south-east, I used to catch the train up the coast to Montgat, fifteen minutes away, where an undiscerning beginner could spend a happy hour or two catching weak waves on the banks in front of the station. Fishing was forbidden between 8am and 8pm, but that didn't deter the gnarled pensioners who lived nearby, and there would often be two or three of them patiently trying to ensnare a surfer, then reacting with outrage when they did.

The beach was a couple of miles long, but with unerring skill, they always managed to choose the best – and often only – peak worth surfing. A couple of times I got tangled in their lines, and once was caught by a large hook, which fortunately embedded itself in my wetsuit, not my flesh.

I soon learned not to tangle with fishermen. All that staring out to sea teaches them patience. More so even than surfers. If they are there first, forget it. The peak is theirs. On the other hand, if you're in first, you at least have a moral claim to the peak, even as the weighted lines and barbed hooks start whistling around your ears.

At Marloes it was him or me. I did a cursory warm-up and waded in while he was still unrolling his rod. Much like Montgat, the waves were more playful than thrilling. Strong winds were on the way and the heralds of the hurricane to come made the waves messy and fat. But there were rides to be had if you caught them early, stayed in the pocket and kept a weather eye out for rocks in the crystal-clear water close to shore. The fisherman moved on and I had the pretty cove to myself, enjoying the sunshine and a pleasant, if unchallenging session. By mid-afternoon the wind had stiffened, blowing force six or seven, followed later by driving rain. Yet again, I was glad to have got one in the bag.

WAVE 79: Broad Haven

The following morning was no better. It was still raining and a brisk force seven was blowing south-south-west, so anything vaguely south-facing was unsurfable. I continued to west-facing Broad Haven, where a reasonable wave was breaking whenever a set came through. It was never going to be an epic surf, but given the conditions, it was the best I was likely to find. It certainly wasn't a day for sitting around in the van admiring the view. I plunged in, the only person on the beach, while two razorbills bobbed around in the line-up, looking smug and weatherproof in the Welsh rain.

My initial thought was to catch three waves and get out, my duty discharged. But it was more fun than it looked, despite the rain and the relative mediocrity of the waves. And surfing with seabirds is always more interesting than surfing alone. I caught three waves very quickly.

'I'll just get another three,' I thought. And did. Then another three. And another, until, about an hour and seventeen waves later, I finally decided it was time for a second, well-earned breakfast.

Broad Haven wasn't pretty enough to hang around, and I continued up to the vast expanse of Newgale, a long, windy beach stretched between two deep headlands. I expected it to be too windswept, but I wanted to take a look before dropping down to Manorbier again. When I got there, though, distinctive lines were coming through, not too troubled by the wind. Lunch could wait. There was surfing to be done.

WAVE 80: Newgale

In theory, I should have been celebrating at Newgale. It was my 80th wave. I had reached my target!

I didn't celebrate, though, and not because I still had several breaks and several hundred miles ahead of me. No, the sad truth is that I had miscounted. I thought I still had three more waves to surf before I hit my target. So, entirely oblivious to the significance of this beach, I blithely got on with surfing it.

Getting down to the beach was treacherous. The path disappeared among a scramble of dice-like crags that were tricky to negotiate with a board, particularly in a gusty wind. But down on the beach, the waves were bigger and better – and less affected by the wind – than they had appeared. And after a tricky entry though the whitewash, the water was deliciously crisp and clear. A gannet was patrolling just above the line-out, which is always a good sign.

The sets were around shoulder to head high. A bit fat and slow, but when they walled up, there was a decent, smooth face on them that peeled well. Some though, just went flat and soggy, so you had to keep an eye on them as you paddled, and then really commit to the take-off. And because you were watching what they were doing, you found yourself looking straight ahead, down a head-high, vertiginous drop, rather than along the line of the wave. So it was quite a heart-stopping, last-minute take-off each time. But then the wave seemed to fatten up a little. Once you had caught it, you felt as if you were riding a large mound of moving water, almost like snow-boarding over a smooth hillside, dramatic and exhilarating and really satisfying to ride.

The tide dropped and the wind freshened. I was thinking of calling it a day when a large set appeared, crumbling and then reforming before it reached me. I turned and paddled hard, and was on my feet fast, taking a giddy drop left, with plenty of clean, shoulder-high wall ahead. Then round a section that started to crumble and out onto green face again for a really satisfying final ride to end a satisfying session, one that had been unexpected, shapely, sizeable and challenging – and very different to the drizzle-fest at Broad Haven a few hours earlier. I couldn't have been happier, even if I had known I should have been celebrating.

I had covered my miles and surfed my waves for the day. I stayed where I was for the rest of the afternoon, as sunshine drove the squalls away and later rewarded itself with a brilliant, beautiful sunset beneath a clear sky.

The following morning was sunny and serene. The tide was far out, and the waves messy and unconvincing. I no longer had the luxury of repeating waves in mediocre conditions. I pressed on.

WAVE 81: Whitesands Bay

It was still early when I reached Whitesands, but the weather had worsened, and the wind picked up. A stiff cross-shore breeze was blowing, but at beach level it was funnelled a fraction off-shore by the surrounding hills. Decent waves twice the height of the two surfers surfing them were crashing in. By chance, I had stumbled on the right place at the right time.

I warmed up, and headed to the northern corner of the beach, where a handy rip sucked you out past the rocks, and through the howling waves into the line-out.

From sea level, the waves were intimidating – large and disorderly, and for a while, I was rather overawed by their size and savagery, and by a couple of unpleasant-looking close-outs. But the remaining surfer didn't seem too concerned, and I didn't want to look like a coward. I tried to ignore the nagging doubts.

Once again I fluffed my first wave, and was pitched over the falls as I paddled into it. Not paddling fast enough, as usual, no matter how many times I had repeated the mantra. I fell down the face and into the depths, hitting the sandy bottom before kicking back up and paddling towards the rip to try again. But the ducking hadn't been too desperate, and it restored my confidence a little.

Big, fat mountains of water were swilling through, and when a promising wave approached, I paddled again, harder this time, making sure not to look down into its jaws, but along the line as it drew itself up. Immediately, I found myself on a generous launch pad that soon transformed into a huge wall. I was amazed to find myself high up on the face, standing above a lovely, long slope of water that didn't appear to be moving too fast, giving me time to enjoy it. It felt like the wave I had seen a fellow surfer ride at Bantham, huge and elegant and shaped like a dream wave. I surfed it carefully, making a couple of gentle turns, trying to keep my movements smooth and elegant – though I suspect elegant isn't the first adjective an on-looker would use to describe my surfing.

Emboldened by this success, I realised that if you selected wisely, the waves were very makeable. So of course, I messed up my next wave. Not by going over the falls, but by attempting to grab the rail too abruptly, which yanked the tail round and plunged me straight into the face. After that, though, I got the hang of the large waves, and caught a couple of nice rides on long faces, taking an easy drop into a lovely wall as it wound forward majestically for twenty or thirty metres, and then surfing up into a floater as it crashed down towards the beach.

I was having a fabulous time, a really phenomenal, exhilarating hour in dramatic conditions as everything at last came together. There was just one minor irritant – the air was reverberating with the high-pitched whine of outboard engines: five RNLI ribs were buzzing around the bay like racing cars, bouncing off the waves as they practised picking up shipwrecked sailors in the pounding surf.

I have nothing but admiration for the people who voluntarily put out to sea in terrible conditions to rescue hapless seafarers. What they do is genuinely heroic. And of course, they need to train and practice. But surfing alongside them was like standing in the paddock at Brands Hatch. The noise soon started to grate.

The Saturday morning crowds were arriving, the swell was dropping, and I had caught some fabulous waves. Better to save my energy for another surf later on. In the car park, I got talking to Duncan, a local surfer with impressive dreadlocks, who taught IT nearby. He suggested I try Abereiddi, a little further north. So as the coach parties rolled in, I rolled out, glad to escape the infernal buzzing.

Abereiddi is tucked away in a fold between two hills, surrounded by disused quarries and a labyrinth of steep lanes and pretty cottages. The beach itself resembles a quarry yard, strewn with smooth stones that pour over onto the foreshore like a lick of foam. It feels unstable and precarious, as if the stones might slip back into the water at any moment, taking everything else with them. The weather was closing in, giving the bay an ominous, dour atmosphere, wet and unwelcoming. Against the unremitting grey, the only colour came from dozens of day-glo hikers, and a squadron of school-kids in life-jackets and bright helmets setting off for unspecified activities involving rope and cold water.

Sheltered from the wind, the bay was calm, with a small wave breaking close to the shore, not yet surfable. I sat and watched, in no hurry to leave the warmth of a dry van. A while later, I spotted a familiar shock of blonde dreadlocks: Duncan, who must have had a similar reaction to the crowds and outboards at Whitesands. He and his friend walked along the beach, climbed the steep path at the end and disappeared over the brow of the hill. But instead of cagoules and rucksacks, they had boards and wetsuits. I checked the map. Sure enough, there was another bay, just beyond the headland.

I was faced with a dilemma, or at least a tricky point of surfer etiquette. I didn't want to crash the party if my presence would be unwelcome, but at the same time, I didn't want to miss out on a possible secret spot. I could always go and look for it later, or course. But later, conditions might not be right.

277

WAVE 82: Hidden Bay

I changed and headed in the direction of the hidden bay, not sure what reception I could expect when I got there. Once again, I was barefoot. Once again, it was a questionable decision. The steep path was more or less fine, treading a rasping dance between the rocks, while in the field at the top, mud oozed and squelched between my toes. On the far side, the slippery path flirted with a blustery cliff-top, threatening to push an ill-shod surfer into the void. The wind whistled around my ears, and a sudden downpour stiffened to hail. It's reasonable to expect secret beaches to test your resolve, but this was ridiculous.

I paddled out, and immediately apologised for my villainous intrusion of their privacy. Duncan and his friend Pete couldn't have been more hospitable. They greeted me like an old friend, and immediately included me in their fun and hilarity. Duncan was having a hoot, and was determined we should too. He hollered us into waves, laughing at every improbable catch or frantic wipe-out, mine, his, Pete's – he was just happy to be surfing, and wanted to show it.

The bay was stark and severe, hemmed in by steep, sandy-brown cliffs and scattered with treacherous eruptions of rocks. It was a barren amphitheatre, flooded with trepidation and danger. Corralled into the steep, blind cove, the waves heaved and jostled like cattle. Random energy bounced off the encircling cliffs in all directions, throwing up a lattice of peaks and troughs that were impossible to predict. They broke best at the epicentre of all the action, drawing themselves up from head high to twice that, and by the end of the session, higher still.

It was unlike anywhere else I had surfed. The waves

were troubling, sharp rocks lurked just below the rough surface of your imagination, and when you fell off a wave – either plunging over the falls, as I did plenty of times, or failing to get up in time, which I also did plenty of times – the drop was long enough to lurch your heart up towards your throat. But the singularity of the bay, the unusual, unpredictable nature of the waves, the clarity of the water and the company of my two co-surfers made it a real gem – and all the more so for being uncharted territory.

Alone, I would have been terrified. I probably wouldn't even have risked it. With my new friends, it was exhilarating. Exhilarating but tricky. It was no use being on the shoulder, you had to be right on the peak, right beneath the curl as it started to break, then up and on your feet in a flash, to catch a lightning-quick ride before it exploded in a cloudburst of white. The rides were tricky, intense and over in an instant. But it was a wonder to be on them.

Eventually, as conditions got bigger and rougher, and the energy drained from my arms, my hit-rate dwindled and my nerve started to fail, and I found myself caught in the familiar cycle of exhausted frustration, trying to catch waves I was doomed to miss or mess up. By now, Duncan had gone in, and Pete, a better surfer than me, was having similar trouble. I whooshed to shore on some passing whitewash, and trudged the long path back across the headland, very happy to have surfed such an unlikely jewel.

WAVE 83: Abereiddi Bay

I should probably have stopped at this point. I had enjoyed two challenging sessions that day, and surfed seven new breaks in four days. An eighth should have been a beach too far. On the other hand the slip-sliding walk over the muddy meadow had given me time to recover a little; I thought I was about to complete my 80-wave target; and when I got back to the van, a clean left-hander was peeling across the shingle beach. I was already wet. I might as well go in.

Big mistake. Try as I might, I couldn't catch a thing. It was a fast wave, and I was utterly exhausted. Never a happy combination. I had more chance of catching a lobster. Two hard surfs already that day had wiped me out. Mostly, I was out of position. If not, I went over the falls. Or found myself on my knees. Or missed the footing on my back foot.

I should have gone to get my bigger board, but I was too tired to bother – which suggests I probably should have just gone in. Finally, I caught a decent wave, got to my feet – and in my excitement, spun a bottom-turn around a sixpence that sent me straight into the wall of the wave, face first. Rats.

The tide pushed in and the wave steepened. My burnt-out shoulders burnt with pain, my neck stiffened and ached so it hurt just to hold my head up as I paddled, my arms flailed. The longer I stayed in, the harder it got, and the less chance I had of catching a wave.

Finally, I caught a reasonable right, slicing down the sheer wall like wire through cheese, and catching a brief, clean burst of powerful face. 'That's more like it!' I thought, after this glimpse of redemption. 'That's how you do it!'

So, stupidly, I went out for more. If I could do it once, I reasoned, I could do it again. Incorrectly, as it turned out.

As dusk thickened, I caught a breaking wave that did nothing to salvage my personal gloom. Three new and exhausting waves in one day, after several days of intense surfing, was really at the absolute limit of what my fit but middle-aged body could take.

I was particularly despondent because I thought this had been my eightieth wave. It couldn't have been more of an anti-climax. Like rushing to finish a book you're enjoying, I had gone too fast, and failed to savour the ending. It was only later, when I went through my notes more carefully, that I realised I had miscounted. The real milestone had passed like an unsigned turn-off on a dark country road, unmarked, unseen and certainly uncelebrated.

It made little difference, I had more beaches to surf. Eighty, it turned out, had been rather short of the mark. Either way, the grim, stony beach at Abereiddi in the rain hardly lends itself to celebration. Exhausted, I dragged myself back to the van, ate a horse, drank a couple of quiet drams as token fanfare and had an early night. Tomorrow I had surfing to do.

WAVE 84: West Dale

By morning, the wind had picked up, but so too had my mood. Abereiddi was messy in the sunshine, so after a hearty breakfast and a blustery stroll over the headland to get photos of yesterday's mysterious bay, I decided to head back to Marloes, in search of some shelter. I was in no hurry. My body ached from the marathon I had subjected it to the previous day. And anyway, I had hit my eighty waves.

Marloes was delightful. Small, shapely and breaking nicely across the pretty, rock-strewn beach. But on the way down, I bumped into a local, who said nearby West Dale might be a better option. I was sceptical, given the wind direction, but he was so insistent and so enthusiastic my curiosity was aroused. I went in at Marloes anyway and managed to surf with a modicum of style in the easy surf. But after half an hour I decided to save some energy and give West Dale a try.

Sure enough, at West Dale, the wind was on it, but that didn't matter. It was stunning! You park in Dale, a pretty village on one side of the small headland guarding Milford Haven, and walk over to the other side, up a lush, curving meadow that sits like a saddle between two steep hills. Then over a wooden stile and down a rocky path to a small bay that faces almost due west. It was small, intimate and secluded, and when I left, deserted.

It was a lovely afternoon, the water was clear and the sky blue. The waves were a little fat and formless under the wind, but they were coming in at around shoulder high, and with enough face and enough peel to make it worth the trek. I was tired, but the paddle out was straightforward. Then a decent drop, followed by a race with the pocket, just staying far enough ahead to surf the wave actively to the end. No pressure, no problems, nothing but playful waves and pleasure. As the sun started to sink and the wind eased off, I dripped my way happily back across the meadow to the van.

If I was feeling the effect of days and months on the road, so was the van. To my horror, as I slid the door open, it fell off in my hands. The near corner hit the tarmac with a jarring clunk. A few inches further forward and I would have found myself without a foot, or at least several toes.

I leaned the door against the van, aghast. Scraping the van, on the few occasions it had happened, was traumatic enough. Losing a door was horrible. Somehow it had jumped off its runners, which were dry and choked with sand and grime. I scraped them clear as best I could and manhandled the door back into place with a combination of brute force and raw panic. It took several attempts, but eventually it was back in position, though it rolled with a grinding reluctance that set my teeth on edge.

By now I couldn't face driving too far. Instead I found a lane above the village, near the attractive manor house that grandiosely calls itself Dale Castle. Not the best parking spot in Pembrokeshire, but from my window I could look along the lush meadow I had walked earlier, and out over the sea. As the sun dipped below the horizon, the sky deepened into a panoply of purples and crimsons, framed by the curving meadows and the silhouetted cliffs.

I woke to a still, sunny morning, and should have stayed and surfed West Dale again. But with time running out, Freshwater West was calling me back, though it was a long drive, down pretty autumnal lanes, with the low sun filtering through reddening leaves to slant across mist-filled hollows. The waves, unfortunately, didn't repay the time and effort.

On the way, I visited the beautiful cathedral at St David's, where I discovered that St David is often known as Aquaticus, the aquatic one. One theory is that he used to immerse himself in sea water as a form of penance. This is pretty much what surfing in Britain is most of the time, and makes him my distant forebear. (The other theory is that he only ever drank water, which is not what surfing in Britain is, most of the time, and we are therefore unrelated.)

I continued on to Whitesands, where I woke to a howling mess. But as I watched, a local surfer arrived, straight from a night shift at the oil refinery. He asked me if I was going in. I could hardly decline.

It was rough and ugly. The rip around the rocks was hairy and the waves large and difficult to get into. Or maybe I was too reticent. It's difficult to feign conviction when you're afraid of the consequences. Finally I caught one – a snarling beast, half as tall again as I am. I paddled, taking care to look along the wave, not down its gaping throat, and found myself tucked into the top pocket of a giant that loomed over my shoulder as I sped along its chest. It was closing out ahead, so there was only a short burst of wall, but it was exhilarating and dramatic to be surfing so much power. I angled up to catch a floater as it closed out, and relished the surge of energy as the wave exploded beneath me.

I was still exhausted when I reached Aberystwyth late that afternoon. I parked on the seafront and wandered like a ghost along its Victorian promenade. Four surfers were out, patiently waiting for a brief peak that ambled along for a few metres then faded away. Four was about the right number for the conditions, though it was exhaustion more than altruism that kept me from joining them. The waves were too few, their potential too limited, the effort too great. I simply couldn't be bothered. Tomorrow, I told myself.

I toyed with the idea of sleeping on the sea front, but it looked excessively public, so instead I thought I would tootle a mile or so out of town, then tootle easily back in the morning. The road, though, plunged blindly inland, and didn't glimpse the sea again until Borth, some seven miles later. A handful of dark figures were swooping down glass-smooth faces in the dying light, silhouetted against a tequila sunset. The Aberystwyth wave had been donkey slow. These were gannet fast. I was too tired for a demoralising session in the dusk. The wave would have to wait.

WAVE 85: Borth

Aberystwyth had looked delightful, but not so delightful that it merited a 14-mile detour before breakfast. Not this late in my trip, with the finish in sight and a deadline I couldn't reasonably extend. The pebble beach at Borth didn't look too inspiring, but at least the sun was shining and there was a free shower at the end of it.

In the time it took to put on my wetsuit, though, the weather worsened. Clouds gathered and the wind picked up and swung round slightly, from cross-shore to slightly on-shore. Suddenly it looked even less inspiring. Still, I was in my wetsuit now. I might as well get another wave under my belt.

It turned out to be fabulous! A rainbow appeared out to sea, and the chest-high waves peeled nicely for several long rides, mostly lefts, that flowed smoothly all the way to shore. A rainstorm interrupted the sunshine briefly, dampening down the surface of the sea, making it smooth and matte, pockmarked by rain craters; and lifting a gentle patina of mist so it looked like the view from a mountain top over mist-filled peaks and shifting valleys. The sun returned and eventually I went in for a shower, happy as always that I had forced myself to surf despite the unpromising conditions.

WAVE 86: Llwyngwril

I drove north, scanning the sea, unaware that – with just two days to go – I was in the grip of wave fever. Based on little more than a nameless photo, I stumbled across a series of boulder-bottomed breaks half-way up Cardigan Bay, in a village I could not begin to pronounce but which is written Llwyngwril.

From the road, I could see waves breaking like dominoes, metronomic and scintillating. I needed to check them out. There appeared to be a straightforward path down to the boulder-strewn beach so I decided to risk it. It was part of my job description. Straightforward was the last thing it was: along a gravel track, through a tight gate, across the railway line, over a field and down a muddy gully, with a knotted rope to help you – though it's hard to hold a rope and a board at the same time as you slide down a slippery gully.

The beach bristled with boulders as big as dalmatians, so the walk to the water's edge was circuitous, and increasingly tricky the deeper you fumbled into the silty water. And those perfect waves I had glimpsed from above? Shapely. Regular. Utterly rubbish. A knee-high dribble, thigh-high at best, with no power and no push. I caught the regulation three, feeling rather stupid, added another for luck and headed for shore. Still, I was happy to have tried. If nothing else, I had learned something, though I'm not quite sure what.

WAVE 87: Porth Ceiriad

The road north was stunning, through green mountains and lush fields, across the pretty Mawddach estuary and past Harlech, another blue remembered hill from the happy highways of my youth. The wind was still blowing strong from the south-west so when I reached the Lleyn Peninsula, I headed for Porth Ceiriad in search of shelter.

There was no-one around as I strode across the blustery hillside for a glimpse of the beach. But as I reached the final stile, three schoolboys appeared, bouncing down the grassy hillside on a bizarre vehicle that looked like a golf buggy but turned out to be a quad bike with a four-poster canopy to carry their boards! Driven by a 14-year-old over bumpy Welsh farmland, it looked as precarious as it was improbable.

My body dragged with a familiar feeling of bone-deep weariness. But if they were going in, I was going in.

Weariness, unfortunately, was not the ideal state to be in, especially given the conditions. The bay sat between two short headlands and was backed by steep sandy cliffs. The eastern headland took the brunt of the wind, but the waves were still big, disorderly and unpredictable. Getting out through the powerful shore-dump was tricky enough, and even once you were through, the seething waves were lumpy and formless and nearly twice my height. Worse, it was rolling all over the place, so it felt like being adrift in the mid-Atlantic. Peaks were breaking everywhere, and there was no way of knowing if they were going to fade away or wedge up and close out.

On the other hand, the water was beautifully clear, the sky was scoured clean, and the autumn sun lit up the bay with saturated blues and golds. For a time, while my strength held, it was exhilarating and energising, a glorious struggle with wind and water, pitched and tossed like flotsam. But the surfing was hopeless, even if, early on, I was hoping for more. The waves were too big and too steep and too random. Each time I paddled, I was worried I would go over the falls. And when I did go over the falls, it wasn't fun – a long way to drop, with your board rolling around with you, and a dark pummelling when you got there, followed by a mugging or two as you struggled to get back out.

The three teenagers were having more success. Buoyed by youthful energy and lack of fear, they caught the twitching tails of fading monsters, or took off on suicidal peaks that duly obliterated them in a single bite. I tried to emulate them, but I had none of their energy or immortality.

I struggled for the best part of an hour, an hour of constant motion, heaved every which way in space and time, searching for the chance alignment that would bring me to the right wave at the right instant. The alignment never came. Whenever it looked even vaguely promising, I either pulled back from the sudden precipice, or fell headlong down it.

Increasingly frustrated, I gave myself a stern talking-to. This time I would go, come what may, and to hell with the consequences. But as I paddled desperately on aching arms, the abyss opened up below me – way below – where a whirlpool of churning sand waited to suck me in. I pulled back, my resolve gone. Another stern talking to, and this time, I went – only to be pitched off and rolled around, head over heels, for three glorious revolutions, until I barely knew which way was up.

It was hopeless, and I knew it was time to quit. I caught a consolation broken wave back to dry land, though really it was no consolation. And I still needed a vigorous tussle to get through the shore dump without one last whizz around the spin cycle.

I dragged myself onto the shore, battered and bruised. For the second time in five days, I had proved what should have been self-evident: three new breaks in one day was too much, no matter what my younger self might have to say on the matter.

I retreated to Abersoch to lick my wounds, drink local ale and, finding the chip shop closed, reluctantly cook supper where I was parked, witnessed only by a desultory trickle of incurious tourists who wandered past in the darkness. I slept by the beach and was woken early by a fire-breathing rubbish truck well before dawn. It was my last day. Finally, my time was up. I had to head home and face the future.

Before I left, I was determined to surf once more on the Lleyn Peninsula, then head up to Anglesey, hoping to surf there to complete my circuit. Realistically I knew I would be lucky to find anything so high up, but I had to at least try, for completion, if nothing else. Earlier in the trip, I might have been tempted to have another go at Porth Ceiriad, in search of redemption. Not now. I didn't have the time. I headed instead to Porth Neigwl, or Hell's Mouth as it is also known. Its wide jaws face south-west, greedily snapping up any swell that wanders into the Irish Sea.

To my dismay, it was choppy and weak, with low interval waves washed out of shape by the on-shore breeze. In the car park, a young cow was scratching itself against the notice board while it checked the tide tables, and nearby a flock of curlews floated and landed and floated again. They're my favourite seabird after gannets, elusive and mysterious. But while I would like to believe they presage good waves, most of the evidence is against me. I decided to search elsewhere. It was a peninsula. There had to be decent waves somewhere.

There weren't. Ten miles away, also facing south, Aberdaron was smaller and choppier. To the north, along a lattice of lanes, Porth Oer, or Whistling Sands, was flat, with just a tiny pulse breaking on the shore, though the beach was unspoilt and achingly beautiful. Porth Towyn, another achingly beautiful, unspoilt bay, was slightly bigger. Maybe knee-high; still unsurfable. I would have to head back to Hell's Mouth, wind or no wind.

I jumped into the van and turned the ignition. I used to keep the key on a red boot lace so I could hang it around my neck when I was surfing, but somehow the lace had got caught around the steering column. As I spun the steering wheel, the lace tightened. There was a loud crack. To my horror, the key had snapped off in the ignition. Disaster! So close to the end, and I was stuck.

Fearing a long delay followed by a hefty bill, I inspected the damage. The key had broken off just inside the barrel, so there was no chance of gripping it with pliers, or even desperate fingernails, no matter how much I tried. I was frantic. I was going to be stuck there all day. Maybe all week. There weren't even any waves to surf while I waited for a mechanic.

Then I had a brainwave. There was just enough of a lip at the mouth of the barrel to catch the blade of a screwdriver. With the body of the key still in place, the barrel still turned. So I could simply switch the engine on and off with a slight twist on the screwdriver! Although so could anyone else, of course.

WAVE 88: Porth Neigwl

Relieved to be moving, I returned to Hell's Mouth nearly four hours after I had left, with just a broken key and the fleeting memory of several pretty but flat beaches to show for it. Some days, it's worth turning your back on mediocre surf in search of something better. Some days, it really isn't.

The young cow had gone, as had the curlews. But there was a field of lambs, each with a red love heart sprayed on its side, which made me smile. The waves were still rubbish, though. Sloppy but surfable, with a stiff cross-shore breeze and peaks hitting shoulder height, breaking all over the place, seemingly at random. Weak sunshine peered myopically through the slight haze to create a nondescript glare that perfectly matched the cloudy water. After the pretty bays I had seen that morning, the wide grin of Porth Neigwl was a bit of a dog's mouth.

I paddled out, the morning's frustration getting the better of me, and grumpily got to work, almost determined not to enjoy what surf there was. My body was tired, and I was slow to get up each time, my front foot dragging as it came forward for each drop. Gradually, though, the water worked its magic and I started to relax and make the best of things. They were short rides mostly, and it was a challenge to be up in time. But a few nice waves broke like curls of butter pulled up by a knife, with a smooth pocket, steep and chest high, enough to get the board into for a semi-satisfying session, despite very average conditions.

A surf's a surf, and if everywhere else is flat, you've got to take what you can. As the final surf of a 14-month trek, though, it was rubbish. Unsatisfying waves in an unsatisfying state of mind against an unscintillating landscape.

I wasn't done yet, though. More in hope than expectation, I headed up to Anglesey to complete my loop of Britain. North of Anglesey, Ireland blocks all the swell, so the next recognised surfing was up in Scotland, where I had started. Even if it was tiny in Anglesey, I had to go in. Even if it was flat, perhaps, if only for a paddle around the shallows.

Trearddur Bay was a mill pond. So too was Silver Bay. My final chance lay at Rhosneigr, whose open bay is fully exposed to anything slipping in from the south. It even had a surf shop, which seemed promising. I strolled down to the scallop-shaped bay in sweltering sunshine. It felt like early summer, not mid-autumn. The tide was out and the bay flat, with a gentle, knee-high pulse snaking in, enough to keep a lone kayaker entertained, nothing more. This was no place for a final surf.

I drove slowly out of town rather disconsolate, wondering if it was really worth chasing a non-existent wave. Everywhere was so obviously flat, and all the signs suggested it would be flat from Anglesey to Bangor, and beyond.

As I drove, I caught a glimpse of another bay. With nothing better to do, I thought I might as well take a look. On the far side of a stretch of low, rabbit-grazed dunes was a small beach scattered with clusters of rock. To my amazement, not only was there a small but surfable wave, there were actual surfers surfing it! I didn't have to think twice.

WAVE 89: Rhosneigr

By this stage, it didn't really matter what the waves were like, as long as I could catch one. I would have been happy with anything. But they turned out to be lovely! Not big, not powerful, but nice and sharp, and making up in shape what they lacked in power. The water was clean and crystal clear, the sun shining. I had a peak to myself, and this really was the last wave of my trip. Apart from the fact that it was my final surf, it was perfect.

Following the exertions of the previous days and weeks, my body was utterly washed out. But the waves were relaxing and unchallenging, and after the frustrations of the Lleyn Peninsula, I grew increasingly invigorated as the session went on: fun waves, crisp, clear water and a beautiful blue sky, lit by late afternoon sun.

It felt elegiac, a real end to my odyssey. I lingered longer and longer, not wanting to leave. And fortunately the waves kept coming. Lefts and rights, no more than waist high, but with decent, longish rides – not the longest in the world, but long enough given the conditions and the location, so far up the coast. You could wade out, wait for your moment, and with a couple of well-timed strokes you were up, with enough wall to surf and enough power to keep up with the curling pocket.

There were a few people around, but no one on my peak, and no peak worth swapping it for. I caught wave after wave, just relishing the sheer enjoyment of it, fully aware of where I was and where I had been, and somehow keeping every wave of the trip in my mind at once, every wave that had washed me along to where I was now, physically, geographically, emotionally. I could almost see myself on a map. It felt fabulous. It felt as if I had finally achieved what I had set out to do.

Throughout these long months, alongside the joy of being out on the road, just living to surf, I had felt the weight of my own self-imposed goal, as if I was unable just to bum around without justification, but instead had to complete the trip (and then write about it). Every delay and pause, whenever completion had looked doubtful, had made the task weigh more heavily. Half a circuit made no sense. Half a circuit was just going surfing. Nothing short of completing the circuit would give it meaning. Now that I had completed it, I felt that weight lift. Here I was, several months later than planned, but I had reached my goal.

I didn't want to get out, ever. But eventually my body grew tired beyond retrieval and the waves gradually deteriorated. I decided to catch one final wave. Then after that, another. And then a third, though this time it really was the last.

I walked up the beach, euphoric. My happiness was tinged with melancholy, though. That was it. The end of a beautiful day, the onset of autumn, the close of a chapter. My trip was over. No longer the simple certainties involved in finding somewhere to sleep and somewhere to surf. Karen was waiting. Real life beckoned.

Later, washed and refreshed, I wandered back to the beach to watch other people surfing against the sunset, and to take a few celebratory photos. It was an idyllic scene, as the setting sun shot orange flames along the iridescent sand, and the surfers surfed in silhouette against the silver sea.

My sense of happiness and melancholy increased as I wandered along the sand. Waves of exhaustion and contentment washed over me. It was the kind of warm, tangible melancholy you can embrace and enjoy, but melancholy no less. This was finally it. I had done it.

I had not planned to stay there that night, but it was late and I was exhausted, and anyway, I wanted to hold on to this feeling, this exquisite, bitter-sweet sense of euphoria and completion. I bought celebratory fish and chips, and drove round to where all the surfers parked, in among the dunes. One by one they packed up and left. I was alone once more, sleeping by the beach for the last time.

I woke early, my body still washed out and weary. I had no plans to surf. The swell was dropping, and I didn't want to lose the glorious sensation of contentment on mediocre waves. I strolled down to the beach anyway, just for a look, and was delighted to surprise a flock of curlews breakfasting in the pale dawn light.

Sure enough, the swell had dropped. I was almost relieved. It wasn't worth the effort. I was excused! I wandered back to the van. A short while later, I wandered back again. I couldn't stop myself. I just had to check in case anything had changed. But no, the waves were still small and weak.

Even so, the pull of the water proved irresistible. I didn't want to break the spell of the previous evening, but nor did I want to leave without going in again. Eventually, at the very last minute, when it was almost too late, almost despite myself, I submitted to their Siren call. Just enough time to revel in the clear, cool water, and catch two insubstantial rides before the tide was too high. It wasn't a real surf, but I knew I couldn't have left without going in that one last time.

I cooked a bowl of porridge, packed up and pulled out. The trip was over. That was it. I just had one last destination before I could head south. Crosby, and the Anthony Gormley installation of a hundred human figures staring out to sea. I had started out from there, fourteen months ago. I had to return to complete the circle, to complete my circuit of Great Britain.

When I got there, the tide was in, so only a few of the figures appeared above the water. Small waves in clean lines were slapping around them, and they looked like swimmers about to plunge in. Or surfers, staring out to sea, still waiting for the next wave.

Finally, I dragged myself away. It was time to go home. I was still filled with melancholy that it was over, but also a sense of enormous satisfaction. I had done it. I had surfed everywhere, and I had a million memories – of waves, of people, of places, of waking up in the van each day somewhere new and full of hope. I was a different surfer, a different person. Looking at a map of the British Isles would never be the same again.

Glossary

BACK-HAND: Surfing with your back to the wave. Slightly trickier than surfing on your fore-hand.

BARREL: When the wave folds over to create a tube.

BIC: A durable plastic board used by beginners.

BLOWN-OUT: When on-shore wind whips the sea into an unsurfable mess.

BODYBOARD: A short length of foam used for getting in the way of surfers.

BOTTOM-TURN: A turn at the bottom of the wave, to set up the rest of the ride.

BREAK: A place to surf. Also SPOT.

CATCH: The moment the wave picks you up.

CLOSE-OUT: When the wave collapses along its length. Not good for surfing.

COVER-UP: A wave that briefly covers a surfer riding it.

CURL: The part of the wave that is breaking.

CUT-BACK: Turning your board back towards the curl.

DUCK-DIVE: Pushing your board beneath an on-coming wave so it doesn't drive you backwards.

FACE: The smooth, unbroken part of a wave.

FIN: A thin slice of plastic attached to the bottom of the board to stop it slipping sideways in the water.

FLOATER: Surfing along the breaking lip of a wave.

FORE-HAND: Opposite of BACK-HAND.

GLASSY: Smooth and unruffled. Ideal for surfing.

HEAD HIGH: As high as the top of my head. Wave measurement is notoriously controversial, so all sizes are given in relation to a 5'10" surfer surfing the wave.

IMPACT ZONE: Where the waves detonate.

INTERVAL: The time between two waves. Long is good.

LEASH: The strap that attaches the board to your ankle.

LINE-UP: Where surfers wait for the next wave.

LIP: The top edge of the wave.

MUSH: Small, weak, rubbish waves. Also SLOP.

OFF-SHORE WIND: Blowing from land to sea. It grooms the waves, making them clean and good to surf.

ON-SHORE WIND: Blowing from sea to land. Makes the waves weak, choppy and often unsurfable.

OVER THE FALLS: Dragged over the front of a breaking wave. Like Niagara.

PEAK: The highest point of a wave and the first part to break. By extension, the best place to catch a wave.

POCKET: The steep, clean face just ahead of the curl.

RAILS: The edges of a board.

REEF: A patch of rock below the surface, where waves break regularly and powerfully. Also available in coral.

REFORM: When the wave gets it shape back.

RIP: A strong, narrow current. Good for getting out into the line-up. Bad for getting swept out to sea. Under no circumstances try to paddle against it. You won't win.

SET: The bigger, cleaner waves that arrive in each cycle.

SLOP: Small, weak, rubbish waves. Also MUSH.

SUP: Surfer Unable to Paddle. Best avoided.

SWELL: Waves.

TAKE-OFF POINT: The point where you catch the wave.

TAKE THE DROP: Swoop down the front of a wave.

WHITEWASH: The pummelling white mess after a wave has broken. Also known as WHITE-WATER.

6'5": A board that is 6 foot 5 inches long.